W9-ABY-138

WITHDRAWN

Gramley Library
Salem Academy and College
Winston-Salem, N.C. 27108

August Wilson

AUGUST
· ·
WILSON

Completing the Twentieth-Century Cycle

EDITED BY ALAN NADEL

UNIVERSITY OF IOWA PRESS, IOWA CITY

Gramley Library
Salem Academy and College
Winston-Salem, N.C. 27108

University of Iowa Press, Iowa City 52242
Copyright © 2010 by the University of Iowa Press
www.uiowapress.org
Printed in the United States of America

Design by April Leidig-Higgins

No part of this book may be reproduced or used in any form
or by any means without permission in writing from the
publisher. All reasonable steps have been taken to contact
copyright holders of material used in this book. The publisher
would be pleased to make suitable arrangements with
any whom it has not been possible to reach.

Cover art by Romare Bearden, *Mill Hand's Lunch Bucket*, 1978.
Collage on board, 13 ¾" × 18 ⅛". Estate of Romare Bearden,
© Romare Bearden Foundation/Licensed by VAGA, New York, NY.

The University of Iowa Press is a member of Green Press
Initiative and is committed to preserving natural resources.

Printed on acid-free paper

Library of Congress Cataloging-in-Publication Data
August Wilson: completing the twentieth-century cycle /
edited by Alan Nadel.
p. cm.
ISBN-13: 978-1-58729-875-2 (pbk.)
ISBN-10: 1-58729-875-9 (pbk.)
1. Wilson, August — Criticism and interpretation.
I. Nadel, Alan, 1947–
PS3573.I45677Z565   2010
812'.54 — dc22   2009038141

This book is dedicated to my wife
Sharon Kopyc

to Constanza Romero
and to all those
who loved August Wilson

Contents

· ·

August Wilson

Introduction

· ·

A t a turning point in his career, August Wilson was faced with a crucial decision. He had won the National Playwrights Conference competition, which gave his play, *Ma Rainey's Black Bottom*, a staged reading at the Eugene O'Neill Theater in Connecticut. The conference director, Lloyd Richards, who at the time was also dean of the Yale School of Drama, wanted to do the play at the Yale Repertory, but Wilson was more attracted to a lucrative Broadway contract. When he read that contract closely, however, he discovered he would be signing away control over the play. *Ma Rainey's Black Bottom* — a play about about the role of black music in a white industry, the problem of artistic control, and the conflict between communal production and commercial — concerns not only how the products of the black community have been altered by their conversion into white commerce, but also how the community itself has been damaged in the process. In other words, the play, like Wilson's *The Piano Lesson*, explores the different inflection property rights have when framed by black American history, with its origins in chattel slavery.

Conflict over the meaning of property — implicit, arguably, in all of Wilson's drama — becomes particularly cogent in the last two plays that Wilson completed, *Gem of the Ocean* and *Radio Golf*. These plays culminate the writing of Wilson's ten-play, twentieth-century cycle, and, set in 1904 and 1997, respectively, they also bookend the time span that the cycle chronicles. In *Gem*, a black man has died in order to prove that his life is worth more than a bucket of nails, and in *Radio Golf*, another black man abandons his mayoral aspirations to affirm the property rights of a Pittsburgh home once owned by his great aunt that legitimately belongs to his cousin. In *Ma Rainey*, in other words, even before Wilson had fully envisioned the cycle that would trace the arc of black ownership in the twentieth century, he grappled with some of its basic issues. These entail the relationship of human worth to human labor to human production to physical property, as all of these factors are weighed on the imbalanced scale of America's racial history.

Clearly, the Broadway producers who wanted to acquire *Ma Rainey's Black Bottom*, who wanted to put their own property rights above those of August Wilson, didn't understand the property they were pursuing. When Wilson raised objections, he was told that the contract wasn't that important: "In this industry," they said, "we go a lot on faith." "As long as the words don't mean anything," Wilson responded, "why don't you write the contract my way?" The producers told him to call his agent; instead, he called Lloyd Richards, and together they mounted a production at Yale that eventually, under Wilson's careful artistic control and Richards's equally careful direction, went to Broadway, where it won the New York Drama Critics' Circle Award. Two years later, in similar fashion, the two brought *Fences* to Broadway, then *Joe Turner's Come and Gone*, *The Piano Lesson*, and *Two Trains Running*. These plays, the first five in the cycle to reach Broadway, amassed two Drama Desk Awards, five New York Drama Critics' Circle Awards, an American Theatre Critics Association Award, a Tony Award, and two Pulitzer Prizes. As a group, those first five plays have garnered the greatest body of critical attention, including the essays in *May All Your Fences Have Gates: Essays on the Drama of August Wilson* (Iowa, 1995), the companion piece to this collection.

The other five plays completing the cycle — in order of their New York productions: *Seven Guitars*, *Jitney*, *King Hedley II*, *Gem of the Ocean*, and *Radio Golf* — not only give that cycle some new dimensions, but also provide an overall shape that converts the cycle from an anthology to a loosely structured epic.

Several factors effect that shift. The first is the revised *Jitney*, converted from a solitary play written in the historical present of the 1970s to the play Wilson used to represent the 1970s decade in the ten-play project that Wilson conceived after *Jitney* was first written and performed regionally. As the play that reunites the cycle with the history of its own origins, therefore, it multiplies the historical dimensions of the cycle as a whole. In that play, we see many of the Wilson archetypes — the ambitious young man, the rebellious warrior, the wheeler-dealer, the responsible entrepreneur, the oral historian, the crotchety old man — struggling with their personal demons in a world of economic naturalism. From this pragmatic world will emerge the struggles with the spiritual and the ancestral legacies of Christian and African belief — struggles essential to Wilson's plays after *Ma Rainey*. Although history and legacy inform all of Wilson's work, *Jitney* is more heavily focused on the specific generational shifts in the 1970s, when a post-Vietnam generation of black men begin to assume the role of paternal responsibility or to share it with men who have borne (or neglected) their generational responsibilities in the preceding decades.

In that regard, each of the taxi drivers affiliated with the jitney station has matured in a different decade: the Depression (Turnbo and Fielding), post–World War II (Becker), post-Korea (Doub), the 1960s (Shealy), and the 1970s (Youngblood). In this generational matrix, we can find the incipience of the decade-by-decade progression that will structure the as-yet-to-be-formulated ten-play cycle, here focused narrowly but intensely, as Dana Williams shows, on competing models of male responsibility. None of the models is emphatically privileged; rather, each serves as a generational and ethical modification of its counterpart. In combination, the multifarious perspectives give the specific conflicts of the play their historical dynamics at the same time that these dynamics give the play's conflicts their historical specificity. Because Wilson is simultaneously drawing upon, revising, and undermining racially inflected constructions of black manhood, understanding the nuances of Wilson's enterprise in this play requires, Kimmika Williams-Witherspoon makes clear, not only a nuanced production but also an audience attuned to the nuances of the play's "hidden transcripts"— the use of "musicality, call and response, and African American Vernacular English." Recognizing the hidden transcripts requires a cognizance of cultural competency. These transcripts allow Wilson to communicate with a black community while forging a theatrical community — an audience — capable of reinvesting traditionally racialized stereotypes with new cultural and historical significance.

In this way *Jitney* becomes an important counterpoint to *King Hed-*

ley II, which takes place in the decade immediately after *Jitney* but is separated by six plays and was written nearly twenty years later. As *Jitney* subtly portends the cycle, *King Hedley II* just as subtly shapes and unites it. The direct sequel to *Seven Guitars*, it emphatically connects the historical aspects of the cycle to the generational, thus weaving the play's themes to those of *Jitney* in the same way that it ties its events to *Seven Guitars*, so as to give the cycle a coherent fabric of themes, names, and neighborhoods that function in several disparate — sometimes even contradictory — ways to inform and structure Wilson's dramatic enterprise.

I once asked August if he was acquainted with the Samm-Art Williams play, *Home*. "No," he said. Then after a pause he added, "It's about one person, isn't it?" In Wilson's dramatic world, nothing is ever about one person. Even when the focus seems to be on a single character, that character remains in dialogue with ancestors and social obstacles, with artifacts and songs, with spirits and gods, with the face of destiny and the force of opposition to it. Even as singular a character as Troy Maxson never soliloquizes; in his loneliest of moments, he is in direct dialogue with Death.

Because community is so central to Wilson's understanding of the human, of the historical, and, more specifically, of the African American condition, Aunt Ester, the spiritual leader of the Pittsburgh Hill community where all but one of the plays is set, becomes a key figure, as the cycle moves toward completion, symbolizing the entire duration of African American existence and the multifarious strategies for resisting or transcending its multiple forms of oppression. She is the oral historian who recollects African Americans across four centuries. Also a pragmatist, she is a woman who instructed runaway slaves on the Underground Railroad in the strategies of escape and the tactics of survival. At the same time, she serves as a teacher explaining the stories of those who failed to survive to those who must learn, from those stories, how to endure.

Drawing equally on the terrestrial and extraterrestrial to function, she is, as Barbara Lewis explains, a double presence, merging the temporal present that requires a specific corporeal identity with a role that can be assumed by a series of women who accept the call of the community, in all its history and legacy. At the same time, to the extent that that identity unites a series of historical people to comprise a single transcendent spiritual persona, she is a derivative of Mammy Wata, an androgynous African female water divinity empowered by the "lore and healing power of the ancient continent." She is also, Yvonne Chambers and Vivian Gist Spencer demonstrate, a Christ figure whose life and death are inextricably related to the cycles of ritual sacrifice so prevalent in the second half of Wilson's cycle. Aunt Ester's own death, which takes place offstage in *King Hedley II*, Wilson's most tragic play, thus implicates every aspect of the African American tradition with this ritual while creating a void that prompts Sandra Shannon to ponder the apocalyptic implications toward which, by this eighth Wilson play set in the century's eighth decade, the cycle seems to be pointing. In that play, King's death, Soyica Diggs Colbert argues, "revises the worldview expressed throughout the play and clarifies the destructive and productive, psychic and social facets of violence."

The "Lazarus Complex," as Donald Pease has so brilliantly named and explained it, is Wilson's unique understanding of the unrepresentable void that separates a spiritual violence doomed to its own reproduction from the blues that such violence produces. By pointing out that the resurrection of Lazarus is not a miracle of reward but a miraculous punishment, Wilson relegates the story of Lazarus, Pease makes clear, to the realm of vengeance: the act of forcing Lazarus to relive his death. That vengeance replicates itself when men are forced to reenact the killing of their fathers in retribution for the cycle of violence from which their fathers found no escape — a cycle initiated by the involuntary capture, transatlantic transportation, and New World servitude of Africans, all of which began at the moment of Aunt Ester's birth.

Pease's insight places *King Hedley II* in a focal relationship to the entire Wilson cycle, providing the moment when Wilson can release his own cycle from the same complex that has entrapped his characters. The very first murder in the history of the cycle's composition — Booster's killing of the white woman who lied about him (in *Jitney*) — effects the actual death of Booster's mother and the spiritual death of his relationship with his father. And so it goes through the generations of Wilson's plays, as it did through the centuries that compiled the Middle Passage's sunken City of Bones, and through the centuries in which people crossed the ocean under which that city was buried: Troy Maxson, Boy Charles, Crawley, and the ghosts of the Yellow Dog walk in the shadow of Lazarus — not to mention both King Hedleys, Floyd Barton, and that other nominal king, Leroy Slater. Only after King's refusal, in *King Hedley II*, to participate in the cycle of retributive violence can Wilson's plays move past his own drama's restaging of that complex. *King Hedley II* ends therefore not with the death of King but with the rebirth of Aunt Ester, as signified by her cat's meowing and, more important, as demonstrated by her informing presence in Wilson's final two plays, her flesh, as represented in *Gem of the Ocean* and, in *Radio Golf*, her spirit. In both plays, she is thus the anti-Lazarus: the presence, as Pease makes clear, embodied instead by and in the blues community.

That community represents everything productive about pain that excludes dying again — everything that makes it possible for Cory, Raynell, and Gabriel Maxson to become the family that facilitates and witnesses Troy's ascent into Heaven. Nothing demonstrates more extensively the pervasive, intricate, rich role of blues mode and blues history than Steven Tracy's elaborate explanation of how the blues function in *Seven Guitars*. As Tracy's detailed discography (*Appendix*) for the play indicates, the play is a virtual American Bluesography, surrounding, informing, interpreting, and transcending the lives of the seven principals, all of whom, Tracy demonstrates, are figured as blues artists. Like the number seven itself, which Wilson uses "to juxtapose and unify his ideas of sacred and secular, sexuality, death, chance, bad luck, and the vernacular music tradition in the text, regularly relating the number to the African American vernacular tradition to reinforce its centrality to their lives, and to emphasize the struggle of African American existence," the blues figures and the blues tradition, Tracy shows, unify the sexual invitations, double entendres, relationship to spiritual figures, and quest for wealth and power in the play.

Refiguring that quest for wealth and power, the blues community in *Seven Guitars*, Herman Beavers explained, consecrates the liminal space, significantly outdoors, according to Beavers, where "the plays enact, then, the dilemma of characters trying to locate the proper site to perform the act of consecration and trying to determine who should benefit from the act of renewal." In the relation between the two plays, Wilson explores the effects of urban decay, masquerading, ironically, as urban renewal. If several of the essays in this collection locate *King Hedley II* in the shadow of the spirit of Aunt Ester, the maternal figure who unites African and Christian ritual, Beavers makes clear that the violence of paternal bonds operates equally under the specter of Reaganism. If Aunt Ester is the Christ figure whose death portends the apocalypse, in other words, Ronald Reagan is the antichrist of that apocalypse. Despite the cycles of violence, the repeated struggles for consecration, and the tortured and tortuous bonds of paternity that unite *Seven Guitars* and *King Hedley II* as plays of the outdoor urban environment — a space Hedley thought of as his plantation — they are also separated by the radical difference between the 1940s and the 1980s, "particularly in terms of the amount of faith the black community invested in the idea of achieving an equitable community."

The investment of the community, however, is not only an issue of faith but also of capital, as Nathan Grant insightfully explains. The cultural capital that accrues to a blues musician such as Floyd Barton allows him a legacy, but one that his progeny — real, potential, or figurative — cannot capitalize. The tension between art and capital, epitomized by Floyd's and Hedley's riffs on Buddy Bolden's lyrics — glossed extensively by Tracy — also make clear, Grant points out, a concern over the role and meaning of capital, as it affects what African American fathers may leave their progeny.

To some degree, this represents a shift from Wilson's earlier plays. The figures in *Joe Turner* are searching what they have been left in order to find a new start. The dramatic arc of *Ma Rainey*, of *The Piano Lesson*, and of *Fences* relies on Levee, Boy Willie, and Troy each inheriting from his father a warrior spirit that can then be converted into a blues legacy. (Boy Willie's confrontation with Sutter's ghost, we should remember, does not earn him the piano that he views as capital, but rather resurrects the piano as a productive musical instrument.) From *Two Trains* on, however, with growing significance, the capacity — thwarted or realized — for the father to bequeath capital connects the contending forces of the African American communities that Wilson chronicles. Thus, Grant shows that *Gem* and *Radio Golf* "speak across the cycle to issues of capital and its abuses to characters in each play."

By the 1990s, however, the cycle has come full circle, and Harmond, the central character of *Radio Golf*, has indeed inherited a great deal. If the sets of *Seven Guitars* and *King Hedley II* mark the time span from the 1940s to the 1980s by replacing a domicile with an empty lot, the indoor set of *Radio Golf*, an office high above the ground-level or two-story sites of Wilson's other plays, provides an overview in which space is property, and both are capital. Harmond, therefore, because he has a different relationship to capital, occupies, as David LaCroix explains, a radically different relationship to time. If masters owned the slaves' time, then one mark of emancipation should be the ability to control one's own time, but in a world where time can also be construed as money, this is not necessarily the case. If *Radio Golf* seems, therefore, to be a struggle about property rights — the right to demolish Aunt Ester's house, the right to build a specific type of "urban renewal" project, the right to reap the profits from that project — it is pervasively, LaCroix makes clear, about control over time in all its manifestations: as legal and social control, as legacy, as ancestry, as history, as the struggle between finitude and continuity.

LaCroix thus helps explain Wilson's choice of golf to focus the new playing field on which the figurative and literal descendents of Aunt Ester and Caesar Wilks have arrived in Wilson's last play. The sport of vast space and limitless leisure time, golf, Anthony Stewart explains, defines masculinity in terms of cultural capital, such that wealth and power stand in for the "masculine" virtues — speed, strength, aggressiveness — demonstrated in the sports where African American athletes have traditionally been distinguished. (Consider, for example, what Joe Louis represents for the characters in *Seven Guitars*.)

In this light, *Radio Golf* makes it impossible to recognize that the acquisition of capital — of time and money — puts African Americans on a different kind of playing field. If sports, in *Fences*, is just one more mechanism of white discrimination, in the rest of the first nine plays — aside from the radio broadcast of the Louis-Conn match — sports doesn't exist. Stewart shows, however, that in *Radio Golf* there is a new game in town — one that puts competing understandings of loyalty in conflict. Harmond can exchange his capital for loyalty to the African American community, while his partner, Roosevelt, conversely can turn his African American identity into capital for white investors who need a black face to get redevelopment money: "This sense of competing loyalties makes *Radio Golf* so compelling, as the play reflects the ambivalent and, at times, ironic nature of the progress made by African Americans over the century chronicled by Wilson's plays."

Looking at that progress through the lens of the Obama election, Harry Elam, Jr., explains the significance of *Radio Golf* as it culminates not only Wilson's cycle but the era in which August Wilson, the most performed playwright of the 1990s, was the dominant sensibility in American drama. His twenty-first-century play about a well-educated, financially successful black man with unprecedented political opportunity is, Elam demonstrates, both a prelude to what Elam calls the Age of Obama and a retrospective that reminds us of the role that race must continue to play in that age. In the same way that Tracy delineates the extensive allusions to the blues in *Seven Guitars*, Elam traces Wilson's allusions in *Radio Golf* to the other plays in the cycle: "Wilson's willingness to repeat and revise his own dramatic texts foregrounds his awareness of the cycle of history within his history cycle." Based on the history that informs Wilson's cycle and the history internal to it, *Radio Golf* "argues that black identity is not simply biology or the result of prescribed agendas but about active choice, engagement, doing in the moment informed by history." As a result, Harmond, as the culminating person in the cycle and in the history, is connected to the earliest figures by blood, by money, by history, and by spirit. These things, which the cycle has consolidated out of African American history and *Radio Golf* has consolidated out of the cycle, enable Harmond, according to Elam, to determine "a new course of action that is at once cultural, spiritual and political."

The work of this play, then, becomes the work of the cycle: to connect the economic conversion to the spiritual and social conversions that enabled it. To accomplish this, Wilson points relentlessly to the cycle's penultimate play, *Gem*, which is also the cycle's temporal origins. In this way, I point out,

Gem is "an initiation written in retrospect and also a retrospective condensation of the properties of capitalism that produced the unresolved confusion of human rights and property rights, a confusion all too extensively — albeit not exclusively — operating in the interest of racial privilege."

Because the public streets compose the communal thoroughfare, that is, the right to move freely, the streets both in Wilson's retrospective beginning, *Gem*, and the cycle's initial play, *Jitney*, become sites of contested rights and identities. The jitney drivers, who disdain the figurative practice of putting one's business in the street, earn their living by doing that literally, and the characters who pass through Aunt Ester's house all have contested relations with the streets and the rules determining who may pass freely upon them. The arrest warrants in *Gem*, like the law of eminent domain in *Jitney*, threaten to destroy the familial arrangements based not on bloodlines but on communal responsibility.

The question of the requirements of the state — as they on one hand assault the African American community and on the other hand ignore it, as they open new doors to African Americans at the cost of the communal legacy that makes it possible for some African Americans to walk through those doors — consolidates in *Radio Golf* the impetus of Wilson's two beginnings: that of writing the cycle, with *Jitney*; and that of chronicling the century, with *Gem*. If the gap is greater, moreover, between the actions of the characters in *Gem* and those of their progeny in *Radio Golf* than between the generations in *Seven Guitars* and *King Hedley II*, it is not just because the gap traverses a longer time span — the entire cycle — but because it spans the time it takes human beings to change from the potential to *be* capital to the potential to *own* it, and, equally, the time it takes for property to transform its owners.

In some ways this is also the history of August Wilson himself, who, in the last twenty-five years of his life, changed his name and his destiny. But the real history of August Wilson lies not in his biography as a high school dropout, cook, poet, political activist, museum script writer, playwright, contest winner, Pulitzer Prize winner, and resident of Pittsburgh, Minneapolis, and Seattle. The real history of August Wilson lies in the content of the plays, where his pride and endurance, his love of language and music, his passion for respect, and his understanding of how adversity can foster triumph all reconnect with the three hundred years of black experience on this continent, from which that love and passion and pride and understanding were forged. Completing the cycle, Wilson gives that experience historical status in much the same way John Coltrane, in his version of Rodgers and Hammerstein's "My Favorite Things," recalled the superannuated American musical theater to the vitality of its ignored origins in nineteenth-century black performance, while at the same time making something totally new and important out of those repressed origins —making musical history.

The real history of August Wilson, in other words, starts before his birth in 1945; it starts with the historical conditions that surrounded that birth —conditions largely overlooked or marginalized by the American establishment. These conditions were not adequately recorded in formal documents —particularly during the first two hundred years —but recorded instead in the song, the dance, and the story; preserved in the community rather than the museum; revealed in the moments of community action and collaborative improvisation that only recently —because of the contributions of people like August Wilson —find some space in American textbooks or under the spotlights of the "legitimate" theater.

If legitimate history thus belongs to whoever owns the erasers, Wilson's responses to those producers who wanted to aquire *Ma Rainey's Black Bottom* can be seen as a perfect gloss on the difference between the history that Wilson was taught in textbooks and the history he is trying to teach in his plays:

> "As long as the words don't mean anything, why don't you write the contract my way?"
> "We hold these truths to be self-evident, that all men are created equal and endowed by their creator with certain inalienable rights."
> "Give me your tired, your poor, your huddled masses yearning to breathe free."
> "As long as the words don't mean anything, why don't you write the contract my way?"

Gramley Library
Salem Academy and College
Winston-Salem, N.C. 27108

If the state has never answered that question, it remains ever more important to ask it in this Age of Obama, lest we have to restart once again the act of remembering and reconstructing the sorrows produced by the blank spaces in our history. Completing the cycle, therefore, should be viewed not as the culmination of Wilson's enterprise but as its initiation, the beginning of the way drama can call us to the ongoing question of the social contract — ever in tension, flux, and crisis as it collides with its own ideals. Wilson's was a life whose work had just started, even as it was constantly starting over. A person who would never complete anything before he knew how his next work would begin, Wilson was a relentless collector of fresh starts. That was the warrior in him — always fixed simultaneously on the horizon and on the past.

In light of the unavoidably elegiac aspect of this collection, therefore, I want to end this introduction as improbably as Solly Two Kings, in *Gems of the Ocean*, quoting a white American poet's nineteenth-century poem, "Thanatopsis," with my quoting words fashioned by a white Victorian poet, Tennyson, as he tried to voice the relentless aspirations of an aging warrior, Ulysses, part of whose monologue, when we think of August Wilson, is all-too-uncannily apt:

> The lights begin to twinkle from the rocks:
> The long day wanes: the slow moon climbs: the deep
> Moans round with many voices. Come, my friends,
> 'Tis not too late to seek a newer world.
> Push off, and sitting well in order smite
> The sounding furrows; for my purpose holds
> To sail beyond the sunset, and the baths
> Of all the western stars until I die.
> It may be that the gulfs will wash us down:
> It may be we shall touch the Happy Isles,
> And see the great Achilles, whom we knew.
> Tho' much is taken, much abides; and tho'
> We are not now that strength which in old days

Moved earth and heaven; that which we are, we are;
One equal temper of heroic hearts,
Made weak by time and fate, but strong in will
To strive, to seek, to find, and not to yield.

"And that's the way that go."

ALAN NADEL

Beginning Again, Again

Business in the Street in *Jitney* and *Gem of the Ocean*

The foreboding presence of Herald Loomis that haunts *Joe Turner's Come and Gone* is explained, finally, in terms of spiritual, material, and historical deprivation. Loomis has been deprived of his song, his labor, and, most important for my purposes, his start. A start — a beginning — is a temporal marker, quite distinct, as Edward Said has made clear, from an origin (Said, 6), an important distinction in understanding the work of August Wilson, whose opus is steeped in multifarious temporalities. As I have noted elsewhere, for Wilson, it's all about time.[1] It's about time, for example, that Memphis Lee reclaimed his land and that Boy Willie finally owned the land made fertile by the sweat of his ancestors. It's about time Troy Maxson finished his fence and Hambone got his ham and Risa found a man, and that Ma Rainey and Floyd Barton got to their respective Chicago recording studios; it's about time that Ma Rainey signed away her voice and that Levee got his chance to solo. And the difference between Levee's version of the blues and Ma Rainey's version is all about time. The play *Ma Rainey's Black Bottom*, moreover, is about the time when the value of music ceased to be its performance and became instead the record of its performance.[2]

At any given time, since the beginning of recorded time, the record separates a "before" from an "after." Troy Maxson, therefore, is not in the record books as a home-run hitter because, his friend Bono explains, "You just come along too early," to which Troy responds, "There ought not never have been no time called too early" (9).

And this is something Wilson proves when he brings into the second half of his cycle the play *Jitney*, a play he wrote that came along too early. Thus, like Troy Maxson, Wilson with *Jitney* was reconfiguring the before/after relationship that informed his history by giving us the beginning of the cycle before it began. Because there are always two trains of thought running through his plays, however, Wilson also gives us, with *Jitney*, a culmination: the moment when the historical past represented in the cycle meets the present from which that history is recorded. From the moment of *Jitney*'s inclusion in the cycle, all of Wilson's plays will take place roughly in the present day — meaning roughly in a moment contemporaneous to their writing — with the exception of *Gem of the Ocean*, the play that provides the cycle's alternative beginning. Written after the end of the century that it, in Wilson's dramatic world, begins, *Gem of the Ocean*, like *Jitney*, is simultaneously a culmination and an initiation, for the dramatic world of which *Jitney* is the first instance will give birth to Aunt Ester, while the historical trajectory initiated by *Gem of the Ocean* will lead us to the crumbling inner-city neighborhoods of the post-1960s, the world where human dignity must continually reinvent itself in the face of decaying and confiscated property.

Jitney, set in the 1977 jitney taxicab station in the Hill section of Pittsburgh, thus reenacts the antebellum conflict between human rights and property rights. Space here does not allow even a cursory investigation of the multifarious and profound ways in which this conflict is intertwined, in the first half of the nineteenth century, with the Gordian knot of transcontinental nationalism. A few obvious points must, however, be stressed. First, the Union, in order to expand, needed not only to acquire territory but also to convert that territory into states — states that would participate as equal members in the complex system of legal reciprocity that allows the unimpeded flow of commerce and secures the universal sanctity of ownership. This process of reciprocity, which composes the legal concept of comity, becomes dysfunctional when specific states have laws such as those surrounding slavery that directly contradict one another. To resolve this contradiction by invoking the rationale of states' rights requires another contradiction: that the federal government has to enforce those states' rights; that is, that the innate rights of states was dependent on the

supplementary power of the federal government. Under the instrumentalist philosophy of jurisprudence that dominated in the first half of the
nineteenth century, a virtual mandate arose to protect the commercial and
economic interests of the nation, which meant that, as the legal resistance
to slavery rose in the non–slave states, so too did the federal impetus to
protect nationally the states' rights of slaveholding states. So strong, in fact,
was this impetus that the decisions emanating from the strongly proslavery
Supreme Court in the 1850s gave rise to fears in many — including Lincoln
— that a pattern of decisions would lead to the de facto nationalizing of
slavery.

As Kermit Hall succinctly points out, "As long as respect for the property interests of slave owners overshadowed the abhorrence of slavery, or
concern for peaceful relations was greater than repugnance of the 'peculiar
institution,' interstate comity, of course, could have provided a viable solution to the problems created after 1780 by the abolition of slavery in the
North." But as the "property rights" of slaveholders came under increasing
threat from the personal liberty laws of non–slave states, and as the principle of comity became more and more impracticable, interstate commerce
became more and more fragile. That fragility extended, needless to say, to
territories that not only created new sites of contestation but also threatened to alter the legislative balance. Thus national interests merged with
slaveholding interests so long as those interests privileged property rights
over personal liberty, and, even more important, so long as blacks — slave or
free, South or North — remained silent and invisible in defining "national
interests"; that is, in creating and delimiting the nation's public space.

In light of these legal disputes, the act of emancipation, by voiding the
pending slavery-related cases, in effect precluded judicial affirmation of the
primacy of human rights. In other words, emancipation was not a moment
of liberation but a moment in which a formerly enslaved population was set
loose in a world where human rights were usually contingent and property
rights usually absolute. As the legal history of the last century-and-a-half
has shown, property rights continued unabated to distribute and define
liberties — so much so, in fact, that our laws now hold that a corporation
can be treated as a person (Supreme Court, *Santa Clara County v. Southern Pac. r. Co.,* 118 U.S. 394 [1886]), while people have fewer and fewer

safeguards on the public regulation of their private lives.[3] Therefore, to cite one of numerous examples, the massive corruption of subprime lending, as a regrettable trait of the *private* sector, falls outside the purview of prosecutors, while the Patriot Act enables the Department of Justice to scrutinize the sex lives of public figures.

From one perspective, emancipation could be viewed as the action that prevented the nation from grappling with the implications of giving legal primacy to property, because it removed from the docket the most cogent test of property rights: the case of chattel slavery. This was in part what Ralph Ellison meant when he argued that, in the antebellum period, the Negro represented the moral burden placed on the democratic ideals that justified, in Lincoln's succinct phrase, "a new nation conceived in liberty and dedicated to the proposition that all men are created equal." With the end of Reconstruction — what Ellison has called the counterrevolution of 1876 — the moral burden was not lifted; it merely went underground, became invisible.

That invisible world is Wilson's starting point, as it is manifest in every aspect of the jitney station, surrounded by vacant properties and empty lots that represent the lot of people who have descended from property — descended, that is, from a condition in which they constituted the capital that they were not allowed to acquire. Mark Twain summarized this dilemma concisely when Jim, referring to the $800 reward for his capture, says to Huck, "Yes — en I's rich now, come to look at it. I owns myself, en I's wurth eight hund'd dollars. I wisht I had de money, I wouldn' want no mo.'"

The historical conditions of *Jitney* thus become the starting point for Wilson's dramatic cycle examining the conditions of history that produced that start. David Krasner marks *Jitney* as the source of the Wilson dramatic opus, the play that "evolved into the 10-play cycle" (159). As such, the play shares with all the historical dramas that will follow the recognition that history has been full of false starts — the first of which was the start of slavery in the New World, which itself was the false start of capitalism, invested as it was in the primacy of property, the supremacy of the marketplace, the heroicizing of trade.[4]

That start was concurrent with the birth of Aunt Ester, the matriarchal

figure and spiritual leader whose presence informs the locale and sensibility of most of Wilson's plays written after 1992. Although her birth thus
symbolizes the beginning of a specific Anglo-American economic practice,
she was born in a very different place than that of the peculiar institution
to which Wilson connects her birth. Her birthplace, we should remember,
had to be Africa — not America — in that the practice of slavery was the
necessary precondition for turning her from African into African American. Therefore, her African American identity was contingent upon a practice of slavery she did not initiate, but her initiation into slavery marked
the beginnings of her African American identity. Once again, therefore,
Wilson has doubled the beginnings. Aunt Ester marks the beginning of
the peculiar institution that will culminate with the moment in which
Gem of the Ocean will begin the chronology of plays that will dramatize
the twentieth-century aftereffects of that institution.

If Aunt Ester marks the start of the slave trade, let me emphasize again
that her origins, geographically and temporally, were elsewhere. She was a
victim of the transatlantic traffic that subsumed her in an exchange system,
subordinating her freedom and her identity to commercial interests that
antedated her birth — commercial interests that mapped the New World
as claimable property and the residents of the Old World as that property's
managerial class. Thus began a set of special circumstances in which Africa
became a way station in the flow of commercial traffic, never eligible, as
America was, to assume its management. By the same token, as Krasner
points out, Wilson's plays suggest that "to succeed, African Americans . . .
establish specific locations in which they can flourish" (160). This leads
me to two initial points: one being that, in this sense, the jitney station is
Africa, and the second, that Aunt Ester's home at 1839 Wylie is the jitney
station.

Let's start with Aunt Ester's home, as it reconfigures the way station
that is Africa at the start of a century that has rid itself of slavery's issues
but not of its vestiges and implications. One in a line of lost souls — think
of Sterling and Memphis in *Two Trains Running* — Citizen Barlow will
thus visit Aunt Ester's house in order to get his start. But to go forward,
Barlow will have to go back. Like Loomis and all of the Wilson charac-

ters who have had their song stolen, he will have to go back because if he does not find his start in the past, he is likely to confuse it with his finish. For this reason, Barlow, using a boat made out of Aunt Ester's bill of sale, will travel again the Middle Passage, this time not as a superficial crossing of the sort registered in a shipping corporation's commercial log, but one that takes him under the surface to the sunken City of Bones in a manner that confronts the slave trade by invoking the combination of African and Christian traditions and rituals that characterized the postbellum African American church. "For Barlow," Harry Elam explains, "going to the City of Bones is a ritual act of cleansing in which the spiritual, the political and the historical all combine" (*Gem* 84).

In this way, *Gem of the Ocean* is our initiation into the forces that produced the world from which Wilson initiated his historical cycle. But, notably, *Gem of the Ocean* is an initiation written in retrospect and also a retrospective condensation of the properties of capitalism that produced the unresolved confusion of human rights and property rights, a confusion all too extensively — albeit not exclusively — operating in the interest of racial privilege. That condensation starts with the Middle Passage, the re-experiencing of which becomes essential to Barlow's initiation rites. In this construction, *Gem of the Ocean* is positioned not as the initial play of the cycle but as the culmination of a journey that must be compulsively reinitiated. Since Barlow's departure point is the New World, however, he does not so much repeat as retrace the Middle Passage. He takes it backwards, in other words, so that he may *take it back* in both senses of the phrase: to retract it, and also to use it to find his path back to the present moment — the present place of departure for him, for the twentieth century, and for the Wilson cycle.

The scene of death by drowning, which the City of Bones memorializes, also returns us to the start of *Gem of the Ocean* in that the play begins when Citizen Barlow attempts to see Aunt Ester so he can expiate his guilt over causing the death of Garret Brown. Brown had jumped into the river because he was falsely accused of stealing a bucket of nails actually stolen by Barlow. Rather than be punished for a crime he did not commit, Brown chose to stay in the water until he drowned. Brown did this, as Aunt Ester explains to Barlow, because, he had said, "I'd rather die in truth than to live a lie. That way he can say that his life is worth more than a bucket of nails" (45). Aunt Ester thus sees Brown's decision as replicating the Middle Passage's disruption of the slave trade's economic logic. Brown was, in effect, refusing to allow his body to enter into an exchange system that could equate it with property.

This is the exchange system that Caesar advocates in the play, when, as constable, he justifies shooting a boy for stealing a loaf of bread: "He was a thief! He was stealing. That's about the worst thing you can do. To steal the fruits of somebody else's labor" (36). A quintessential capitalist, Caesar describes at length the legal and semilegal ways he accumulated capital, clearly differentiating stealing from conning or swindling. Thus, the fact that he never stole anything in his life justifies his killing a man for stealing bread; at the same time Caesar sees his own overcharging for bread as a public virtue:

> Yeah, I sell magic bread. Got a big sign that say you only have to eat twice as much to get twice as full. And I charge one and a half times as much for it. You don't understand I give the people hope when they ain't got nothing else. They take that loaf of bread and make it last twice as long. They wouldn't do that if they didn't pay one and a half times for it. *I'm helping the people.* (36; emphasis added)

In making this distinction, Caesar seems to be refuting directly the Marxist doctrine that property is theft by turning Christ's miracle of the loaves into a capitalist parable, wherein not the bread but the profit from selling it is the magic multiplication Caesar's enterprise produces. This perverted miracle perpetrated against black people turns the miracle of capitalism into a black magic and Caesar into a form of antichrist, one who insists that the law is everything.

Figured this way, we can say that Caesar represents the state; that is, the law that makes Barlow free — that allows him to be a citizen. But as a constable, Caesar also rules the street, the public thoroughfare, the means and ways of traffic and transaction, the social and economic space where Citizen Barlow is citizen in name only. As Barlow explains, when he left

Alabama only four weeks earlier, "They had all the roads closed to the colored people. I had to sneak out." These roads, closed at the beginning and at the end of the play, make the free black no longer the property of a specific master, but the universal property of the state.[5]

Instead of bestowing the freedom to travel, the public roads convert the stamp of blackness into currency in the same way that the official mark of the state has, since the inception of empire, converted first ore — silver — and then promissory notes — silver certificates — into money. On the coin of the realm, the face of Caesar is always and everywhere the inscription of the state on the entire state of economic affairs; the face of Caesar makes wealth real and reduces the material on which that face is imprinted to a substance used to bear the Emperor's sign. The value of thirty pieces of silver is thirty pictures of Caesar. The face of Caesar is the foundation of capital in that it performs the miracle of converting not water into wine but matter into money; that is, Ceasar's image makes the pieces a medium of standard exchange. In this way, Caesar is to money what blackness under slavery was to human beings: the sign of commodification. It is important to remember that unlike slavery in antiquity, slavery in America was a racialized condition valorized by genetics, even as the visible signs of the gene pool diminished. A fair-skinned "Negro," therefore, could circulate under slave law the way a well-circulated coin, from which Caesar's image had all but faded, could still pass as legal tender by allusion to the conditions under which it was minted. Thus the features of a face, the tints of a complexion — even when diminished to hints — bear the signs not of race but of history, of the historically specific circumstances that commodified human subjugation in accordance with specific commercial practices and legal standards. Slavery, like money, functioned on the basis that specific markings certified the stamp of history as the apparatus of the state.

That is why the Caesar of *Gem of the Ocean* ironically misunderstands the nature of money when he says, "Money ain't got nobody's name on it" (33). In the system that has made Caesar wealthy and powerful, currency with nobody's name on it is worthless. In other words, all money has Caesar's name on it, in that it is tender of the realm. Money that has no name on it is shit, or, as Solly Two Kings calls the dog shit he collects to sell to tanners, "pure." Invoking a water metaphor, Caesar explains to Solly his belief about money: "It's floating out there go on and grab you some." Named after Old Testament kings David and Solomon, who were never subjects of the Roman Empire, Solly shuns the legal tender that, unlike his "pure," bears the brand of the state: the figurative image of Caesar.

Similarly, Solly will later reject that which is "floating out there" so he can attend instead to that which is sinking. Noting the failure of emancipation to deliver what it promised, he describes the current state of affairs: "They wave the law on one end and hit you with a billy club with the other. I told myself I can't just sit around and collect dog shit while the people drowning. The people drowning in sorrow and grief. That's a mighty big ocean. They got a law tied to one toe. Every time they try and swim, the law pull them under." The law, in Solly's view, has thus replaced the Middle Passage in populating the City of Bones. The same rule of law that manufactures legal tender, that legally tendered in human cargo, and that legally emancipated the slaves, is thus connected to the force of law that drowned Garret Brown. And ultimately the refusal to serve two kings, to render unto Caesar what Caesar claims as his, will cost Solly Two Kings his life.

Just as Solly must grapple with his names, whatever the consequences, Citizen Barlow must grapple with his. As Solly points out to him early in the play, "It's hard to be a citizen. You gonna have to fight to get that. And time you get it you be surprised how heavy it is" (27). The site of citizenship like the site of commerce is the street, and *Gem of the Ocean*, set one year after W. E. B. Du Bois proclaimed the informing problem of the twentieth century to be the color line, can be seen as initiating one aspect of what Sandra Adell (*Double Consciousness*) has defined as the double bind of double consciousness; in this case manifest in the conflict between the state and the street.

This conflict thus connects Wilson's two beginnings, because both of the sites of *Gem of the Ocean* and of *Jitney* — havens sheltering families formed by mutual affiliation rather than bloodlines — feel the encroachment of the state, manifest in *Gem of the Ocean* as a set of arrest warrants and in *Jitney* as eminent domain. These two issues converge in the play that serves both as the cycle's end and as Wilson's last play, *Radio Golf.* At the same time, both *Gem of the Ocean* and *Jitney* are about taking one's business into the streets.

At the outset of *Gem of the Ocean*, Barlow is living on the streets just as Solly is making his living from what he picks up off of the streets. The black workers, moreover, have taken *to* the streets. Because of Brown's drowning, "they was," Caesar states, "all over at the mill rioting." As Caesar sees it, this putting their business in the streets, which threatens to close the mill, will end up putting hundreds of black people on the streets — as loiterers, prostitutes, and disturbers of the peace. In that all of these activities are criminal, Caesar regards the streets for black people as pathways to jail.

But despite all of Caesar's attempts to enforce the law, the street and the state govern by different rules, and it is in that space of difference that the emancipated but not yet free black person must, in Wilson's world, negotiate the means for liberation. That is why Citizen Barlow must repeatedly take his business into the street. That is why his admission to the City of Bones must be the two shiny new pennies he finds on the street, not with the face of Caesar but of Lincoln, the newly minted shiny man; not the color of silver but of copper, a new coin with the datemark of the new century.[6] These new coins connect the Middle Passage to every place the street will lead: to the Great Migration, to Marcus Garvey, to the civil rights movement, and to the black power movement.

In this initial moment of the twentieth century, Wilson thus uses the Middle Passage to juxtapose Aunt Ester's initiation into slavery with Barlow's into citizenship, that is, into the century that would equate freedom with free markets, into the entrepreneurial system that brought Aunt Ester to America as property and will bring Aunt Ester's property values to the present conditions of urban decay and urban renewal that inform *Jitney*, *King Hedley II*, and *Radio Golf.* Thus, urban renewal becomes one more restaging of the search for a new start effected by the conflict between property rights and human rights, between money and history: the conflict of serving two kings.

As this was the problem from the beginning of Christianity and from the beginning of slavery, it is also the problem we find at the beginning of

Wilson's dramatic enterprise, where the jitney station is situated between the laws of the state — which license legitimate taxis, control property through eminent domain, and prosecute murders — and the rules of the street, which are always contingent and negotiable — the product of what Michel de Certeau has called the practices of everyday life. Thus the jitney station is the unauthorized car service, controlled by "Becker's Rules" that dominate the station, the set, and, even in their violation, the tenuous world of the jitney drivers. This is a world where the law has little say, because in the 1970s the case is still that, as Wining Boy said in the 1930s, the difference between a black man and a white man is that "the colored man can't fix nothing with the law" (*The Piano Lesson* 38).

Instead the black men in *Jitney* must fix things with one another through a series of negotiations, codes, and deals — none backed by the heft of legal sanction or the threat of police enforcement. Thus, if the set, with "Becker's Rules" written prominently on the wall, suggests a rigid world, the actions of the play make clear from the outset that we are in a world based not on rules but on deals. The play begins, in fact, with Youngblood and Turnbo arguing over the rules of checkers: "How you gonna jump him with the man sitting there!" (11). Youngblood says to Turnbo, "I got a man sitting there! Is you blind?" to which Turnbo responds, "Then put him where he belongs" (12). This is the first of Turnbo's many attempts in the play to put men where they belong, but the game disbands when Youngblood subsequently accuses Turnbo of cheating. Because rules, unlike laws, require mutual consent, and because the space of consent is also the space of negotiation, everyone in the station is trying to interpret the rules so as to cut some sort of deal for himself.

The "deal" thus not only defines the station's purpose — to facilitate an agreement struck between a driver and a caller — but delimits all activities that intersect there. Part of Turnbo's deal with a customer, for instance — another way he puts people in their place — is that, as he constantly stipulates, he won't wait; Youngblood, similarly, won't haul things he thinks will sully his car. The drivers make deals with one another over who will take the next call or under what circumstances they will accept the ride. Turnbo even argues with Youngblood about whether or not they had a deal about coffee. "If you're going next door," Turbo says, "bring me back a cup of coffee," to which Youngblood responds, "I ain't your slave" (23). When Youngblood nevertheless returns with the coffee, Turnbo refuses to pay him for it, fomenting a vicious argument about whether Turnbo and Youngblood had, in effect, entered into a deal. The argument evokes Caesar's concern, in *Gem*, over the need for limiting black freedom — "It's Abraham Lincoln's fault," Caesar asserts, "He ain't had no idea what he was doing" (34) — in that Youngblood and Turnbo are arguing about the conditions under which Youngblood is or is not a slave.

The alcoholic driver, Fielding, similarly, must negotiate the way he is or is not a slave to the bottle. Thus he leaves the station to drink, and on his return argues with Becker about whether he has broken the "no drinking" rule and, further, if he has, whether that allows Becker to return his dues and break his agreement with the jitney station. Like so many in the Wilson canon, Fielding is not interested in getting his money back; he is interested in having his contract honored, because his status as equal party to a contract distinguishes him *from* property, making his humanity a fact of law. "This is a free country!" he shouts, "I'm a free man! You can't tell me what to do! This is the United States of America!" (50), asserting both his right to be a jitney driver and to drink. By evoking the name of the nation, Fielding is, like Citizen Barlow, making his business in the street an issue of the state — converting a rite of passage into the rights of citizenship.

Similarly Shealy, the numbers runner, may take numbers at the jitney station and get messages there, but, by Becker's rules, may not use the station to operate his business. This situation puts him in constant negotiation with Becker, even while Becker is placing a bet with him. Shealy's entire enterprise exemplifies the tenuous world of contingent rules, in that his business is based on verbal exchanges and relationships of implicit trust for which there are no legal recourses. The irony of Shealy's double bind, therefore, is that while one of his rules is that "I don't be putting nobody's business in the street" (15) — his own business, like those of the jitney drivers, is always in the street, because that is the place where they can — where they have to — make their living and deal with their lives.

Because putting business in the street turns private life into public property, however, it is also the process whereby the street acquires proprietary rights over individuals. This is why Turnbo puts others down for putting their business in the street, and, at the same time, it is why others accuse Turnbo of putting *their* business in the street. When Turnbo spreads the word that Youngblood is carrying on with his wife Rena's sister, Turnbo justifies his gossip on the grounds that Youngblood, by driving around in public with Rena's sister, had turned his life into public property. The conflict, restaging the earlier conflict between Youngblood and Turnbo over the coffee, pivots on the circumstances under which Youngblood's life is legitimately Turnbo's property. The business in the street, in other words, is the business of slavery.

Cigar Annie, the evicted woman standing in the middle of the street cussing out everybody from God to the gas man, although never actually seen in the play, serves to consolidate the confusion of property rights and human rights that business in the street produces. With "her furniture and everything sitting out on the sidewalk" (22), she is indistinguishable from her own property—a point she emphasizes by repeatedly raising up her dress, because, as Doub says, "that's all anybody ever wanted from her since she was twelve years old. She say if that's all you want . . . here it is" (22). By disowning the commercial rights to her own body—"here it is"—she not only replicates the landlord who is putting her personal property on the street but also the slave auction that, too, rendered a slave's body a property that she had no business controlling. But in her double bind, Annie's control of her body comes not from ownership but from using the street to stage its disowning, so as to restage the business in the street as a slave market. Annie has thus replaced the commercial laws of the slave trade with a personal deal that violates the conventional rules.

In light of Annie's double bind, Becker's "rules" can be viewed as an attempt to impose order where the law has failed. But if Becker runs the station—and his life—according to Becker's rules, those rules have not produced for him the deal he had hoped to get: "You look up one day and all you got is what you ain't spent. Every day cost you something and you don't all the time realize it" (36). A man who has for twenty years tried to manage rules for the business in the street not surprisingly figures his life in economic terms, a perspective affirmed, after his death, by his son: "He ain't got out of life what he put in it" (96).

The point I am making is that the street, in *Jitney*, comprises a private social and material economy authorized by the community, not the state. It is the composite of negotiation, rumor, and myth, where people construct the alternative history that Wilson will subsequently narrate back to the start of the twentieth century when he sends Citizen Barlow out into the street, in defiance of Caesar's authority. That is why the *fear* of putting business in the street and the *necessity* of doing so are inextricably linked in *Jitney*. If the street is the antithesis of the private property and private lives that the characters crave, it is also the lifeline that allows them to pursue their dreams.

In pursuit of his dreams, Shealy, our quintessential agent of the street, has also made an elaborate deal with himself regarding women. After he was dropped by Rosie, a prior (albeit brief) love, he said to himself, "I was gonna find me another woman. But every time I get hold to one . . . time I lay down with them . . . I see Rosie's face. I told myself the first time I lay down with a woman and don't see her face, then that be the one I'm gonna marry." Although this has never occurred —"with that little yellow gal works down at Pope's I seen Rosie's face . . . but it was blurry" — and despite the fact that this has encouraged Shealy, the new "yellow gal" will not respond to Shealy's calls. Shealy's blurry face deal thus becomes a comic exaggeration of the ostensibly one-sided, unenforceable deal Becker had made with someone *he* loved. Becker had invested everything in Booster, his gifted, talented son, who broke the deal while in college years earlier, when, as Becker sees it, he threw his life away dating a rich white girl. As Turnbo tells it:

> One day see her father was up here in the neighborhood, looking for one of them whores. He find one and she tell him to drive up the dead-end street there by the school, so she can turn the trick in the car. Don't you know they pulled right up in back of this gal's car where her and Booster done went to fool around! Her father recognizes the car and he goes over and looks inside and there's Booster just banging the hell out of his daughter! Well that cracker went crazy. (41)

All of the power relations that inform the business of the street in 1957 consolidate around what it means for the rich white father, as opposed to, for example, Cigar Annie, to "go crazy" in the street. Whereas the disempowered Cigar Annie, figuratively, and perhaps literally, the whore whose business twenty years earlier had brought the father to that alley, can only be regarded as mad — meaning insane — when she puts her business in the street by breaking the rules, the father's unruly behavior is *mad* — meaning manifesting the full force of appropriate anger — because, like Caesar, he can bring the law of the state down on the business in the street so that the police, accepting the girl's story that Booster had kidnapped and raped her, arrest Booster. On his first day out on bail Booster kills the girl, because, exactly like the drowned Garret Brown in *Gem of the Ocean*, Booster refuses to live a lie. And the lie — the big lie — rejected by the numerous warriors in Wilson's cycle, is ultimately the lie that one can be conflated with property.

This is the lie that Citizen Barlow must dedicate his life to fighting if he is to earn his name. Thus, Wilson's penultimate play takes us back to the paradox with which he started, nearly twenty years earlier, in *Jitney*. Barlow's reenactment of the Middle Passage that allows him to commune in the City of Bones with the spirit of his ancestors enables him to proclaim himself the heir not only of those who survived the Middle Passage — and thereby made slave traffic profitable — but also of those whose lives were thrown away, those whose deaths denied the property rights of the slave traders and the profitability of their trade. This is one of the great ironies, I want to conclude by suggesting, with which Wilson's history struggles: that the business in the street serves repeatedly, and often tragically, to remind us that it was the warrior — who fought on in the face of the impossible, who survived the Middle Passage and the ordeals of slavery — that made the slave system work, that made it profitable. If everyone had died in transit, the slave traffic would have died with them, but some impossibly endured and, in ways small and large, even triumphed, ever confirming the high value of human property, the great value that slavery brought to American history.

Notes

1. See Nadel, "*Ma Rainey's*," 102–112.

2. See Shannon, "The Ground on Which I Stand."

3. One particularly ironic aspect of this legal trend is that the basis for treating a corporation, i.e., property, as a person is the Fourteenth Amendment, which was designed to differentiate people from property. As David Korten points out: "The doctrine of corporate personhood creates an interesting legal contradiction. The corporation is owned by its shareholders and is therefore their property. If it is also a legal person, then it is a person owned by others and thus exists in a condition of slavery—a status explicitly forbidden by the Thirteenth Amendment to the Constitution. So is a corporation a person illegally held in servitude by its shareholders? Or is it a person who enjoys the rights of personhood that take precedence over the presumed ownership rights of its shareholders? So far as I have been able to determine, this contradiction has not been directly addressed by the courts" (186).

4. See Eric Williams, *Capitalism and Slavery*.

5. In chapter 1 of *Invisible Criticism*, I discuss the implications of the postbellum shift of surveillance and discipline of African Americans from the personal master to the impersonal state.

6. In actuality, the Lincoln penny was not minted until 1909, five years after the events of *Gem*. Nevertheless it seems to me fruitful to read this as a Lincoln penny, making the reference to the penny one of Wilson's anachronisms, akin to his having the characters in *Seven Guitars* listen to the Joe Louis-Billy Conn fight, although neither of the two Louis-Conn fights took place in 1948.

DANA A. WILLIAMS

Contesting Black Male Responsibilities in August Wilson's *Jitney*

According to August Wilson, the function of black theater, not unlike that of white theater, is "to create art that responds to or illuminates the human condition" (Shannon and Williams, 191). American theater in general, he argues, has the power to hold the mirror up to truths it has "wrestle[d] from uncertain and sometimes unyielding realities" (Wilson, *Ground* 53). If each of the plays in Wilson's ten-play cycle meets this function and exhibits this power perpetually, of signal importance in each play is the construction and reconstruction of black male identities. While a number of critics have interrogated the comparative lack of women who take center stage in his plays,[1] few critics have investigated the sociocultural implications of Wilson's pointed choice to write male-dominated, male-centered plays. A notable exception in this regard is Keith Clark, who, in *Black Manhood in James Baldwin, Ernest J. Gaines, and August Wilson*, examines Wilson's reconfiguration of the black male dramatic subject, hinting at the sociocultural implications of that reconfiguration. Examining how Wilson "dissects the codes of conduct that govern blacks' relationship to each other," Clark emphasizes Wilson's "black men's excruciating attempt to gather together in the name of individual and collective affirmation" (99): "In situating a panoply of black male voices in central roles, Wilson envelopes his plays with multiple perspectives to convey the multifaceted nature of post 1960s black male dramatic subjectivity, a discursive figuration far more complex than a simple replication of Anglo-American patriarchal subjectivity" (101). *Jitney*, originally drafted long before Wilson conceived of the cycle, typifies, even at that stage in his career, Wilson's use of multiple and varied perspectives on black male identity. In this essay, I examine the way these perspectives contest seemingly stable notions of black male responsibility by complicating black male dramatic subjectivity.

Though it did not have its Broadway premiere until April 2000, *Jitney* is actually one of Wilson's earliest plays. Prior to *Jitney* he had tried his hand at poetry, and at least two of his plays were staged: *The Homecoming*, which was staged for Kuntu Repertory Theater in Pittsburgh in 1976, and *Black Bart and the Sacred Hills*, which was given a staged reading at Los Angeles's Inner City Theater in 1978 and then produced as *Black Bart* at Penumbra Theater in St. Paul, Minnesota, in 1980. But *Jitney*, first produced in 1982 at Pittsburgh's Allegheny Repertory Theatre, marked Wilson's declaration of himself as "a playwright" (Savran, 291). Inspired by his experience of Pittsburgh's actual jitney services, the play presents one jitney station in particular, run by Jim Becker and operated by four other drivers: Youngblood, a young Vietnam War veteran; Turnbo, a nosy instigator; Fielding, a former tailor whose life is now more defined by his dependency on alcohol than on anything else; and Doub, a level-headed Korean War veteran. Becker, the "boss" of the station, is a former mill worker who is well respected in his community by blacks and whites alike. (He is able to get the white foreman at the mill to hire new black workers on his recommendation alone.) Although other men frequent the station, as does the play's only on-stage female character, Rena, it is these four drivers (Doub, Turnbo, Fielding, and Youngblood), Becker, Booster (Becker's son), and the discourses these male characters raise that render the play such fertile ground for a meaningful discussion about black manhood and responsibility.

In response to the varied critiques of his focus on male characters, Wilson contends that he writes about black men because he is a black man, and it is the view from which he perceives the world (Shannon, *Dramatic* 222). In *Jitney*, he tells Sandra Shannon, he "simply wanted to show how the station worked, how these guys created jobs for themselves and how it was organized. . . . [H]ow these guys could be responsible" (56). David Krasner picks up on this theme, arguing that "the play's main ethical theme is responsibility" (159). Whether one agrees with his interpretation or not,

Krasner's repeated invocations of black male responsibility in the essay engage highly charged and often-problematic contemporary conversations on the same topic.

According to Krasner, Rena and Youngblood must "learn the importance of responsibility" (162); "The play . . . highlights characters possessing a sense of responsibility" (163); "Despite Turnbo's meddling, an important point about responsibility is made in criticizing young men for their lack of commitment not only to spouses but also to the community"; and *Jitney* "is meant to teach us that community and social responsibility must take precedence over selfishness" (167). That the black male (and the issue of responsibility as it relates to his success or failure) has been the subject of much "study" as of late is perhaps an understatement.[2] We can even include under this rubric Barack Obama's 2008 Father's Day speech at Apostolic Church of God in Chicago.

Reactions to Obama's speech, which focused on black male responsibility as it relates to fatherhood, were mixed at best. While people apt to argue that the absence of black male responsibility is the chief impediment to black male progress tended to approve of the speech, more progressive listeners were less enthusiastic. They argued that the speech and others like it diminish the sociopolitical and economic realities that limit or obstruct black male progress. These reactions suggest that conversations about black male responsibility must be as complicated as the issue itself. In its representation of black male identity as complex, varied, and understood through layered perspectives, *Jitney* adds an important dimension to the commentary on this aspect of black life and culture.

Wilson's revision of *Jitney* over the years reveals the centrality of that issue. As Joan Herrington notes in "Jitney," Wilson "barely touched" (113) the play's structure when he began to rewrite it. Adding only one scene, he focused instead on "the creation of much richer portraits of his characters . . . by illuminating the details of their lives and increasing the complexity of their relationships with one another" (114). The later versions of the play also reveal the effectiveness of the method of rewriting Wilson developed while working on the Goodman Theatre production of *Seven Guitars*. During that production, he discovered that he could rewrite a play during rehearsals with the same — if not more — effectiveness than if he rewrote scenes and lines in isolation. Rather than rewrite *Jitney* from its latest draft, before rehearsals began, Wilson rewrote the play during rehearsals "in close collaboration with the director, and inspired by the art, life, and response of the actors" (113).

For years, Wilson worked almost exclusively with Lloyd Richards as the director of his major productions. When Richards was hospitalized as the Chicago production of *Seven Guitars* began, Walter Dallas stepped in to direct the play. Unlike Richards, who directed whatever Wilson wrote without much interrogation, Dallas was fully engaged in the rewriting process, and he allowed the actors to pose questions to Wilson and to make suggestions for changes in the script. Perhaps Richards and Wilson had worked together so long that they trusted each other enough not to question one another's choice, or perhaps Richards believed that the play is the playwright's, and the director's job is simply to interpret and direct. Whatever the case, the change in directors from Richards to Dallas (and then to Marion McClinton when Dallas was not available to direct the Pittsburgh production of *Seven Guitars*) generated a spirit of collaboration that served Wilson well. Like Dallas, McClinton worked extensively with Wilson during rehearsals to make changes to the script. An actor himself, McClinton, who had played Fielding in *Jitney*'s 1985 production, also encouraged input from the actors. This method of collaboration facilitated Wilson's desire to create richer portraits of his characters, and this enrichment, in turn, enhanced his ability to dramatize certain aspects of black male life.

Herrington notes, "As [Wilson] rewrote *Jitney* in the rehearsal room, his contact with the actors encouraged and significantly influenced his writing of the stories they told" ("Jitney" 120). Insisting that each character be portrayed as fully as possible, the actors encouraged Wilson to add small details to their characters' stories. When Wilson gave Doub the phrase "just like I tell my boys" and included the word "railroad" in front of "pension," Doub became both a father and a railroad man. "That made him somebody," Wilson explained. "That little thing made Doub somebody. The railroad, the army, has two kids. The character prior to Pittsburgh didn't have that, he was just a guy" (Herrington, "Jitney" 120). Wilson's interest in making Doub "somebody" speaks to his commitment to creating characters that transcend stereotypes, providing a sense of authenticity that helps the audience *sense* what is important rather than *hear* what is important. Herrington argues that Wilson's reliance on characters rather than plot to develop his story line highlights his maturity as a playwright and his confidence in sophisticated dialogue.

The commitment to representing the complexity of his dramatic situation inevitably increased the structural challenges that plagued *Jitney*. At least some of these challenges can be attributed to the fact that it was one of Wilson's earliest plays and that he wrote it in ten days. He tells Herrington: "When I started *Jitney* I didn't know you weren't supposed to write it in ten days. I just sat down and wrote it and didn't make a big thing about it. When I go to it now I go to it as a skilled craftsman" (Herrington, "Jitney" 130). As the "skilled craftsman," Wilson was confident enough in his abilities as a playwright that by the time *Jitney* premiered in its final form, he had become equally confident in his own aesthetic. Accordingly, he had few qualms about focusing on character and dialogue development rather than on unity to enhance the play's credibility, despite critics' frequent critique of his plays as structurally flawed in the sense that they seem disinterested in being traditional, "well-made" plays. As Clark notes, "Wilson's multiple dramatic discourses . . . are rooted in black men's retrieval and voicing of personal histories, which inform the plays' thematic and formal configurations. Hence, personal story takes precedence over the erection of a seamlessly crafted dramatic story" (97). And even as his characters and their stories are dramatic fictions, they are often truer to life than stories of real people when those stories are presented in the abstract or packaged in the form of archetypes and/or stereotypes.

The diversity of the male characters in *Jitney* thus allows Wilson to reject all variations of the "fiction of archetypal masculinity" (Clark, 100). Throughout the play, Wilson reveals the inauthenticity of this fiction and has his characters reject it both because of and independent of the "virulently hostile hegemonic culture" (100) that precludes conformity to idealized archetypes. Rather than employ an archetypal hero, *Jitney* allows multiple characters and their stories to compete. This allows Wilson to present layered and varied facets of black male identity and to interrogate the experiences that have shaped his characters' identity formation rather than to present their experiences out of context or in isolation.

Becker and Booster's father/son relationship and the experiences that inform it offer the most fertile ground for analysis in this regard. From the moment Becker enters the stage, Wilson indicates that Becker is responsible. Shealy says to him: "Say Becker, I been meaning to ask you. I got a nephew that's trying to make something of himself. You reckon you be able to get him on down at the mill?" (Wilson, *Jitney* 21). While Becker cannot guarantee anything, if the mill is hiring, he knows some people who "will be able to take care of [Shealy's nephew]" (21). For young men trying to "make something" of themselves, Becker seems to be the man to go to. Becker is equally responsible to his wife and shows no interest in Turnbo's attempts to get him to look at a woman in a *Playboy* magazine. When Turnbo and Youngblood argue over Turnbo's unwillingness to pay Youngblood for the coffee he bought at Turnbo's request, Becker squashes the argument, and later, when Turnbo actually pulls a gun on Youngblood, Becker settles that skirmish, too.

But Becker's quiet, responsibly lived life is more complicated than it seems. Eventually we learn that Becker's son, Booster, is being released from prison. Until Booster was imprisoned for murder, he had been Becker's pride and joy. A star science student on scholarship at the University of Pittsburgh, Booster was doing well until a white girl he was dating falsely accused him of rape when her father caught her with Booster. When the father reacted aggressively, Booster, not knowing that the man was her father, beat the man nearly to death. The same day Booster was released on bail, which Becker had posted, Booster killed the girl. Youngblood, hearing this story, responds, "Served the bitch right! . . . Served her right for lying!" (41–42). Unlike Turnbo and Becker, who see Booster's actions as hasty and unequivocally irresponsible, Youngblood and Booster, two of the youngest men in the play, seem to believe that Booster acted appropriately. Although Booster believes that he deserved to be punished, he preferred the consequences of his actions over being known for a rape he did not commit.

Wilson is careful not to privilege one perspective over another. Because

Becker believes that they could have fought the rape charges, he chastises Booster for not allowing the justice system to run its course: "We could have fought the lie. I had already lined up a lawyer . . . together we could have fought a lie" (55). Booster, who knows how unlikely it is that a jury would have believed him over a white girl or would set him free after he had beaten up a white man, defends himself by saying that a lawyer would not have made a difference: "I wasn't going the penitentiary for nothing. I wasn't gonna live a lie" (56). When Becker claims that two wrongs don't make a right, Booster retorts, "Sometime they do. Sometime you got to add it up that way. Otherwise it's just one wrong after another and you never get to what's right. I wasn't gonna hang no sign around my neck say 'rapist'" (56). Not coincidentally, Booster's rationale sounds a lot like Becker's concession to Doub that some things can't be understood: "After Coreen died I told myself I wasn't gonna ask no more questions. Cause the answers didn't matter. . . . I thought that would change but it never did. . . . I'm tired of waiting for God to decide whether he want to hold my hand" (36). Although both Beckers have given up on things being the way they ought to be, the elder Becker cannot understand Booster's recklessness, especially after that recklessness destroyed the dreams he had for Booster's life and after that recklessness killed Coreen, Becker's wife and Booster's mother, who decided to quit living after Booster was sentenced to death.

Wilson is careful to provide a context for both men's versions of their own reality. Booster claims that he grew up thinking that his father was "a big man" and wanting to be a "big man" too. Booster confesses to his father: "Everywhere you went people treated you like a big man. You used to take me to the barbershop with you. You'd walk in there and fill up the whole place. Everybody would stop cussing cause Jim Becker had walked in. . . . I wanted to be like that" (56). Booster's childhood vision of his father was shattered, however, when he overheard their landlord, Mr. Rand, yell that he should put Becker and his family out on the street "where they belong." In shaping the perception of Becker as ultra responsible, Wilson makes it clear that the family was unable to pay the rent because Becker had to help pay for the funeral of Grandma Ada. Booster, however, had expected Becker to demand that Mr. Rand get off of the family's porch.

When Becker, instead, "just looked at [Rand] and promised [he] would have the money next month" (57), Booster, no longer seeing his father as big, swore to himself that if he ever got big, he wouldn't let anyone make him small. To Booster, being responsible means being big at all times and at all costs. As he explains to Becker, killing the girl was answering to a sense of responsibility: "I thought about you standing there and getting small and Mr. Rand shouting and Susan McKnight shouting out that lie and I realized it was my chance to make the Beckers big again. . . . I thought you would understand. I thought you would be proud of me" (57).

Becker, however, rejects Booster's belief that a man should be big when being big threatens responsible action. Becker rejoins:

> you want to come in here and ridicule me cause I didn't knock Mr. Rand on his ass. You wanna know why? I'll tell you why. Because I had your black ass crying to be fed. Crying to have a roof over your head. To have clothes to wear to school and lunch money in your pocket. That's why! Because I had a family. I had responsibility. . . . I swallowed my pride and let them mess over me, all the time saying, "You bastards got it coming. Look out! Becker's boy's coming to straighten this shit out! . . . Becker's taking this ass whipping so his boy can stride through this shit like Daniel in the lion's den! . . . And what I get, huh?" (58–59)

Wilson presents both men as having equal justification for their actions. When Becker accuses Booster of killing his mother since she refuses to eat, talk, or move once she hears his death sentence (which is later reduced), Booster claims that it wasn't her refusal to live long enough to see him die that kills her. Rather, as Booster sees it, she shuts down because Becker, "clinging to [his] rules," turns his back on her (60). In short, their relationship is far too complex to be simplified into dichotomies of right and wrong.

Wilson refuses to choose sides or to resolve the tension between the men even at the play's end. Becker dies in a freak accident at the mill, after having worked there for years without incident. And while Wilson admits that he took the easy way out in resolving *Jitney* by having Becker die at the end (Shannon, *Dramatic* 63), he nevertheless was willing to forego the well-made, unified play for the sake of honoring his dramatic situation's complexity. Notably, however, Wilson does not have Becker die before his evolution begins. As Herrington notes, as *Jitney*'s drafts evolve, so does Becker's willingness to stop clinging to the rules for their own sake. Eventually, he "adopts some of Booster's defiance as his own" ("Jitney" 127). Only after he disowns Booster, however, does Becker become rebellious. Having resolved to fight against the station's being boarded up, he tells the drivers, "When I first come along I tried to do everything right. I figured that was the best thing to do. Even when it didn't look like they was playing fair I told myself they would come around. Time it look like you got a little something going for you they change the rules" (Wilson, *Jitney* 85). He claims that he was willing to play by the rules because he was counting on Booster to "straighten it out." Rejecting that possibility, he adopts Booster's spirit of defiance and vows to fight the city. And even if his defiance is tempered (he plans to get a lawyer and to fight legally), we see the influence Booster has had on him. As a consequence, we begin to view their relationship as less destructive and mourn Becker's death and the strained father-son relationship on Booster's behalf.

Becker and Booster's relationship is not the only interaction that encourages *Jitney*'s interrogation of responsibility as a posture that is easily recognizable or that is definitively "right." Youngblood, like Becker, tries to play by the rules. He accepts his civic responsibility when he is drafted and sent to Vietnam "to be shot at" (65), despite the racial inequality he knows he will face upon returning home. And he accepts his familial responsibility when he works two jobs to buy a home for Rena and their son. But when he learns that the jitney station is being boarded up in two weeks, he complains to Doub: "White folks ain't got no sense of timing. They wait till I get in the position to buy me a house and then they pull the rug out from under me!" (64). Doub, then, becomes the mouthpiece for black male responsibility: "You keep thinking everybody's against you and you ain't gonna get nothing. I seen a hundred niggers too lazy to get up out the bed in the morning, talking about the white man is against them. That's just an excuse. You want to make something of your life, then the opportunity is there" (65). Assuming the role of father figure, Doub tells Youngblood, "Like I tell my boys, the world's opened up to you" (66). When Doub suggests that Youngblood get Becker to try to get him work at the mill, responsibility's gray area rears its head again. How open is the world really when after telling Youngblood that he can be anything — "a pilot or a engineer or something" (66) — the last option Doub presents to Youngblood, perhaps the only real option, is to work at the mill? Youngblood tells Doub, "I don't want to work in no mill. I done seen what the mills do to people and I swore I'd never work in no mill. The mills suck the life out of you. . . . I'll do anything but I don't want that" (66). Doub's only response is that "it ain't all the time what you what. Sometime it's what you need. Black folks always get the two confused" (67). Both men are right — Youngblood must be responsible to his own well-being — yet Youngblood must not confuse his wants with his needs. And Doub must not confuse the idea of opportunity with its reality. The fact that he concedes to the confusion of needs and wants rather than insists that opportunity and responsibility can go hand in hand highlights his own awareness that being responsible sometimes means accepting limited opportunities.

As he does with all the plays in the cycle, August Wilson uses *Jitney* to explore black culture — a culture that carries with it its own set of complications and its own desire to have these complications interrogated with authenticity and sophistication. This is why his call for black theaters is an appropriate one, for it is largely, though not exclusively, in black theaters that black actors and black directors will nudge black playwrights to reject simplified portrayals of black people and black culture and to depict both as complex and multidimensional instead. And it is in black theaters and in the American theater informed by black theater that we will find the power "to bring the light of angelic grace, peace, prosperity, and the unencumbered pursuit of happiness to the ground on which we stand" (Wilson, "Ground" 503).

Notes

1. Consider Sandra G. Shannon's "'Ain't I A Woman?' Sojourner Truth's Question Revisited in August Wilson's Female Characters," Shannon's "The Ground on Which I Stand: August Wilson's Perspective on African American Women,"

Harry Elam, Jr.'s "August Wilson's Women," and Tara T. Green's "Speaking of Voice and August Wilson's Women."

2. Among the many analyses on the subject are the National Urban League's *The State of Black America 2007: Portrait of the Black Male*; Demico Boothe's *Why Are So Many Black Men in Prison?*; Bruce Western's *Punishment and Inequality in America*; Earl Ofari Hutchinson's *The Assassination of the Black Male Image*; Jewelle Taylor Gibbs's *Young, Black, and Male in America: An Endangered Species*; Ronald Mincy's *Black Males Left Behind*; Mark Anthony Neal's *New Black Man*; bell hooks's *We Real Cool: Black Men and Masculinity*; the *Washington Post*'s 2007 series on the black male and the series's corresponding book *Being a Black Man*, and, most recently, CNN's documentary "Black in America: The Black Man," which first aired July 24, 2008.

KIMMIKA L. H. WILLIAMS-WITHERSPOON

Challenging the Stereotypes of Black Manhood

The Hidden Transcript in *Jitney*

The media and popular culture propagate the myth that each medium is value free — without judgments or bias. As Michael Parenti suggests, however, what popular culture gives us through theater, literature, and media is "something that is neither purely entertainment nor purely political. [Rather] it is a hybrid that might be called political entertainment" (Parenti, 3). In much the same vein, Ralph Johnson explains that "beliefs, attitudes and values are more palatable and credible to an audience when they are molded and reinforced by characters" (R. Johnson, 200).

Problematic definitions of "black manhood" are not new in American popular culture's attempts to choreograph reality (Pieterse). Sterling Brown postulated in 1933 that there were, in fact, seven categories of popular stereotypes of African American characters that had helped to shape the perception and (in many cases) misconception of "real-time" African American life (Gates). In the continuum of "imagined images," Brown's list included the contented slave "Tom," the comic "Coon," the brute, and the tragic mulatto — stereotypes that are now all easily recognized for their pejorative, subliminal messages about blackness (Gandy, 27–34).[1]

Donald Bogle, in *Toms, Coons, Mulattoes, Mammies, and Bucks*, outlined some of the pejorative African American characters that have become iconic in the American cultural consciousness. That seminal work explored the historical, socially constructed manifestations of race and maleness that were first created by white writers in so-called enlightenment literature. Among the other stereotypes Brown identified that Bogle did not are the "exotic primitive,"[2] "the wretched freeman," and the "local color Negro." The blueprint for the wretched freeman type grew out of the legacy of enslavement itself—"natural sons of unnatural fathers," as W. E. B. Du Bois would call them (Du Bois, "Talented Tenth" 520). Those blacks typically made up a black aristocracy with greater access to opportunity or what Oscar Gandy calls "life-chances" (Gandy, 46–48) and, with those chances, the ability to gain an education and professional skills.

As a polar extreme, the local color Negro was meant to depict the large number of darker-skinned laborers who sold their muscle and lived the blues. These characters struggled—despite the limitations of blackness—under the eyes of random but regular acts of deadly racism. Unlike the coon, who was the butt of every joke, the local color Negro allowed white audiences—in their comfort zone of the public transcript—to snicker at the nerve of black perseverance, against the steady onslaught of racialized misfortune.

If those stereotypes were initially created by a cadre of white performers and playwrights who sought to romanticize black life and culture during minstrelsy, today paternalistic and pseudoscientific explanations of race and cultural difference are still replicated, even in the work of black writers, precisely because audience members have come to expect them. In the political economy of African American arts production, the stereotypes compose a necessary staple of popular culture in a world where the logistics of minority arts production—accessibility to mainstream venues, production cost, advertising, media attention, public sentiment, industry concessions and fear of group reprisal (Gandy, 54)—has curtailed, exploited, and in some cases even sabotaged the cultural production of African American arts. As a result, a "hidden transcript" often operates in these social sites (even the seemingly benign ones) that contests overarching power relations. That hidden transcript uses musicality, call and response, and African American vernacular English so that recognizing the hidden transcript requires a cognizance of cultural competency (Williams-Witherspoon, 164) and of the importance of active and social rituals. With these hidden transcripts black writers such as Wilson can communicate encrypted or coded meanings in juxtaposition to a public transcript that replicates the ideological assumptions of the dominant culture. In this context, such contemporary stereotypes as unsuccessful black men and dysfunctional fathers — even the "coon" and the "brute" — can acquire new use-value.

In Wilson's work, because race and its meaning are constantly negotiated, many male characters oscillate between acting like the wretched freeman and the local color Negro. By linking these characters to the historical distribution of "life chances" (Gandy, 35), Wilson allows us to redefine black manhood — and by extension, black people as a whole (Harrison, *Drama of Nommo* 164) — in contrasts, oftentimes, to the burden of black image-making that fueled their struggle for survival. It is necessary, therefore, to foreground the hidden transcripts in Wilson's drama to understand how his work breaks down black stereotypes to reveal the complexity of the black man's experience.

. . . .

Set in 1977, when young black men were returning home from Vietnam full of hope and possibility, *Jitney* looks at the changing face of the African American community in the post–civil rights era. In urban areas such as Pittsburgh's Hill district, however, residential segregation was still a very real factor for African Americans. Hiding behind the dubious legality of government-constructed empowerment zones, gentrification has begun to rear its ugly head, and for black men in America, jobs and life chances were limited. For a group of African American men in a small jitney cab station, life chances and manhood are continually tested while, all around them, small black businesses are forced to close because of impending redevelopment. In this setting, *Jitney* presents some of Wilson's most positive understandings of black manhood.

In *Jitney*, much of the African American population is still living in traditionally segregated neighborhoods that haven't completely lost their interdependent sense of community, despite the failure of public transportation. In the midst of sociopolitical maneuvering, a group of hardworking men struggle to hold together a jitney cab company as an alternative survival strategy. In this context, the names posted on the chalkboard suggest a hidden transcript at work in the play.

Becker presents an aspect of black masculinity that beckons the audience to understand the history of black progress, to lead by example, and to work tirelessly to give children access and opportunity. Turnbo's name suggests *turncoat* or *turnabout*; though he means no harm, he has two faces, and his behavior indicates that dealing with duplicity may be one of the greatest challenges for African Americans. Turnbo raises the question of whether black men have been forced to play the Janus role — one side brute and one side coon — for such a long time that the perception of black men has become fused to the mask.

Fielding uses his alcoholism to *field* off the hurt of loneliness. We are never told why he and his wife are separated. We only know that he is loyal and that being able to add his name to the roster on the chalkboard is a privilege of belonging while he fights against addiction. Doub, like *dub*, personifies grateful reason. "It ain't all the time what you want," he says. "Sometimes it's what you need" (67). Duplicating the ancestors' voices, his story reframes the history of many African American veterans who never had their stories told. Doub mediates. Like Becker, he won't give up on Fielding and, in the end, signifies perseverance. Shealy is the *shield* for a vast underground illegal employment strategy that, at one time, operated out of the African American community by African Americans for African Americans. If Shealy is simply a numbers runner, the play's hidden transcript recognizes him as "good guy" who provides alternative modes of production and sources of capital. (As my 63-year-old older brother would say, "Black men have to huck a buck.")

Youngblood represents the *young blood* of the community, and his relationship with Rena provides the impetus for hope. If Rena doesn't grow hard from her choice of loving him and if Youngblood can only stick to the code — put family first, go back to school, as Doub suggests, and curb the spontaneity of youthfulness — his story may be as successful as Becker's with his second wife, Lucille. As Becker admonishes, *"It ain't all gonna flow together all the time. . . . When you look around you'll see that all you got is each other. There ain't much more"* (78). Here, Wilson offers his audiences the primal truth rather than the paradox: black men need black women, just as black women need black men.

Not just the names on the chalkboard but the act of checking in reveals a hidden transcript, making that act a ritual that undoes a time when all a black man could do was make his mark as anonymous labor in a world that valued a black as three-fifths of a white man. This is one of many rituals that contributes to what Carlton Molette calls the collective, "commonality" of culture (Molette, 24).[3]

One important ritual that helps to give meaning and work to the men who eke out a living in Becker's jitney station is the answering of the phone, which allows the men to tap into and contribute to the cultural pulse of their community. By being a pulse point of their community — ferrying residents back and forth along the arteries of their neighborhood — the men in Becker's jitney station build a niche of service into a mode of production. For the men of *Jitney*, maintaining the lines of communication and the connection to community keeps each man grounded, despite his personal torments. As Doub says, "Every man in here depending on this station for their livelihood" (36), to which Fielding responds "You got to have somebody you can count on you know" (52).

If the jitney drivers often play games around the ritual of answering the phone, they also ritualize the playing of games. In other plays (e.g., *Seven Guitars*) Wilson uses card games as ritual, and game-playing is almost always an element in his work. In *Jitney*, checkers is more than the way men jockey for approval, power, and dominance. At the jitney station (and for Youngblood in Vietnam) checkers reflects the political and economic position of many black men in their negotiations in and around notions of identity and in their demands to be treated as men rather than merely as strategic game pieces.

The male ritual of incarceration is also significant in *Jitney*. Doub's and Booster's references to penitentiary time versus "real time" speaks to a ritual that historically evokes the brute stereotype of the black man as being forced to give up — to lose time and to do time. Although *Jitney* does not represent visually the regimented dynamics of incarceration or indicate the huge percentage of African American men forced to waste caloric and intellectual output in a nonproductive community, the repeated references to the twenty years Booster spent in prison represents incarceration as a negative end product consistent with one stereotype of black manhood.

Jitney also reflects the gun culture and concomitant acts that are associated in the public imaginary with the black male brute. When Turnbo pulls a gun on Youngblood — in part over the price of a cup of coffee, in part for stepping out of line and hitting his elder — the gun becomes part of a ritual reflecting the testosterone-induced male-butting games in which many men, regardless of culture, engage. In the African American community, however, as the gun makes clear, this ritual is often volatile. The hidden transcript of this scene references the turning point in the African American community when disputes were no longer settled "like men" — with fists — but rather with knives and guns.

When the fighter persona or the mythology of athleticism is no longer believed to offer black men a way out of the limits of their oppression (as with Youngblood believing himself to be unbeatable like Muhammad Ali), the accessibility, the neutrality, and the potential fatality of guns is believed to even the playing field. When Turnbo points a pistol at Youngblood and says "Comeon! You young punk. Comeon! Hit me again! . . . Jump at me and I'll blow your ass to kingdom come" (44), Wilson makes the audiences recognize what the culture of guns evokes.

In contradistinction to the rituals of prowess, Fielding's alcoholism, although still a consequence of the social rituals of alienation, loneliness, and "anomie" (Durkheim), serves as a negative ritual — unlike Shealy's numbers-running, an entrepreneurial and strategic alternative mode of production made positive as it solidifies the cultural fabric of the community. While Fielding's alcoholism reflects a sociocultural response to the limited life chances for black men in America, Shealy's running represents a second job, a street job, a hustle that could provide the necessary seed money for the upward mobility of a whole cadre of those Sterling Brown would call "local color Negroes."

. . . .

Wilson also blurs the lines between public and private space. The private spaces of Wilson's plays — the back porch and yard of *Fences*, the large utilitarian kitchen that serves as a common space for borders in *Joe Turner's Come and Gone*, and the equally large and expansive living room that opens out into the kitchen of the Charles home in *The Piano Lesson* — allow his audiences to catch his characters when they are putting on their best behavior and when they are rawest and most vulnerable.

Even Wilson's most public spaces, such as the studio in *Ma Rainey's Black Bottom* or the diner in *Two Trains Running*, always hint at a sense of enclosure, creating tight though public spaces — spaces where Wilson's characters get to know each other intensely. This compressed space — social, political, and economic — forces the characters into revealing discoveries about themselves, their space, and their place as black folks in America. This compression often creates moments when one or more of the characters expresses deep inner rage. In those moments the ceremonies, rituals, and activities of the public sphere, as Sandra Barnes writes, reaffirm the reality that "social space . . . stands between the private (domestic or familial) spheres of society and the state" ("Yoruba," 44).[4] In that public space, then, "the defining quality of the public sphere is the ability of people to criticize, oppose, influence or inform" (45). The jitney station is that kind of public environment, in which Wilson questions the duplicity of city administrators by suggesting that urban renewal is tantamount to urban removal. Turnbo suggests as much when he says, "Told me they was conducting a survey. . . . They won't be satisfied until they tear the whole goddamn neighborhood down" (38).

Wilson uses the intensity of these spaces to reformulate black stereotypes. When Becker moves between Turnbo and Youngblood, he disrupts the gun culture with a contrasting image of black manhood: putting his own life on the line to diffuse a potentially volatile moment. Becker is demonstrating an alternative understanding of the warrior stance so many black men inevitably assume. In this pivotal interchange, the idea of not being afraid to die serves a mediational rather than an inflammatory end.

Although Turnbo, Youngblood, and Becker provide salient evidence that being able to adopt the warrior stance at any given moment is an element of black manhood, the culturally competent audience member understands that having to adopt the warrior stance is as much a consequence of the legacy of enslavement as it might be a consequence of biology or contemporary culture. While insensitive staging might represent this scene as a stereotypical public discourse on gun games in our community, when staged with a sensitivity to the political economy of African American culture, the scene enacts the hidden transcript that critiques the consequences of anomie — a social condition whereby individuals develop apathy toward human life as a socio-psychic side effect of prolonged poverty — and limited life chances (Gandy, 35), or, as Durkheim would suggest, being disconnected from the product of one's labor (Durkheim; Giddens, 82–104). While the discourse on the pervasiveness of rituals of violence in the black community cannot be eclipsed by Becker's standing between Turnbo's gun and Youngblood's volatile youth, the hidden transcript suggests that African Americans must continue to defy the odds — even when at risk of personal injury — as a counter-hegemonic strategy.

Forced into mediocrity, many African American men find themselves sinking into a "blinding hopelessness" (Madhubuti, 16). Engaging that problem, *Jitney* attempts to redefine black manhood. Using hidden transcripts to explore the variables and rigors of social conditions and political economy, the play suggests that black manhood must be defined by voice, a sense of responsibility, friendship, and a commitment to home and family.

In urban culture a "booster" is a shoplifter, one who steals. Claiming the warrior stance by murdering the white woman who had lied about him, Booster inverts images of black men like Emmett Till who were murdered because of those same "white" lies. By demanding Susan McKnight's accountability, however, Booster stole his own life at the expense of his mother's will to live and his father's love. But in a pivotal moment at the end of the play, Booster steps up to the challenge when he takes up his father's mission and "boosts" himself to take back his own life.

Notes

1. Much can be said about the negative effects of the pervasiveness of those images of "blackness" consistently perpetuated in drama, literature, the media, and popular culture, which foster white *expectation*. That "white expectation of blackness" that is nurtured, encouraged, and "fostered" by the ready replication of stereotypes in the media and popular culture is then *imposed* on African Americans in work, education, and social settings. In some cases, after a series of unsuccessful attempts to counter those expectations, some African Americans

take the next step in the vicious cycle by beginning to take on the characteristics of the stereotype, in what I call *resigned resignation*.

2. Sterling Brown's stereotypes of blackness would painstakingly separate the exotic primitive from the tragic mulatto. As he saw it, the exotic primitive was the romanticized character sought out for the negative valuations of "Negroid features," like the so-called Hottentot Venus (Hernton, 84).

3. Molette, "Ritual Drama in the Contemporary Black Theater."

4. Barnes, "Yoruba: Political Representation in Old States and New Nations."

The Holyistic Blues of
Seven Guitars

Over the years, August Wilson has used remarkably consistent language in interviews in his commentary on the relation of blues to his work. For Wilson, the blues is "the African American's response to the world before he started writing down his stuff" (Savran, 26). It is the "book of black people" that contains "the African American's cultural response to the world" (Livingston, 58) with "a philosophical system at work" that demonstrates that "there was a nobility to the lives of blacks in America" (Moyers, 63). The attitudes and ideas, Wilson asserts, have been transferred from the blues "over to all the ideas and attitudes of [his] characters: these come directly from blues songs" (Sheppard, 110). As such, "the blues are life-affirming music that guides you throughout life; the blues teach you the morality of the culture" (Sheppard, 111). He calls the blues "my primary influence" (Shannon, 156), "the bedrock of everything I do" (Rosen, 198), and demonstrates how it serves an important function in the lives of African Americans: "The music is ours since it contains our soul, so to speak. . . . We need it to help us claim this African-ness and we would be a stronger people for it" (Savran, 37).

Supernatural elements in Wilson's plays indicate a deep interest in spirituality as well, but a worldly spirituality that eschews the sacred-secular dichotomy in favor of a spirituality that is of this world, firmly rooted in the daily particulars of the lives of African Americans and accepting and partaking of the spirit of the blues as a valid philosophical system. In *Seven Guitars*, Vera tells Floyd, for example, that the dress she was wearing was colored "two different kinds of blue" (12) when they first met, emphasizing that the blues experience is neither monolithic nor unidimensional.

Indeed, many commentators see blues and gospel music as different sides of the same coin in terms of the source, description, and performance of experiences. Asked about references in his plays "that seem to indicate that God has forsaken the black man" (Sheppard, 110), Wilson responds with a philosophical discussion of the nature of divinity:

> Well, it depends on what God you are talking about. When Africans were brought to this country, they were denied their language, their gods, customs, all the rest. Toledo in *Ma Rainey* says, "We forgot the names of the gods." But I have a very simple viewpoint toward that — when you look in the mirror, you should see your God. If you don't, then you have somebody else's God. Because there is not a people on the planet who have a God that does not look like them. . . . So what happens in *Joe Turner* is that Loomis rejects not just the idea of God, but the idea of salvation coming from outside himself. He says, "I don't need anyone to bleed for me, I can bleed for myself." So it is an acceptance of his responsibility for his own salvation, and by way of that, an acceptance of his responsibility for his own presence in the world. (Sheppard, 110)

It is a resolution of the dilemma explored by Countee Cullen in his poem "Heritage," a poem that itself uses the symbol of blood to emphasize the vital importance of relating to one's own gods.

In *Seven Guitars*, August Wilson explores the lives of seven characters in relation to their notions of identity and love and how the two intertwine, considered in the context of their sociopolitical status in a racist society. Through a deft and subtle use of African American vernacular music, especially blues and gospel music, Wilson delineates the culture from which his characters come in the context of the larger culture in which they subsist. Further, he exposes the ways in which that spirituality and culture inform and sustain their lives — makes them seven instruments, seven guitars with stories to tell, formed and plucked by the cultures that shape their music — and the ways that philosophy dovetails and clashes with the master narrative of the dominant culture of the land. Out of the polyphony of voices in the play emerges a sense of the diversity and unity of their world — imbued with a sacred and secular dialogic that reflects African and African American spirituality — that informs the efforts of a determined blues man, Floyd "Schoolboy" Barton (at least two recorded blues men used that nickname: Schoolboy Cleve and John "School Boy" Porter), to learn to take a chance on his own destiny, to determine his own future, to learn from the "book of black people," even as the world in which he lives gravitates against him. This desperate hope in the face of adversity exemplifies one of the main philosophies of the blues, expressed in one of its best known stanzas:

> Sun gonna shine in my back door someday.
> Oh, the wind gonna rise, and blow my blues away.
> (House, "Delta Blues")

Seven Guitars exemplifies Wilson's comments about the importance of blues to his work, but also shows that gospel music has an important role as well. Altogether, Wilson makes explicit references to a dozen blues and gospel songs in the play, five blues — "Anybody Here Want to Try My Cabbage," "That's All Right" (originally recorded as "Ora Nelle Blues"), "Buddy Bolden's Blues," "Good Rocking Tonight," and "Sixty Minute Man" — and seven from the gospel tradition — "Death Don't Have No Mercy," "God Don't Like It," "If I Could Only Hear My Mother Pray Again," "Old Ship of Zion," "De Blind Man Stood on De Road and Cried," "Ain't No Grave Can Hold My Body Down," and "Satan I Will Tear Your Kingdom Down." Further, when one takes into account people, phrases, and themes that are common in blues and gospel songs, there are over fifty different echoes of blues and gospel music — mostly blues — throughout the play, down to the names of Floyd's idol Muddy Waters (McKinley Morganfield, 11) and of the club in which Floyd plays at the end ("Blue Goose" refers to the African American section of town in Jesse "Baby Face" Thomas's "Blue Goose Blues," and, very likely, to the convict cage at a prison camp at Sugarland in James "Iron Head" Baker's "De Blue Goose," with the obvious association of Floyd's life with imprisonment) (74).

Of course, it can be difficult to say where some phrases known to blues fans first occurred — in the music or simply in everyday speech — since one would expect the music to reflect speech patterns of the oral tradition. But their common usage in blues and gospel songs and Wilson's own comments about the importance of the vernacular music tradition to his work suggests that he is drawing strongly on the blues tradition for his portrayal of the lives and philosophy of his characters. It is a tradition, indeed, formed out of the lives of the masses of African Americans and, appropriately, many songs are frequently presented in musical performance mode in the play by Vera, Floyd, and Hedley, though it is Red Carter who sings "Jump Back Dooley" (53–54), the lyrics of which were recorded by Little Walter in 1954 as "Mellow Down Easy." Some of those echoes are the incomplete or modified reproductions of previously existing recordings that are performed and adapted, as the oral tradition of the blues frequently is, to the varied experiences of individuals. What this emphasizes is the simultaneous functioning of blues on the levels of both first person singular and first person plural experiences, connecting the individual to the ancestors and cohorts with whom the performer identifies, from whom the performer draws strength and knowledge, and after whom the performer expands the purview of the song through the additional personalized experience.

Three songs, "Anybody Here Want to Try My Cabbage," "That's All Right," and "Buddy Bolden's Blues," are prominently placed for maximum effect — in these cases, at the beginnings of the first three scenes of act 1, respectively. The references to "That's All Right" and "Buddy Bolden's Blues" are used multiple times and figure prominently in the text, including both at the beginning of act 2 and "Buddy Bolden's Blues" at the very end of the play. These three prominent blues songs each make important contributions in a variety of ways to the style and meaning of the text, and they demonstrate Wilson's knowledge of the oral blues tradition. All three songs emphasize orality and performance through use of the words "hollering," "telling," "saying," and "hearing," clearly investing the atmosphere with orature, its appropriate milieu. Finally, Wilson's employment of what he calls a distinctive "philosophical system at work" resonates through the content and performance of the lyrics, as the performances themselves ring out in the air.

As the song that opens up the universe of these seven characters to the audience, "Anybody Here Want to Try My Cabbage" plays a particularly important role in introducing important textual themes. While some — perhaps many — people might consider it to be a sacrilege to sing a stanza from a song that celebrates sexual promiscuity upon arriving home with other guests from a religious funeral service, and judge Wilson's placement of the words as the first heard in the entire play to be character critical (once one finds out a few lines later that the characters are returning from a funeral), in the context of the entire play the song is not meant to comment on characters in that way at all. The song itself is a Fats Waller-Andy Razaf composition recorded first by Maggie Jones with Louis Armstrong in 1924 in New York City, followed by versions by George McClennon's Jazz Devils in 1925, Mildred Austin in 1928, and Lil Johnson (titled "Anybody Want to Buy My Cabbage") in 1935. While some commentators have found the lyrics to be trite, even "corny" (Oliphant, 63), Wilson finds them to be appropriate to begin his play, and, according to the stage directions, "a much-needed affirmation of life" (1). Recognizing that the song is "bawdy" (1), Wilson sees this blues as functioning as a release from the heaviness of the funeral service and inevitable memento mori thoughts that accompany it. The biblical "ashes to ashes, dust to dust" passage performed during funeral services and which is referenced in the text itself (70, 107) as well as in relation to the money that Buddy Bolden gives Hedley (24, 70, 107), can also be used in the African American folk tradition to refer to sexuality — when one gets one's ashes hauled, one is having good sex:

> Hey, Hey, I wonder where my ash hauler gone.
> Hey, Hey, I wonder where my ash hauler gone.
> I've got ashes in my bin, Lord, them things been there so long. . . .
>
> That's all right I've got a woman, she's got a wagon with a great
>   big bin.
> That's all right I've got a woman, she's got a wagon with a great
>   big bin.
> Yes, she said she'd haul my ashes, that's the last word I heard
>   her say. (Broonzy)

Thus, the recourse to sexual thoughts following the final placement of the physical body in the ground reinforces the continuation of life and celebration of the physical in the face of extreme reminders of mortality, a reminder to continue to experience and celebrate intensely and personally in this life while it lasts. Near the end of the play, when Vera and Floyd seem nearly reconciled, Floyd's ritualistic performance of Roy Brown and Wynonie Harris's "Good Rockin' Tonight" ("Tonight she'll know I'm a mighty, mighty man") and Billy Ward and His Dominoes' "Sixty Minute Man" (fifteen minutes each of "teasin'," "squeezin'," "pleasin'," and "blowin' my top" (101–102) comprise both a public performance and a private sexual message to Vera. This she hears and understands and prepares to carry out once the formal show is over. It is a physical culmination of their spiritual reconciliation in the play. Canewell, too, provides illumination on the lighthearted sexual playfulness post-funeral as well: "See, all Jesus done by raising him from the dead was to cause him to go through that much more suffering. He was suffering the pain of living. That's why the Bible say you supposed to rejoice when somebody die and cry when they come into the world" (26). Canewell exposes the dilemma of the man caught between conflicting imperatives: "Many a time I felt like God was calling. But the devil was calling too, and it seem like he call louder" (45). The blues world, like that of the gospel performer, is a vale of tears and suffering, whose nature is ameliorated by the embracing and performance of African American modes of existence and performance.

Commentators on the blues have identified relationships between the blues tradition and spiritual matters that shed light on Wilson's intentions here. As early as 1926, Carl Van Vechten described Bessie Smith in performance as an "elemental conjure woman" performing "strange rites" (Tracy, *Blues Reader* 316). In 1966, Charles Keil departed from this somewhat primitivistic and mystical description to draw more serious parallels between blues singers and preachers: "Blues singers and preachers both provide models and orientations, both give public expression to deeply felt private emotions, both promote catharsis — the blues singer through dance, the preacher through trance; both increase feelings of solidarity, boost morale, strengthen the consensus" (164). Rod Gruver feels that "the poetry of the blues also became a religion" (Tracy, *Blues Reader* 224), attempting to "balance the supernaturalism of Christianity" and "oppose the imitation of white society by the black middle class" (Tracy, *Blues Reader* 225), primarily through the use of sexual attitudes and behaviors:

> Blues poets made a religion of the blues by distilling behavior into the single point of sex, by creating a sacred realm of charged atmosphere conducive for the appearance of Men and Women, the gods of the blues. By creating a song-type with Woman as one of its chief characters, blues poets created a mythology that unifies opposites and offers a new religious orientation. (Tracy, *Blues Reader* 229)

As quoted above, Wilson described in relation to the ideas in *Ma Rainey's Black Bottom* how one should be able to look in the mirror and see one's god, reinforcing the notion that the god ought not to be outside oneself. This relates directly to Gruver's assertion about human beings being the gods of the blues. James Cone builds on this emphasis on men and women in the blues by asserting that "the affirmation of self in the blues is what connects them theologically with the spirituals. Like the spirituals, the blues affirm the somebodiness of black people, and they preserve the worth of black humanity through ritual and drama" (Tracy, 236). Wilson himself commented similarly in an interview with Bill Moyers: "After I discovered the blues, I began to look at the people in the house a little differently than I had before. I began to see a value in their lives that I hadn't seen before. I discovered a beauty and a nobility in their struggle to survive. . . . The mere fact that they were still able to make this music was a testament to the resiliency of their spirit" (64).

While not all commentators, Christians, or blues performers are willing to categorize the blues as a religion, the idea that it functions in ways similar to the black Christian church and its leaders can be quite valid. And while one might hope to avoid approaching a stereotype of African Americans by overemphasizing "distilling behavior into the single point of sex," the fact is that sexual activity is in fact prominent in the blues and does provide an affront and antidote to middle-class attitudes about appropriate sexual behaviors that can be quite liberating, if sometimes shocking. Lucille Bogan sang in her 1935 unexpurgated version of "Shave 'em Dry:"

Now your nuts hang down like a damn bell clapper
And your dick stands up like a steeple
Your goddamn asshole stands open like a church door
And the crabs walks in like people.

Bogan recasts the church in the form of male genitalia and environs, and the song worships at the throne of sex quite forcefully, if sometimes cynically, throughout its text. Besides crossing that "boundary," this section of the song is a parody of a children's hand game, transforming the ritual from one thing—"here's the church, here's the steeple, open the doors and see all the people"—into something altogether different, and shocking in innocent children's hands. Similarly, Harlem Renaissance author Nella Larsen's depiction of the "Bacchic vehemence" of a storefront church service being "penetrated" by the "wild appeal" of the "orgy" in which the women were "like reptiles," "sobbing and pulling their hair and tearing off their clothing," and "dropping hot tears and beads of sweat upon her bare arms and neck" (113–114) acknowledges quite clearly the sexual element of religious fervor.

The notion of unifying opposites by bringing men and women together certainly dovetails with Wilson's emphasis on unity in this play. Wilson's use of the number seven—the number symbolizing the universe, the macrocosm, completeness, perfection, security, synthesis—at several points in the play emphasizes his concentration on unifying parent and child, men and women, sacred and secular in the text.

The play's title, *Seven Guitars*, refers to the number of characters in the play, six of whom—like the six angels at the cemetery—are alive at the chronological end of the play (2); Canewell refers to six or seven men having gotten killed when he hears of George Butler's death (21); in the guitar "battle" between Floyd and Hedley, Floyd plays a six-string guitar while Hedley plays a one-string (49); when Floyd describes his options for action, he says he "had seven ways to go" (81); and Red Carter counts seven birds sitting on a fence as he recounts his tale of bad luck (82).

The number seven is also associated with the number of sacraments in the Catholic Church and devils cast out by Christ, as well as the number of deadly sins—again demonstrating associations between sacred and secular.

There are also seven notes in the common heptatonic scale, reinforcing the musical connection. Another musical connection comes through the reference to the seven days of the week and Red Carter's reference to having had seven women, calling them "Friday woman," "Sunday woman," etc. (38–39). These kinds of designations also occur in the blues tradition — for example, in some of the hyperbolic boasting songs in the blues tradition — with references to having different women for each day in the week in Papa Harvey Hull and Long Cleve Reed's "Gang of Brownskin Women," Jim Jackson's "My Monday Woman Blues," Pink Anderson and Simmie Dooley's "Every Day in the Week," and Joe Turner's "I Got a Gal":

> Got a Friday Friday girl, she brings me a bottle of beer,
> Got a Saturday one, well, she better not catch me here. (Hull)

Wilson uses the number seven, then, to juxtapose and unify his ideas of sacred and secular, sexuality, death, chance, bad luck, and the vernacular music tradition in the text, regularly relating the number to the African American vernacular tradition to reinforce its centrality to their lives and to emphasize the struggle of African American existence.

The lyrics of the opening stanza of Maggie Jones's "Anybody Here Want to Try My Cabbage" that Vera performs comment on the text in several ways. First, as a teasing invitation to sexual activity, the lyrics acknowledge the playful element in sexual attraction that is part of the "game" experienced by a variety of couples in the text. It is not even clear that a real invitation to sexual contact is implied, since the song is part of a ritual being enacted in this setting, as it had been enacted on record and on stage previously. The "game" calls for movement ("step this way") and speech ("just holler Hey"), and evokes, as African and African American performance is frequently intended to do, a response, which she gets from a playful Red Carter. Thus, at this point the performance itself depicts and promotes responses from the living in the aftermath of Floyd's death, and does so in an affirmation of the value and validity of the African American performance aesthetic, which uses antiphonal elements to promote involvement and community — life.

Second, in its use of sexual euphemism, the song is entirely consistent with the element of creative sexual double entendre common in the blues and hokum elements of African American music. Genitalia have been referred to in blues lyics as "pigmeat," "stew meat," "hot dog," "tuna," "barbecue," "jelly roll," "gravy," "biscuits," "yams," "apples," "peaches," "plums," "bananas," "potatoes," "tomatoes," "lemons," "coffee," "sugar," "pudding," and "candy," to mention only the appetitive euphemisms (Tracy, *Langston Hughes and the Blues* 194). This element — allowing one to be able to say something without saying it — is of course important in an African American tradition where speaking one's mind can be a great danger and liability, on the one hand, whereas on the other hand avoiding the disapprobation of the middle class and its notions of sexuality can at least be somewhat ameliorated, if not avoided (although this tactic can also be a nose-thumbing at the middle class as well). The blues tradition itself has its own well-known lyric — "You don't know my mind, when you see me laughin', I'm laughin' to keep from cryin'" (Viola McCoy) — that acknowledges the strategy. This ability to say without saying, to speak indirectly and protect oneself from repercussions, features prominently in African American history and communication, especially signifying.

Third, the reference to offering some sexual favors to a welcoming parson is entirely consistent with portrayals of preachers in the secular song and blues tradition as abundantly human, sexual creatures whose motivations and actions must at times be considered separate from the "ideals" of the societal based religions they represent:

> Now when I first moved to Memphis, Tennessee,
> I was crazy about the preachers as I could be,
> I went on the front porch just walkin' about,
> Invite the preacher over to my house,
> He washed his face, combed his head,
> Next thing he want to do was slip in my bed,
> I caught him by the head, man, kicked him out the door,
> Don't allow preachers in my house no more.
> Don't like 'em, they'll rob you
> Take your daughter, take your wife from you,
> Take your chickens, take your money. (Stokes)

Some folks say that a preacher won't steal,
I caught three in my cornfield,
One had a yellow, one had a brown,
Looked over in the middle one was gettin' down.
Now some folks say that a preacher won't steal,
But he will do more stealin' than I get regular meals.
    (Kansas Joe and Memphis Minnie)

Thus, the lyric introduces a healthy and direct amount of skepticism regarding the ability of humans to live up to religious tenets and makes room for the practical philosophy of the blues in the spiritual life of humans. And since the preacher is portrayed as a willing participant in sexual activity after the funeral, if he is a moral and spiritual leader of the community his actions in Vera's song at least sanction this type of affirmation of life. In fact, the offertory here becomes a repayment for sexual favors, connecting the church and its congregation to this act as well. Many in the community, of course, would have been outraged by the use of the offering in this way — and that is part of the outrageousness of the act — but the notion of the preacher sanctioning the event with the church's money does communicate something about the value of sexuality in human life. Perhaps bawdiness is not as bad as it is made out to be, and the blues take a clear-eyed look at the way things are in order to counter a guilt-riddling church philosophy that pins a fig leaf on the genitalia of human survival.

Fourth, in the vernacular tradition "cabbage" refers not only to genitalia, but also to money. Though the song makes it clear that sexuality is implied here, one cannot overlook the monetary aspects of the lyric. After all, Lil Green did record the song substituting "buy my cabbage" for "try my cabbage," and the action of the preacher in the lyric does suggest a certain commodification of the act as well. In the play, of course, the quest for money by both Floyd and Hedley as a means to the end is an element on which the plot turns, and in this the song also connects to the "Buddy Bolden" lyrics also featured prominently. Floyd must get money to get his guitar out of pawn in order to go to Chicago and make another record, put a gravestone on his mother's grave, and become a big man — a hero like Joe Louis. This would help bring him back together with Vera.

Significantly, Hedley wants to buy his own plantation so he can run things the way he thinks they ought to be run. This is also an interesting echo of an idea in the blues tradition: as Blind Lemon Jefferson sang in "Broke and Hungry," "I'm goin' away to build me a railroad of my own." Son House, in a variant on the lyric in "Preachin' the Blues Part 1," sang, "Oh I wish I had me a heaven of my own / Then I'd give all my women a long, long happy home," and Wright Holmes echoed in "Alley Blues," "One of these here days I'm gonna build me a heaven of my own." In all three instances the intention is to gain some power or control over one's life by gaining or creating one's own power base or idealized environment. Whereas Jefferson's immediate referent is in this world — significantly a means of mobility important to a large part of a group historically deprived of geographical movement during slavery — House and Holmes want to have or to create their own heaven, a place traditionally associated more with spirituality and eternity. However, just in case one mistakes House and Holmes for Christian saints, the remaining stanzas refer to sexuality: House with a veiled reference to the length of his penis and sex being associated with home, and Holmes describing how he is going to get a gang of brownskin women to gather around his throne.

It is also important that House sings his version in a song titled "Preachin' the Blues Part 1," in which he portrays his own tortured ambivalence with regard to his status as both a Baptist and a blues singer. Those in the church would likely classify House as being on the side of the devil — playing the devil's music — and Part I of the song dramatizes his conflict as he portrays himself as alternately cynical ("I'm gonna be a Baptist preacher, and I sure won't have to work"); entrapped ("I'm gonna do like a prisoner, I'm gonna roll my time on out"); embattled ("The blues came along and it drove my spirit away"); and sexually ebullient and celebratory ("Then I'd give all my women a long, long happy home"). This brings us back to the issue of religion and sexuality discussed earlier. The two clearly do not see sexuality or promiscuity as being inconsistent with heaven as it might be to the middle class — indeed, "heaven" is sometimes used as a euphemism for vagina — much in the way that the blues song and its use in this text does not envision the activity described as incongruous or sinful. Indeed House finds himself agonizing over the decision between the Christian sacred and the blues sinful as it is defined by the church, feeling the strong pull of his sexual urges that he finds difficult to deny. He is seeking a way to be his whole self — to use all of his power — and he expresses it in his blues. Of course, the desire to build a plantation of one's own, charged as that is with racial overtones, is different from — even antithetical to — the implications of the railroad and heaven of the blues songs. Both of those references would be liberatory — the railroad offering mobility and choice to previously restricted slaves; the conventional notion of heaven providing freedom from sin, oppression, and suffering. However, the newly empowered owner of the plantation provides the possibility of righting early wrongs, even eliminating their practice altogether.

Hedley's dream is a significant key to his character. African critic Jan-heinz Jahn suggests that the blues singer sings the blues "not because one finds oneself in a particular mood, but because one wants to put oneself in a certain mood" (Tracy, *Blues Reader* 30). The blues singer asserts the right to "an intact 'perfect' life," termed by Jahn *magara*, or "the life force one possesses, which one wants to increase, and which can be diminished by the influence of others" (Jahn, 172), and increases his or her power by exercising the nommo or life force through the music. This is, of course, exactly what Louise is attempting to accomplish at the beginning of the play. Interestingly, Hedley wishes to run his own plantation — to see himself as a king and a powerful man in the tradition of Toussaint (40, 86–87), Garvey (40, 68, 71), and especially Buddy Bolden (23–24, etc.) — to return, in a sense, to the scene of the crime, and to subvert the prevailing historical, social, and aesthetic order by installing a proud, knowledgeable, jazz-identified black man in a position of power.[1]

Wilson reinforces notions of power and royalty in a variety of locations in the text. References to King Buddy Bolden (67), King Hedley (67), King Edward cigars (36), the rooster as "king of the barnyard" (61; also a common sexual reference in the blues), the black man as "king" (61), and Louise as Queen Ester and Vera as the Queen of Sheba (96) emphasize concretely the notions of hierarchy implied by such terminology. References to a symbol of royal wealth in the name "Dr. Goldblum" (27), Old Gold cigarettes (16), and the goldenseal plant (19) all serve to reinforce issues of the measure of importance in a hegemonic society. Hedley is awaiting his money from Buddy Bolden so he can be the "King" he was named for at birth (with his jewel Ruby as his Queen, 89) — another significant jazz and blues music association. Of course, jazz and blues "royalty" abounds in the music business: there's the Empress of the Blues (Bessie Smith), Queen of the Moaners (Clara Smith), Queen Victoria Spivey, Queen Elleezee (Lizzie Miles), Queen of the Blues (Susie Edwards and Sara Martin), Queen Bea of Blues Singers (Wee Bea Booze), the Uncrowned Queen of the Blues (Ida Cox), Princess of the Blues (Olive Brown), King of the Jukeboxes (Louis Jordan), King of the 12-String Guitar Players of the World (Leadbelly), King of the South/King of Zydeco (Clifton Chenier), King of the Blues (B.B. King), Harmonica King (George Smith), the Queen of Gospel Song (Mahalia Jackson), the Queen of Gospel (Albertina Walker), the King of Gospel (James Cleveland), King Solomon Hill, King Kolax, Count Basie, and Duke Ellington, to name a few, though some were likely invented by record companies for promotion. Many songs in gospel music refer to Christ as "King Jesus" as well.

Such references emphasize the ability of the "lower classes" to assume an exalted status, though frequently the "value" is comparative or illusory. The evocation of Joe Louis in the play is instructive. Several recorded blues songs refer to Joe Louis as the King as well: "King Joe," "Winner Joe (The Knock-Out King)," and "Champ Joe Louis (King of the Gloves)" are among the over forty songs relating to Louis composed in the African American vernacular tradition in his lifetime. Louis was a great champion and icon, especially following his defeat of Max Schmeling. However, the King was also hounded by the U.S. government for much of his postwar life when his generous voluntarism and role as spokesman and star recruiter for the armed services was repaid by unreasonable, virtually usurious tax demands. Louis was indeed king in the ring, but ultimately his royalty did not translate to social equality, or even appreciation in the face of the pursuit of money.

That pursuit, of course, drives the marketing of products that seek to draw us to their images. Wilson explores those illusions that pass as realities by employing prestigious symbols in an argument over cigarettes in the play. Hedley recommends Chesterfields, the name associated with elegance and urbanity, while Louise pushes for Old Gold, with its associations with inherited wealth and power. Both are just cigarettes — perhaps somewhat different — but their values are in the lips and lungs and minds of the would-be puffer, neither inherently nor objectively superior to the other, even though that image attempts to convince otherwise.

Other comparisons abound. Alabama, Georgia, and Mississippi roosters are all different (60); Canewell talks about different kinds of beer (5). The King Edward cigars are cheap, though there are better versions of the King Edward cigar (36). In fact, none of these images have much to do with reality. Miss Sarah Degree (probably an evocation of gris gris), the goldenseal plant, and Doctor Goldblum are among the cures offered for Hedley's illness, each generating its own believers. However, as Canewell points out, Goldblum gets his medicine from plants like the goldenseal and the ones Sarah Degree uses, so Sarah does have a legitimate "degree" of power based on her use of those elements, as well as the image she projects that convinces Hedley that "she got a big power" (19). Finally, while these references to gold are used to connote value, the value of money is certainly deflated in Hedley's dream of getting money from Buddy Bolden, whose cash turns to ash of no value (24, 70). Significantly, Hedley refers to the language of the burial service that stems from Genesis 3:19 to characterize the origin and value of money — and life. It is a line frequently paraphrased in blues and hokum songs, including W. C. Handy's "St. Louis Blues," Blind Willie McTell's "Southern Can Is Mine," and Blind Boy Fuller's "I Crave My Pigmeat":

> Ashes to ashes and dust to dust
> Show me a woman that a man can trust . . .
> Ashes to ashes and sand to sand
> Show me a woman ain't got a back door man. (Fuller)

Once again, cynical references to sexual fidelity form a central part of the meaning of this blues lyric — as they form a central concern in Wilson's play — here in relation to Hedley's illusory dream about a windfall of money that will allow him to buy a plantation and wield his much-desired power.

The stanza from the second prominent blues song performed in the text — nearly the entire first stanza of "That's All Right" is sung by Floyd in seven locations throughout the play (6, 16, 65, 78, 90, 101, 104) — is also from an actual blues recording that has reached the status of a standard. It was first issued on record as "Ora Nelle Blues" by Othum Brown for the Ora Nelle record label in Chicago in 1947 and was later recorded in better-known versions by Jimmy Rogers for Chess (also in Chicago; 1950), Junior Parker on Duke (1957), and Junior Wells on Vanguard (as "You Lied to Me," also in Chicago; 1966); nobody named Floyd Barton actually recorded the song, and it apparently never appeared on the Savoy label. This places the song in the time period of the play as opposed to the fifteen to twenty-five years that "Cabbage" was removed from that era. By drawing on songs from two different eras — the first a lighthearted sexual entertainment from the infancy of the blues recording era; the second a hard-edged and cynical lament from the urban electric postwar blues infancy, a period that reflects the rise of the independent record label — Wilson is able to span three decades of the recorded blues tradition. In contrasting the eras, Wilson emphasizes the consistency, constancy, variability, adaptability, and value of the blues. Indeed the oral tradition adapts to survive, retaining elements of social and cultural history that have sustained previous generations while adjusting to the demands, in this case, of increasing urbanization, industrialization, and modernization that force adaptation and new techniques — such as the uses of amplification — to maintain relevance in a changing world. This negotiation of past and present allows the blues to be both group referential and individually adapted: first person singular and plural.

The song reflects a certain cynicism toward interpersonal relationships even as it communicates ambivalence through its wistful longing for a more lasting association. The title itself, "That's All Right," clearly does not mean what it says in relation to the lyrics — it is not "all right." Replacing the playful commodification of sexuality of "Cabbage" is another, more tragic side of relationships that sees the notion of fidelity in this instance as a kind of fairy tale: "You told me, baby. *Once upon a time* / You said if I would be yours / You would sure be mine" (6; emphasis added). The repetition of the pronoun "you" here is almost accusatory, especially when paired with "said" and "told" and with the conditional "if" as a fulcrum and the adverb "sure" as the emphatic central focal point of the phrase. The irony is that the relationship is not a sure thing at all, especially since it is already conditional at best. The refrain of the song replaces the illusory telling and saying speech of the earlier lines with the first person *knowing* of the singer — "But that's all right / I know you in love with another man" — framed with the identical phrase introduced by a coordinating conjunction: "But that's all right" (7). Like many traditional fairy tales, of course, hardships intervene to create complications, which, in the case of this blues song and in Floyd's life, prevent one from living "happily ever after," as more genteel versions of fairy tales sometimes end.

Interestingly, Wilson does not include the entire refrain of the original song in the play. Following "I know you in love with another man but that's all right" in the original song is "Every now and then I wonder who's lovin' you tonight." Those familiar with African American culture would be expected to know that the twelve-bar lyric is not completed, and might even be expected to know this final line of the song since it is a blues standard. By using this modernist fragmenting technique, Wilson underscores the importance of the knowledge of African American vernacular culture and the nuances of the language and philosophy of the blues in interpreting African American lives and texts. But we must question further why Wilson does not have his character perform the entire twelve-bar stanza. In a sense by employing (and having his character actually performing) an actual blues song with verifiable lyrics, Wilson allows the cognoscenti to complete the stanza — which has already been generated, completed, and performed in reality and by Floyd on his record — with the realization that something is missing that may or may not fit in directly with this particular situation. It is an invitation to active reading, and to an exploration of how the folk tradition operates. In the final refrain line of "That's All Right," a speaker who has resigned himself to the inevitabilty of infidelity and of fleeting relationships casts a wistful eye on what he has lost. The attempt to seem nonchalant — "every now and then," he sings — is undercut by the fact that he has couched his story in timeless fairy-tale language and has taken the time to compose a song about a seemingly casual experience. Thus the singer caresses the hope, sadness, and longing of the experience, and encapsulates his interaction with each in his mind. In the play, does Floyd wonder at all points when he sings the song whether Vera is being loved by someone else? Or does he at some point develop faith in her? Will that faith be repaid, or will the lyric at some point revert to a situation of doubt? The indeterminate gap leaves the door of possibilities open for the next improvisatory experience.

The third prominent blues song is a paraphrase of a snatch from "Buddy Bolden's Blues," a song Jelly Roll Morton recorded twice in 1938 and again in 1939, claiming it was the composition of legendary and pioneering New Orleans jazz cornetist Bolden. The opening stanza of his Library of Congress version, based on a bawdy old riverfront folk song sometimes called "Funky Butt," goes: "I thought I heard Buddy Bolden say, 'You dirty, nasty, stinky butt, take it away.'"[2] Much more direct and derogatory than the playful double entendre of the "Cabbage" song, it is also not a song of longing or occasional desire for reconciliation — as "That's All Right" is — but a song of humiliating disparagement and personal and sexual rejection. In other words, it is another take on the spectrum of interpersonal relationships — a vigorous, foul, and funky declaration of independence slung into the beautiful and durable spittoon of blues music. Wilson, though, does not retain the theme of the song as Morton sang it a decade before the time of Wilson's play — rather, he excerpts just the first line — though he does have Hedley sing his own couplet lines along with the Bolden line in the play, which demonstrates perfectly how Wilson highlights the adaptability of the blues tradition. It is reasonable to expect that the characters in the play would have had some familiarity with the song as a composition and performance unto itself; however, in the play the song refers to image and monetary concerns expressed by Hedley, Floyd, and Canewell in a variety of places in the text. Hedley's concern for his status and power in the world is expressed in his response line, "Soon I be a big man some day" (65, 66); perhaps "a god" (which is what Hedley's father felt Bolden was [67]) or Jesus Christ, "the Son of the Father" (68). This may also reflect a sexual element in the play, since Hedley's need to be a big man by having sex with

Ruby (89–90) and ultimately by thinking he has impregnated her with a son she vows to name "King" (96) indicates that Hedley expresses his need for power and control in patriarchal terms, especially in light of Hedley's skirmishes with his own father.

Additionally, the difference between the response lines spoken by Canewell and by Hedley capture the tension that Hedley feels in his relationship with his father, and that Floyd feels in his relationship with his mother and with Vera. These together reflect the larger relationship of the black man with American society and the call-and-response nature of African American vernacular music. Hedley always completes the line "I thought I heard Buddy Bolden say" in relation to money with an offering of money to himself: "Here go the money, King, take it away" (16, 70) or "Come here. Here go the money" (106). Floyd (23, 39) and Canewell (106) claim that Bolden actually said, "Wake up and give me the money." It is the difference between having someone acknowledge that you deserve money and having to take what you think you deserve. Hedley desires reconciliation with his father, and Floyd does what he has to in order to get what he feels he deserves. He wants a fair chance at stardom, a decent relationship with Vera, and an honoring of his mother, all of which are blocked by racism in an American society that holds him down and kicks him. With the money both will be able, they think, to fulfill their dreams of being important men. Hedley wants to be the son of the father and to be called by the name his father has given him. Floyd tells Hedley, "I need someone to say that to me" (70) — to offer him the money — but he cannot imagine, as Hedley can, someone making that offer to him.

In the end, with Floyd dead and the crumpled bills falling from Hedley's hands "like ashes" (107), their lives and dreams are in shambles; both men have become criminals who have destroyed themselves and each other as a result of the limitations placed on them as black men in America. Hedley has not been able to reconcile with his father; Floyd has not been able to find the interpersonal relationship that will complete him. In response to Vera's telling him, "You got to believe in yourself," Floyd counters, "A man that believe in himself still need a woman that believe in him. You can't make life happen without a woman" (13). This has a meaning different from Hedley's assertion "that you know a woman need a man" (19): Floyd means not just some kind of practical and spiritual relationship, but actually producing a vital impulse. The blend of African American vernacular music traditions provides the opportunity for a physical consummation and spiritual attachment that allows people to see the god(s) in themselves.

In the end, Wilson leaves us once again with a fragmentary lyric, as he had employed only part of a stanza of "That's All Right" and part of the song "Anybody Here Want to Try My Cabbage." While Wilson had employed only part of the "Buddy Bolden" lyric earlier, he had at least filled in the heard message with his own words. At the end, Hedley is left stuck on the first line of the performance, "I thought I heard Buddy Bolden say," singing it three times. This may have reference to the three different completions of the couplet offered in the play. On the other hand, the presence of the ellipsis suggests that there are perhaps more repetitions of the line, acknowledging that it is a song that others may complete individually in different ways. In this reading, it functions almost as an incantation and invitation as "the lights go down to black" (107); clearly it is a reference both to Floyd's demise and the end of the play. With Floyd now dead — the money of Hedley's dreams partly responsible for that and now turned to ashes — it is left to the strong African American oral tradition to provide some ritualistic strength and wisdom to complete the stanza. Still looking to Buddy Bolden, the King, the great black man, for wisdom and guidance — for affirmation of life in the midst of suffering and struggle — this is also going down to "black" as well. The surrealistic vision of Floyd floating out of his coffin at the graveyard and moving upward is a vision of spiritual resurrection, though not the bodily resurrection like that of Lazarus that is criticized by Canewell as being "against nature" (26). Back on earth, Floyd would only go through more hardship and suffering that would threaten to disintegrate him, with only his music to help try to bring unity to all that chaos.

In "A Note from the Playwright" preceding the text of the play, Wilson provides another reference to the number seven — a list that emphasizes his own personal cultural reverence:

I have tried to extract some measure of truth from their lives as they struggle to remain whole in the face of so many things that threaten to pull them asunder. I am not a historian. I happen to think that the content of my mother's life — her myths, her superstitions, her prayers, the contents of her pantry, the smell of her kitchen, the song that escaped from her sometimes parched lips, her thoughtful repose and pregnant laughter — are all worthy of art.

These seven elements that make up the content of his mother's life Wilson finds in African American vernacular music as well, as the tradition reflects the diverse and conflicting content of the lives of African Americans who say it and listen to it in order to persevere. One version might ring out:

> I thought I heard Buddy Bolden say
> The sun gonna shine in my back door

Notes

1. It is worth noting that there were eight versions of an Edgar Dowell song titled "West Indies Blues" that featured a positive portrayal of Marcus Garvey recorded in the 1920s (as early as 1923), and Dowell's "Black Star Line," in support of the Garvey-UNIA shipping venture, was recorded by Rosa Henderson and Hazel Meyers in 1924. Garvey's appeal generally to the masses — as opposed to the intelligentsia of the black middle class — fits well with Hedley's attraction to Garvey in the play. We have no recordings of the legendary Buddy Bolden; only recorded tributes like the one Jelly Roll Morton titled "Buddy Bolden's Blues" when he recorded it for Alan Lomax of the Library of Congress. There was a tradition of tribute songs for blues singers in the blues tradition as well, including tributes to Bessie Smith, Blind Boy Fuller, Blind Lemon Jefferson, Ma Rainey, and Leroy Carr, rendering the use of Morton's tribute here consistent with the blues tradition.

2. Also quoted in a later stanza by Ellison at the end of *Invisible Man*.

DONALD E. PEASE

August Wilson's Lazarus Complex

Although *King Hedley II* is the eighth play in the Wilson cycle, it is the only play that Wilson created as a direct sequel to a previous play. *King Hedley II* repeats scenes, characters, and actions — preparation of a sacrificial animal, ritual murder, burial of the seed, robbing of a store — that Wilson's audience first came upon in *Seven Guitars*. In both plays, the core event centers on a violent confrontation that results in the death of one of the antagonists. In *Seven Guitars*, this violence culminates in a fatal encounter between a blues performer, Floyd Barton, and a West Indian immigrant, King Hedley, whose delusional paranoia induces him to murder Floyd. In *King Hedley II*, King Hedley's son feels compelled to repeat his father's violent actions as the sole means of inheriting his legacy. Instead of a beneficent patrimony, King Hedley II inherits this trauma as the deep truth of his own existence. The "only thing I know about the play," Wilson remarked in an interview about this baneful repetition, is that "his father killed a man. He killed a man. His surrogate father killed a man. He killed a man, and he has a seventeen-year-old son who's getting ready to kill a man" (Bryer and Hartig, 202).

In *Seven Guitars* the blues community transmuted the violent encounter between Hedley and Floyd into an object lesson in folk wisdom, into the subject of everyday gossip and rumor, and into the raw material for the surviving characters' blues performances. But the protagonist in *King Hedley II* becomes subsumed within a vertiginous cycle of violence that threatens to swallow the entire community. Wilson conveyed the potentially catastrophic consequences of King's way of inheriting his destructive patrimony by having it coincide with the death of Aunt Ester, the matriarchal wisdom figure who had accompanied the African community throughout its 366 years in America.

Indeed the site of transition from *Seven Guitars* to *King Hedley II* locates what might be described as the primal scene of Wilson's dramatic epic. The symbolic event that was enacted at this site involved the communal effort to produce a vital cultural legacy for people dissevered from the mainstreams of social life. That event also represents what Wilson described as the original motive for his dramatic project:

> I wanted to present the unique particulars of black America culture as the transformation of impulse and sensibility into codes of conduct and responses, into cultural rituals that defined and celebrated ourselves as men and women of highest purpose. . . . The field of manners and rituals of social intercourse — the music, speech, rhythms, eating habits, religious beliefs, gestures, notions of common sense, attitudes towards sex, and the responses to pleasure and pain — have enabled us to survive the loss of our political will and the disruption of our history. The culture's moral codes and the sanction of conduct offer a clear instruction as to the value of community and make clear that the preservation and promotion, the propagation and rehearsal of the value of one's ancestors is the surest way to a full and productive life. (viii–ix)

King Hedley II dramatizes actions under the aegis of a name that does not name the character responsible for the actions that are represented within it. King believes he is the son of a man named King, but in truth he is the son of the man who died before his mother had met Hedley. Wilson represents the meeting between King and Elmore, the man who killed King's biological father, as a repetitive flashback of two previous fatal encounters: between Floyd Barton and King Hedley I and between Elmore and King Hedley II's biological father, Leroy Slater. Overall, the play confronts King with the violence and the exploitation out of which he was begotten.[1] King's personal drama also allegorizes events that characters in his earlier plays were unable to work through, indicating that they must be worked through to secure the community's viable future.

The play's preface indicates the pivotal status that *King Hedley II* holds in Wilson's epic cycle:

The cycle of plays I have been writing since 1979 is my attempt to represent that culture in dramatic art. . . . From *Joe Turner's Come and Gone* (which is set in 1911) to *King Hedley II* (set in 1985), the cycle covers almost eighty years of American history. The plays are peopled with characters whose ancestors have been in the United States since the early seventeenth century. . . . From Herald Loomis's vision of the bones rising out of the Atlantic ocean (the largest unmarked graveyard in the world) in *Joe Turner's Come and Gone*, to the pantheon of vengeful gods ("The Ghosts of Yellow Dog") in *The Piano Lesson*, to Aunt Ester, the then 349-year-old conjure woman who first surfaced in *Two Trains Running*, the metaphysical presence of a spirit world has become increasingly important to my work. It is the world they turn to when they are most in need. (viii–ix)

If metaphysical presences have played important roles in all of the plays in the cycle (e.g., Toledo's instruction in how to conjure African gods in *Ma Rainey's Black Bottom*, Troy Maxson's rendezvous with Mr. Death in *Fences*, the confrontation with the ghosts of the Yellow Dog in *The Piano Lesson*), *King Hedley II* marks a turning point in Wilson's relationship to the spiritual dimension of his dramatic project: the deadly struggle between King and his father's killer leads to overcoming the specter of black-on-black violence that haunted Africans in America from the period of the Middle Passage to the time of the play's setting in 1980s Pittsburgh. Like the bones Herald Loomis sees in *Joe Turner*, and the bones in the City of Bones that Barlow sees rise up from the sea, this specter positioned the characters in *King Hedley II* within the imperfect past of the Middle Passage. An action might be described as belonging to an imperfect past when the dimension of that past action which cannot be symbolized within available representations continues to haunt present activities.[2]

Hedley's father suffered a physical death without providing his son the opportunity to acquit himself of his feelings of indebtedness. King inherited his father's inability to settle his paternal indebtedness. Because memory could not supplant the void made present by his father's absence, and thus render it to the past, King remained stuck in the terrible spot where his father never stopped killing Floyd. Wilson has described this trans-generational structure of violence that eventuated there as having origi-nated from African Americans' unconscious transference of the collective aggression aroused by an oppressive white supremacist social structure onto black surrogates. This cycle of violence overshadowed present events after the manner in which King's undead fathers haunted the actions of their son. Sharon Holland has persuasively argued that this transhistori-cal structure effected an uncanny propinquity between the living and the dead: "If black subjects are held in such isolation — first by a system of slavery and second by its imaginative replacement — then is not their rela-tionship to the dead, those lodged in terms like heritage and ancestor, more intimate than historians and critics have articulated?" (Holland, 196).

In *Seven Guitars*, Hedley's biological death was preceded by his sym-bolic death, which resulted from his being shut up alive within his dead father's dream. In the final scene of his drama, King and his biological fa-ther's killer, Elmore, come face to face with apparitions who returned from the dead through their conflict. King imagined that by killing Elmore, the man who shot his biological father, Leroy, he would avenge his father's death. But as they reenacted this earlier scene of violence, the spectral pres-ences of Floyd and Hedley arise from the dead to join the ghost of Leroy and the double of the Elmore who committed the murder.

Because the historical location for the reduction of Africans to the imag-ined conditions of death was the slave plantation, Hedley believed that he could become free only by opening up a slave plantation in downtown Pittsburgh, and his putative son, King, believed his given name scripted him to repeat the role of the father who aspired to head a plantation.

Whereas the undead Hedley had lingered in the realm between the living and the dead because he was denied his place in the social order, King's biological father, Leroy, returned to demand that his son render his death legible to a social order that had not taken notice of his life. King's discovery of the truth of his identity, in the form of the suppressed sur-name Slater, alienated him from every family member who raised him. Their "son" became the conduit through which both fathers returned to the social order to relive the retributive violence responsible for their own deaths. The son both of a "King" and of a forgotten dead man, King was completely dissevered from the symbolic order resituated wholly within a cycle of fatal violence. Kinless and natally alienated, King exemplified the condition of social death that Orlando Patterson explains is the juridical fate that the white supremacist order had imposed upon the slave.

Patterson has famously diagnosed the feelings of kinlessness and natal alienation that haunt King as symptoms of what he calls the "social death" African Americans first experienced as slaves. Patterson defined "social death" as the imposition of a juridical and political condition originally intended to dispossess enslaved Africans of their knowledge of or association with history: "Slaves differed from other human beings in that they were not allowed freely to integrate the experience of their ancestors into their lives, to inform their understanding of social reality with their inherited meanings of their natural forbears, or to anchor the living present in any conscious community of memory" (19).

Variations of this motif— social death resulting from the unacted-upon will of a dead ancestor reliving itself through a descendant — appear in all of Wilson's plays. The psychosocial structures that compel these aggressive impulses derive from a self-destructive disposition that, for several reasons, I shall call the "Lazarus complex." Wilson frequently alludes to the biblical Lazarus to allegorize his characters' experiences within American culture, and the figure of Lazarus is explicitly invoked in both *Seven Guitars* and *King Hedley II* to refer to the deadly form of structural violence organizing American culture. Wilson's personification of the cultural memory of Africans' 366 years in America as the character of Aunt Ester, moreover, inspired me to employ "Lazarus" as the name of the allegorical figure who threatens violently to discontinue that memory.

In the New Testament, the name Lazarus identifies the character Jesus resurrected from the dead. When Canewell, a character in *Seven Guitars*, retells this parable, he describes Jesus as having raised Lazarus from the dead so that Lazarus would relive the painful conditions of his death. Canewell intended this redescription to reveal the much more pervasive structure of living death that I have named the Lazarus complex. The Lazarus complex performs the antithesis to Christ's resurrection from the dead. *Rather than lifting men up from what kills their spirits, the Lazarus complex represents the processes through which the dead oblige the living to relive their deaths.*

The Lazarus complex is social as well as psychological in that it operates through a relay of social, political, and juridical institutions that were set in place during the slave trade and that continued to structure the social order after Reconstruction. The white supremacist mentality on which this relay was founded identified Africans wholly with the social order's powers of subjection, such that the subjective "freedom" experienced by whites in taking up their socially mandated subject positions derived from their disidentification from black subjection.

This process of disavowal and subjection connected the psyches of Wilson's black characters with the entrenched relay of social structures that prevented their self-representations from appearing within the mirror of the dominant culture. The Lazarus complex thus names the structure of feeling that induces characters in Wilson's preceding plays to take the aggression that they should have directed against the white supremacist social structure and transfer it onto black surrogates.

Hedley's murder of Floyd displaced his aggression against the white supremacist culture that had demoralized his father: Elmore killed Leroy after Leroy threatened to kill Elmore for destroying his social credibility. Unable to embrace either man in his memory, King remains trapped by these traumatic events, so that the structure adjudicating Elmore's murder of King's father causes its repetitive reenactments. Because King refuses to consign punishment for this crime to the structural violence responsible for its enactment, he instead reperforms a substitute violence that made African Americans stand in both for the white power structure and for that power structure's victims.

King's confrontation with this structure of violence turns, within the same character, the continuity and the discontinuity of the Wilson cycle toward each other and in opposition to each other. In its efforts to produce an identity for a man who did not know his name and a future for a man who struggled to find the resources to work his way through this traumatizing past, *King Hedley II* is about the past and the future of Wilson's theater. The traumatizing trans-generational memory to which King was a respondent constituted the deep truth of the African presence in the Americas. American history could not fill in the void that the historical trauma of the Middle Passage had opened up. The claims to universality of its historical paradigms and the exclusionary processes at work in its representational conventions were both part of the Lazarus complex that induced the trauma.

But Wilson's plays also ensure that his characters' actions and relationships are dramatized before the concerned regard of the blues community, whose culture inspired and whose members composed the ideal audience for Wilson's plays. The white supremacist structure had positioned a dominant white gaze that refused to allow black cultural achievements into the social order. In bearing witness to the profound spiritual significance of African American cultural representations, the blues community displaced this suppressed gaze by adding what was lacking in the visual field. Before they could truly see themselves, Wilson's characters had to learn how to behold the world through the eyes of the blues community that added this second sight. The blues community's second-sightedness ratified the worthiness of characters that the dominant culture had disqualified.

That blues community emerged out of the Great Migration, whose panoramic history supplied Wilson's cycle with its epic scope. The Great Migration is a documentable, historical representation of a mass movement that took place as African Americans migrated from the post-Reconstruction South, from 1895 to the 1930s. But in Wilson's plays, the Great Migration also symbolizes a mythological exodus from slavery to freedom, making the events in Wilson's individual plays, in effect, all part of the collective drama of the Great Migration, which was made inevitable when the first African was forcibly transplanted to America. This is because the Great Migration, as the antithesis to the Middle Passage, names what mobilized the emancipatory aspirations of all of Wilson's characters.[3] In its largest sense, therefore, the Great Migration is both the emancipatory movement in which Wilson's characters participated and the historical force that is interrupted when Wilson's characters fall out of its flow.

As a collective movement, the Great Migration empowered its members to separate themselves from the cataclysmic violence of enslavement by replacing the compulsion to reenact this violence with forms of psychic, social, and spiritual mobility. Wilson's characters obtained access to the spiritual dimension of the Great Migration in moments when they felt as if they could not go on. The ongoing eventfulness of the Great Migration drew upon a repository of wisdom, lore, cultural practices, collective memories, prayers, role models, cooking instructions, conjurings, myths, symbolic rituals, chants, ancestral presences, and songs that have accompanied Africans throughout their 390 years in America. Wilson's characters deploy these spiritual resources to overcome the impediments to their social mobility imposed by the Lazarus complex. The individual and collective performances of music, song, celebration, resistance, backtracking, high-stepping, dance, recrimination, back-talking, and laughter through which Wilson's characters act upon these empowering resources materialize the freedom that the movement conveyed.[4]

The primary means of expression through which Wilson's characters recover their footing within this movement is the blues. The blues, the spirituals, and the folkways of the Great Migration mediate between Wilson's plays and the audiences they address. His blues performers overcome the conditions of kinlessness and social death by enacting improvisatory genealogies that construct surrogate family ties with ghosts from the immemorial past and with strangers from the unknowable future. The affinities the blues effect among performers, music, and the audience in large part presume a simultaneity of experience: the blues singer performs in the presence of and in response to the audience.[5]

In *King Hedley II*, Wilson gives the name Aunt Ester to that individual who embodies the restorative powers of the Great Migration.[6] This 366-year-old matriarch is as old as the African presence in America. Because Aunt Ester personifies the collective memory of the Great Migration, her death renders the ordeal King undergoes in his face-off with Elmore a profound threat to the survival of the blues community. This threat is further evidenced by the fact that Ruby, King's mother, has lost the desire to perform the blues.

This highly condensed account of the actions that take place in the transition between *Seven Guitars* and *King Hedley II* may have induced confusion rather than a clarification of their significance. What follows constitutes an effort to accomplish this clarification by explaining the meta-drama connecting the two plays as the correlation of two profound symbolic actions: the dismantling of the Lazarus complex and the resurrection of Aunt Ester. In the course of this explanation I shall take up several of the topics — the primal scene of retributive violence, the witness to the Lazarus complex, the destruction of the cycle of violence, and the resurrection of Aunt Ester — to which I have gestured in this compressed account of what took place at this turning point in Wilson's epic drama.

. . . .

With the following exchange of refrains, Hedley and Floyd enter into the imaginary space in which Hedley believes that the blues singer Buddy Bolden would hand him his father's legacy:

> Floyd: I thought I heard Buddy Bolden say . . .
> Hedley: What he say?
> Floyd: He said, "Wake up and give me the money."
> Hedley: Naw. Naw. He say, "Come here. Here go the money."
> Floyd: Well . . . what he give you?
> Hedley: He give me the ashes.
> Floyd: Tell him to give you the money. (23–24)

Each time Hedley and Floyd ritualistically repeat these lines they open a site within the symbolic order where Hedley reenters the dream space of his dying father's last will and testament:

> It is my father's money. What he send to me. He come to me in a dream. He say, "Are you my son?" I say, "Yes Father I am your son." He say, "I kick you in the mouth?" I say, "Yes, Father, I ask you why you do nothing and you kick me." He say, "Do you forgive me?" I say, "Yes, Father, I forgive you." He say, "I am sorry I died without forgiving you your tongue. I will send Buddy Bolden with some money for you to buy a plantation so the white man not tell you what to do."

Then I wait and I wait for a long time. Once Buddy Bolden come
and he say, "Come here, here go the money." I go and take it and it all
fall like ash. Ashes to ashes and dust to dust. Like that. It all come to
nothing. (70)[7]

Whereas Floyd hears Buddy Bolden say, "Wake up and give me the money,"
what Hedley hears is, "Naw! Naw! Here go the money." In between the
money that Floyd has imagined hearing Buddy demand and the money
Hedley has contrarily imagined seeing Bolden relinquish, the audience's
field of audibility engages a cycle of retributive violence that cannot be restricted to the dimensions of this refrain. The contours of this cycle become
starkly visible when King adds the following details about his relationship
with his father: "I go home and my daddy he sitting there and he big and
black and tired taking care of the white man's horses and I say how come
you not like Toussaint L'Ouverture, why you do nothing? And he kick me
with him boot in my mouth. I shut up that day, you know, and then when
Marcus Garvey come he give me back my voice to speak" (87).

On the day he stood at his father's deathbed, Hedley said:

"I hope as God is with us now but a short time more that you forgive
me my tongue." It was hard to say these things, but I confess my love
for my father and Death standing there say, "I already took him a
half hour ago." And he cold as a boot, cold as a stone and hard like
iron. I cried a river of tears but he was too heavy to float on them. So
I dragged him with me these years across an ocean. (87)

Hedley had wanted his father to emulate Toussaint L'Ouverture's power
that had overthrown the white power structure. But instead Hedley's father redirected his rage against his son. This internalization of the violence
initially perpetrated upon the members of the black community and then
redirected at his own son constitutes the legacy of Hedley's father, a legacy
that has already mandated Hedley's killing a man for refusing to call him
"King." Hedley repeats this misdirected aggression when he cuts Floyd's
throat with a machete after the blues performer refuses to give him the
money he and Poochie Guillory have stolen from a white-owned department store.

If Hedley's father had suffered a physical death, he cannot undergo a symbolic death until his son, King Hedley, settles his debt to him. In the absence of that settling of accounts, Hedley's father disappears from the symbolic order only to reappear within this dream space in which his son receives Buddy Bolden's money. But his father also reappears through Hedley's compulsive need to reenact the violence his father directed against him.

Hedley's oscillation back and forth between his experience of social death and his own self-destructive drives consign him to this void in the social order where the unacted-upon violence of his (un)dead father overtakes his psyche. When his undead father's violent behavior trespasses into the domain of his living son's body, Hedley imagines himself the head of a slave plantation where he can daily reenact the black-on-black aggression that his father has taught him: "Everything will fall to a new place. When I get my plantation I'm gonna walk around it. . . . I'm gonna be a big man on that day" (24).

When Floyd enters into the imagined space of Hedley's dream in the climactic scene of *Seven Guitars*, he collaborates in materializing the fatal environs of Hedley's imagined plantation. The refrain Hedley reenacts with Floyd there permits Hedley's father to trespass into the domain of his living son. Hedley imagines himself the head of a plantation through which the dead return from the City of Bones and demand the sacrifice of Floyd Barton.[8]

But the site at which Hedley kills Floyd and the social function of the man Hedley murders have violated the conditions of viability of the entire blues community. Wilson invests the scene of Hedley's crime with a quasi-sacred valuation. When Hedley kills Floyd on the plantation he imagines he had inherited from his father's dream, he transfers the death world of the antebellum South back to the material world of a twentieth-century Pittsburgh neighborhood backyard, killing the blues performer who personifies the spiritual resources necessary to liberate the community from that death world.[9]

. . . .

Hedley's murder of Floyd may have been the climactic event of *Seven Guitars*, but the play is primarily concerned with the social processes through which the other members of the community cope with this tragedy. Individually and collectively the characters in *Seven Guitars* searched for lyrics to express their intense grief.

In *Seven Guitars*, Floyd and Hedley enter into Hedley's father's Buddy Bolden blues song to perform the actions expressed in the lyrics. Hedley's killing of Floyd led the blues community to add new refrains to those lyrics so as to liberate themselves from their most self-destructive impulses. After they convert the terrible news of his death into the dozen blues lyrics and seven gospel songs, these performances translate the fatal give-and-take between Hedley and Floyd into the alternative structures of call-and-response, replacing the trauma of Floyd's death with ancillary cultural practices that convert its paralyzing effects into communally revitalizing energies.

In a splendid interview, Sandra Shannon inspired Wilson to articulate the following account of the significance of the blues to his dramatic vision:

> I think that the music has a cultural response of black Americans to the world they find themselves in. Blues is the best literature we have. If you look at the singers, they actually follow a long line all the way back to Africa and various other parts of the world. They are people who are carriers of the culture, carriers of the ideas — the troubadours in Europe, etc. Except in black America — in this society — they were not valued except among the black folk who understood. I've always thought of them as sacred because of the sacred tasks they had taken upon themselves to disseminate this information and carry these cultural values of the people. And I found that white America would very often abuse them. I don't think that it was without purpose in the sense that the blues and music have always been at the forefront in the development of character and consciousness of black America, and people have senselessly destroyed that or stopped that. Then you're taking away from the people their self-definition — in essence, their self-determination. These guys were arrested as vagrants and drunkards and whatever. They were never seen as valuable members

of a society by whites. In fact, I'm writing a play that deals specifically with that.[10]

The blues constitute a way of passing along communal knowledge as sung stories that keep the knowledge memorable enough to be recirculated by successive listeners. Thus the knowledge remains a vital resource in a system of cultural transmission — at work in the oral tradition — that sustains and is sustained by overlapping structures of response. The music provides emotional reference for stories that the community sanctions, and the singing of the song by other members of the community keeps the stories alive, while providing, as well, the means of understanding the significance of the stories to the community's survival.

Blues are not an autonomous idiom; they are interconnected with other idioms that exceed translation and lack definitive signification. The oral tradition includes these pluralized idioms but without a single key that would supply their definitive translation. If blues performers work variations on their idioms' already-established meanings, every variation returns the blues performer to the sources of the idioms in the archival storehouse of the Great Migration. Through these variations, blues performers shift the direction of the idiom on which they are riffing so as to propagate transitions that advance the music's themes. These transitions pivot on the termination of totalizing melodies by embracing a multiplicity of different refrains.

The blues supply Wilson's community with a way of living within an alien symbolic order by providing the resources with which to transform it. The witness names the figure of freedom within the spectator who learns how to view the world from the perspective of the blues community. Wilson's plays add this unfamiliar figure of the witness to the symbolic field. A Wilson play takes hold when the playgoer, exposed to the finitude of his common sense — a set of limitations upheld by the symbolic order — becomes open to an alteration in the order of things.

One of the pieces of knowledge that the blues community of *Seven Guitars* communicates is that, by killing a blues performer, Hedley has destroyed one of the community's sacred regenerative figures. The surviving members of Barton's blues community perform riffs about its significance, which separates the community from what threatens to immobilize it. Wilson's next play represented the drama of Hedley's son in terms of his entrapment within the immobilizing structures. The transition in between the two plays constitutes an impasse for the blues community symptomatized by the fact that King's mother, Ruby, has lost her desire to sing the blues. Without the blues' power to reveal its devastating impact, the Lazarus complex threatens to engulf the community in tidal floods of violence.

In adding the figure of the Lazarus complex, whose structural role has not been allowed visible recognition, Wilson reveals the structures of perception that overdetermine the negation of black cultural representations within the dominant social order. The witness to this structural violence is not limited to African Americans, but in its extensive form Wilson's blues community includes the whites as well as the blacks in his audience. An audience member becomes a witness to this truth when he or she learns how to look at events from the position of this witness.

Because the Lazarus complex is structured in a racist way of looking at the world, Wilson's bearing witness *against* the oppressive visual structures that reproduce that way of looking aspires to annul racist ways of seeing. The witness adds a subjective viewpoint to the members of Wilson's audience. From that viewpoint, they can become cognizant of a framework of visual assumptions. The figure of the witness, furthermore, becomes an additional character, or meta-character, who frames the characters whom the audience re-sees through the perspective of this witness.

The witness produces two figures within the observer (the visualizer and the witness) and within the observed (the visualized participant and the witness). The witness therefore can annul the racist structures of visualization in the observer and can also destroy the figure of racial subjection from within the observed. When Stool Pigeon's witness takes hold of the visual positions that inform the audience's view of the world, this witness reveals the white supremacist gaze as that which blinds the observer to truth of the blues community's perspectives.

Canewell, the one character in *Seven Guitars* who did not benefit from the blues community's restorative displacement of Floyd's murder, also plays a key role in *King Hedley II*. The harmonica player in Floyd Barton's blues band, Canewell brought Floyd's lover, Vera, the medicinal goldenseal plant under the roots of which Floyd hid the stolen money. Canewell also accidentally dug up the money, forcing Floyd to reclaim it. Rather than using the blues to disassociate himself from the site of Hedley's violence, Canewell collaborates in the refrain with Hedley with which the play concludes:

> Canewell: "I thought I heard Billy Bolden say . . . "
> Hedley: What he say?
> Canewell: He say, "Wake up and give me the money."
> Hedley: Naw. Naw. He say, "Come here, here go the money."
> Canewell: What he give you?
> Hedley: He give me this.
> Hedley: (*holds up a handful of crumpled bills*) They slip from his
>   fingers and fall to the ground like ashes. (107)

Canewell is also the character in *Seven Guitars* who invokes the figure of Lazarus to interpret Hedley's relationship to his father: "Jesus ain't had no business raising Lazarus from the dead. If it's God's will, then what he look like undoing it? If it's his father's work, then it's his father's business and he should have have stayed out of it" (25). "I'm talking about you ain't supposed to go against nature. Don't care whether you the Son of God or not. Everybody know that. Lazarus even know that" (25–26). Canewell concludes that Christ's miracle is inappropriate because he believes in the justice of God the Father's law that irretrievably separates the living from the dead. Besides violating God's order, Christ's decision to raise Lazarus causes Lazarus to relive and thereby double the suffering that led to his first death: "When Lazarus was dying the second time—he was dying from pneumonia—somebody went up and got Jesus. Lazarus saw him coming and said, 'Oh no, not you again!' See, all Jesus had done by raising him from the dead was to cause him to go through that much more suffering. He was suffering the pain of living" (26). According to Canewell, Christ had not resurrected Lazarus from the condition of death but resituated the dead Lazarus within the realm of the living.

Canewell is the sole character in *Seven Guitars* who bore the knowledge of the Lazarus complex that had induced Hedley to kill Floyd. But in the transition from *Seven Guitars* to *King Hedley II*, Canewell underwent a change in his nominal status from Canewell to Stool Pigeon. This change was the consequence of Canewell's having testified in court to Hedley's murder of Floyd. His given name "Canewell" was conferred upon him in honor of his slave ancestors who had received the name as an index of the efficiency with which they cut down the harvest on sugarcane plantations. But after Canewell turned into the state's star witness against Hedley, Ruby, the woman who told Hedley she was carrying his child, renames him "Stool Pigeon": "Ruby called me 'Stool Pigeon'. Somehow or another it stuck. I'll tell anybody I'm a Truth Sayer" (15).

In *Seven Guitars*, Canewell provides the state with the evidence it needs to punish Hedley for killing Floyd; in *King Hedley II*, Stool Pigeon becomes the Truth Sayer who bears witness against the structure of social death responsible for Hedley's commission of this deed. Canewell had criticized Christ for disrupting the order of God the Father by raising the historical figure of Lazarus from the death his father had ordained. But Stool Pigeon arrives at a revelation that leads him to reinterpret Lazarus as the figure God the Father had created to personify the relationship between the living and the dead. Stool Pigeon communicates this revelation in the following prophetic saying:

> The Mighty God
> Made the wind
> Mighty is His name
> Who made the water
> Called man out of the dust
> The Mighty God
> Made the firmament
> Called forth Lazarus (80)

When he names Lazarus the figure God called forth after lifting man out of the dust, Stool Pigeon locates Lazarus within the firmament as the personification of death in life. Stool Pigeon also tells King that if he wants "eternal life," he must send Lazarus back to his grave: "For whosoever believeth, then shall I cause him to be raised into Eternal Life and magnify the Glory of My Father, the Lord God who made the firmament. Then shall Death flee and hide his face in darkness. For My Father ruleth over the things in his creation" (69). Stool Pigeon's role in causing the dead Lazarus to flee back into the darkness of his tomb requires that he stand in for the blues community, which the cycle of violence has threatened to destroy, and that he bear witness to the truth of the action that is about to take place.

Rather than continuing its processes, Stool Pigeon becomes the Truth Sayer who bears witness to the white supremacist structure of relations responsible for continuing the subjection and negation of African American culture. His witness culminates in the correlation of King's Lazarus complex with the iniquities of the fathers. To make certain that King understands the gravity of this revelation, Stool Pigeon hands him the machete with which Hedley killed Floyd:

> This is the machete Hedley used to kill Floyd Barton. This is the machete of the "Conquering Lion of Judea." I give that machete to you, and me and Hedley come full circle. . . . The Bible say, "Let him who knoweth duty redeem the house of his fathers from his iniquities against the Lord. And if he raise a cry saying he knoweth not the iniquities of his father then he knoweth not duty for even if the iniquities are great and his father's house be scattered to the numberless winds, if he shall gather it and raise it up then shall it stand even unto the end of time." Floyd was my friend. I give that to you and we can close the book on that chapter. I forgive. That's the Key to the mountain. God taught me how to do that. God can teach you a lot of things. He don't give you nothing you can't handle. God's a bad motherfucker. (62)

Although Hedley had imagined himself in the place of Abraham awaiting the birth of Isaac, Stool Pigeon saw that Hedley had called forth Lazarus. More importantly, Stool Pigeon understands that King can only banish this specter of living death by destroying the Lazarus complex that supports it. When Stool Pigeon hands King the sword with which his father had slain a sacred blues singer, he is challenging King to discover the resources that will end the retributive violence responsible for his father's iniquities. To dismantle the figure who made Hedley feel like Lazarus, therefore, King has to destroy the Lazarus complex within himself.

Stool Pigeon understands that the spiritual figure who can restore the blues community is not the Christ who caused Lazarus to relive his death, but Aunt Ester, whose death has threatened to destroy the repository of cultural resources that has accompanied the blues community throughout its 366 years within the Great Migration. Stool Pigeon's prophetic task also involves performing a ritual that will resurrect the spirit of Aunt Ester. Initially Stool Pigeon believes that this work can be accomplished by sprinkling the blood of her dead cat over the sacred ground upon which Hedley had killed Floyd.

But Stool Pigeon's witness to the actions at the play's conclusion reveals that the killing of Lazarus is the sacred ritual the blues community must perform before it can reconnect to the spiritual resources of the Great Migration. That ritual sacrifice requires that King undergo an ordeal in which he successfully separates the portions of himself that belong to the Lazarus complex from those that descended from the Great Migration.

The blues community in *Seven Guitars* witnesses what the dominant order cannot, namely, the lyrical insights through which it reworks grim spectacle into restorative wisdom. In *King Hedley II*, Stool Pigeon witnesses the deadly cycle of violence to which Ruby had given birth, in her son, and he witnesses as well the threat that retributive violence poses to the entire community. After the horrific encounter, in *Seven Guitars*, between Floyd and Hedley, the blues community transfigures the scene into lessons in survival, but not even the blues community can transform the retributive violence that threatens to renew itself at the conclusion of *King Hedley II*.

The action at the heart of the play revolves around the return of Elmore, who eventually informs King of his true paternity and reveals his own role in Leroy's death. Elmore states that his motives for taking this action were based upon his desire to get King to agree to the justice of the rules of the game that led him to take the life of Leroy: "Tell King I am coming to see him. I know how he had some hard times, I want to see if he learned anything" (44). But Elmore has not in fact returned to find out what King has learned. He has come back to tell King something he could not have otherwise known: "See, when you pulled that trigger you done something. You done something more than most other people. You know more about life 'cause you done been to that part of it. Most people don't never get over on that side . . . that part of life. They live on the safe side. But see . . . you done been God. Death is something he do. God decide when somebody ready. Not you. He decide when he want somebody. God don't like that, you thinking you him. He cut you loose" (73).

Beyond Elmore's ostensible motive for revealing the truth of King's paternity, he also feels obliged to confess his murder so that he can find peace. Instead of covering over the void he caused by taking another man's life, however, his disclosure opens up another void by depriving King of a representable identity.[11]

Elmore's revelation makes him responsible for the deaths of both of King's fathers. He killed King's biological father by shooting him in the face, and he killed King's symbolic father by telling King the secret of his origins. King felt doubly alienated by this news. After losing the name that renders him recognizable to himself, he is renamed after a man who lacks a place in his genealogy.

King discovers his true identity at this fatal crossroads where the violent legacy of Leroy Slater converges with that of King Hedley I. The double of both fathers, King Hedley II has redoubled the loss of name. That redoubled loss signifies his exposure to the sheer contingency of radical anonymity. If the return of the suppressed name of his actual progenitor cost him one name, the name "Leroy Slater" — to which he was now forcibly bound — dissevers him from every known relation.

Hedley had killed Floyd to square his debt to his father; Elmore had killed Leroy for his failure to pay his debt to him. Because King feels compelled to re-perform the violence that has led to the downfall of both fathers, before he can live his own life, he has to settle his biological father's accounts within the symbolic order and to fulfill his symbolic father's wish to transform that order.

This felt need to fulfill their symbolic mandates thus positions King in between the deaths of both fathers in a domain resembling the death world of the Middle Passage, in that it opens up a space within the social order where death trespasses into the domain of life and life crosses over into the region of death. There life confronts its certain death and death lives in anticipation of itself. This death world, which lies under the provenance of Lazarus, also names the place of the imaginary plantation on which Hedley had killed Floyd and the place of life in death where Elmore had killed Leroy. A sacred site, it also names the archaic ground on which the African ancestors of the blues community were violently uprooted from their families and their homeland and were thrown into the slave quarters of the Middle Passage.

Stepping into this domain, King yields his psyche to the Lazarus complex, which demands that he repeat the retributive violence in this cycle of living death. While King's compulsion to settle his father's debts may stir our pity, his drive toward annihilation arouses our deepest fears.

Elmore explains that his deep motive for killing Leroy originated out of a comparable death world. That world had encompassed Elmore's life when Leroy put a gun to his head before an audience of their friends, in a crowded bar. When, instead pulling the trigger, Leroy whispered, "Now you are a dead man," Elmore called forth Lazarus to take up Elmore's place in the social order, and, in keeping with the dictates of the Lazarus complex, Elmore proceeded to relive his own death in the displaced act of taking Leroy's life. Since Elmore had lost a place in the social order, he answered by opening up a void where Leroy once stood. In the concluding act of *King Hedley II*, Elmore returns figuratively to the scene of that crime, wanting King to agree to the justice of the rules which led him to take the life of King's biological father. King instead invents rules that induce the two men to reenact the scene in which Leroy had performed the symbolic killing of Elmore: "Elmore the way I see it . . . Leroy owed you fifty dollars. That was man to man. He should have paid you. You say he's my daddy. . . . I'm gonna pay my daddy's debt. Here goes your fifty dollars. Now we straight on that. But see . . . my name ain't Leroy Slater, Jr. My name is King Hedley II, and we got some unfinished business to take care of" (99).

After repaying Leroy's debt, however, King reproduces the scenario in which his father had incurred the debt by refusing to give Elmore the betting money Elmore thought was owed to him:

> Elmore: Twenty of this is mine. The bet was three to one.
>
> King: When you play the lottery, do the state give you back what you played or do they just give you back what you won? Take that sixty dollars and get out of my face. Unless you want to make something of it. You can take it to the limit.
>
> Elmore: All right. Those are your rules. Those are the rules you wanna play by. Come, let's play. Seven! (100–101)

After Elmore throws a seven, King knocks him to the ground and threatens to kill him with Hedley's machete. But upon taking up the machete that Stool Pigeon has handed down to him, King, rather than killing Elmore, repeats the phrase over the supine body of his father's killer: "Now you are a dead man twice." The repetition of this phrase that Leroy had pronounced to Elmore before refusing to pull the trigger gave expression to King's rationale for his decision not to kill Elmore. Holding up the machete with which Hedley had killed Floyd, King resurrects the memory of his symbolic father at the same instant that he refuses to slay the murderer of his biological father, thereby also declining to reenact his symbolic father's murder of Floyd. By feeling the compulsion to re-perform both acts of vengeance yet declining to do so, King brings two cycles of violence to a close in a single act of rejection. Through the interruption of these cycles of violence, King atones for the "iniquities" of both fathers.

In accomplishing this reparation, King reenters the space where his symbolic father had murdered Floyd and the space where Elmore had killed Leroy, thus making a correlation between the archaic groves in Africa where blacks used machetes to force other blacks into the Middle Passage and the death worlds of white America's plantation slavery.

Ending the succession of violent actions that replenished these death worlds, King II destroys his Lazarus complex, in that the phrase "Now you are a dead man twice" finds its true addressee in the Lazarus complex that had taken possession of both Elmore and King. After Elmore hears the repetition in King's phrase, he recognizes that he has already been living his own death. When he fires his gun into the ground rather than at King, the audience knows that Elmore has sent Lazarus (who personifies the figure "dead man twice") back to his grave. Feeling his father's (and Elmore's) compulsion to kill but declining to act upon it, King disrupts the cycle of living death that originated during the time of the Middle Passage and continues to exact servitude to its destructive imperatives into the contemporary moment.

But King's refusal does not merely result in the sacrifice of Lazarus. In annulling the relay of violence that links his fate to the names of his fathers, King is no longer the son of either man. The settling of his fathers' symbolic debts squares the books and completes the circle that links his birth to their deaths. In de-creating the self who had been fated to repeat the cycle of violence, King can no longer be described as the son of man.[12]

King has accomplished this transfiguration by dissevering himself from the cycle of retributive violence through which the Lazarus complex had taken hold of the African American community. King's transformation cannot be fully accomplished, however, until Ruby kills the Lazarus figure (the "you a dead man twice" figure) within King by accidentally shooting him in the throat. If King's emancipation has removed him from the social order, Ruby's shooting of her son opens up a space within that order through which Aunt Ester returns and restores Ruby's capacity to sing her favorite blues refrain:

> Red sails in the sunset
> Way out on the sea
> Oh carry my loved one
> Bring him home safely to me. (102)

In sacrificing Lazarus, the blues community brings about the dialectical separation between the deadening effects of the complex and what is eternally alive. As the mediator through whom the blues community's connection with the Great Migration is restored, Aunt Ester is the true beneficiary of this sacrificial rite. While alive, Aunt Ester names the medium through whom the blues community receives the spiritual resources of the Great Migration. After her death, Aunt Ester names the ancestor in whose name the Lazarus complex was sacrificed so that she could continue in her service as the blues community's intermediary.

King's ordeal must pass through the matrix of Aunt Ester before it can become transfigured into the unforgettable wisdom that promises to redeem the blues community. Ruby tells Stool Pigeon that Aunt Ester counseled her against an abortion before King's birth, and it is to Aunt Ester that Ruby consigns King's spirit after she brings about his death. The resurrection of Aunt Ester and the killing of Lazarus are co-constituting events. The figure who performs the murder is the blues performer Ruby, whose voice has been silenced by the violence that had overtaken the community. Ruby's song delivers King to Aunt Ester, who has returned to the community to bear witness to the figure who had transformed it.

If the deep action of *King Hedley II* entails the displacing of a cataclysmic cycle of violence by a blues song through which the community has survived that violence, the figure who restores Ruby's voice is Aunt Ester — into whose body King is re-borne. After Ruby sings her refrain, Stool Pigeon sees Isaac rise out of the body of Lazarus, where he is carried into Abraham's bosom. It takes Stool Pigeon to recognize the fact that King's disruption of the cycle of violence has fulfilled Hedley's wish that his son become the Messiah.

> The fatted calf!
> Told Abraham you wanted Isaac!
> Say I want your best!
>
> From the top of the mountain
> You sent the law!
>
> I want your best!
> I want Isaac!
>
> We give you our Glory.
> We give you our Glory.
> We give you our Glory. (103–104)

Notes

1. In order to distinguish King Hedley II from his father, King Hedley, throughout the essay I will refer, as is most commonly done in the scripts of the plays, to the father as Hedley and the son as King.

2. Sandra Shannon drew August Wilson into the following elaboration of the presences of the ancestors from the Middle Passage within the bodies of American Africans: "Loomis's connection with the ancestors — the Africans who were lost during the Middle Passage and were thrown overboard. They are walking around here now and they look like you because you are these very same people. This is who you are" (13). Shannon went on to explain the ghostly revenant of Joseph Sutter in *The Piano Lesson* as a manifestation of what I have called the Lazarus complex: "On another [level] his ghost exemplifies the looming threat of the white power structure."

3. Shannon supplied the emancipatory aspirations of Wilson's characters with historical warrant: "In the face of the South's changing status, many freedmen opted to start a new life in one of the several northern cities and thus escape their history as slaves" (13).

4. Wilson was careful to distinguish the poetic figures within his plays from the sociohistorical referents: "From the beginning I decided not to write about historical events in the pathologies of the black community. The details of our struggle to survive and prosper in what has been a difficult and somewhat bitter relationship with the system of laws and practices that deny us access to the tools necessary for productive and industrious lives are available to any serious student of history or sociology" (*King Hedley II*, viii).

5. In an interview with Herbert Boyd, Wilson described the plot of *King Hedley II* in terms of the disintegration of the family: "So a community under assault begins to take care of itself. It's not so much a breakdown of the family in the play, but a break with the tradition of the extended family. It's the connection with the grandparents that is broken that causes many of the problems in the community" (Bryer and Hartig, 237).

6. She is introduced in *Two Trains Running*.

7. In a preceding passage, Hedley explained that his father named him King because that was his nickname for Buddy Bolden: "My father play the trumpet and for him Buddy Bolden was a God, he was in New Orleans with the boats when he make them run back and forth. The trumpet was his first love. He never forgot that first night he heard Buddy Bolden play. He drink his rum, play his trumpet, and if you were lucky that night he would talk about Buddy Bolden. I

say lucky cause you never see him like that with his face light up and something be driving him from the inside and it was a thing he love more than my mother. That is why he named me King... after King Buddy Bolden" (67).

8. Here is what Wilson has said about the misdirected aggression in this scene: "You see, if Buddy Bolden is bringing some money from Hedley's father, he represents his father's forgiveness. Also, Hedley is going to use the money to buy a plantation, not to get rich, but so the white man doesn't tell him what to do anymore, to become independent, land being the basis of independence. In a way, the play says that anyone who is standing in the way of a black man's independence needs to be dealt with. So it's very necessary that Hedley decides that Floyd, as Buddy Bolden, is the messenger, the courier who would like to keep the money, who will not give him the money so he can buy his plantation. It means it's a betrayal of Hedley's father. Of course the tragedy is he's not Buddy Bolden, that he's Floyd Barton. It's a mistake. It's an honorable mistake, but it is a mistake" (Bryer and Hartig, 193–194).

9. Hedley's murder of Floyd Barton constituted a ritual reenactment of the rooster King Hedley had decapitated. King Hedley had earlier described the rooster as the sacred herald of the black Emancipation Day. Harry Elam has cited Wilson's description of the blues singers as a sacred figure as evidence of this parallel: "I've always thought of them as sacred because of the sacred tasks they took upon themselves — to disseminate the information and carry those cultural values of the people" (Elam, 42).

10. See Bryer and Hartig, 121–122.

11. King's mother, Ruby, recognized this aspect of Elmore: "Something's always missing with him. There's always something he ain't got, he don't know what it is himself. If you gave it to him he wouldn't know he had it. I see him every four or five years, he come through and he always leave more trouble than when he came. Seem like he bring it with him and dump it off, he come and dump off that trouble and then he leave smelling sweet" (45).

12. I want to place my reading into dialogue with that of Harry Elam, who has written the most comprehensive analysis of the play: "Through presenting the machete to King, Stool Pigeon/Canewell closes the book on a cycle of black-on-black senseless violence and the personal trauma of suffering and blame that it causes them." I also agree with his claim that King is "literally the Chosen One who is sacrificed in order to prepare the way for the regeneration of the greater community, for the good of those who live on. His death is a repetition and revision of the sacrifice of the Christian Messiah on the cross who, according to doctrine, dies for the sins of mankind and whose blood is now ritualized as the Com-

munion, blessing those who partake. King, too dies for our sins, and his death offers new life. As a ritualized act presided over by Stool Pigeon, King's sacrifice serves as a beacon of hope, promising a new tomorrow against the bleak backdrop of tragic loss and unfulfilled promise" (87). But I would not describe the figure who is sacrificed as Isaac. The Isaac in *King Hedley II* is liberated through Ruby's killing of the Lazarus figure in King.

SOYICA DIGGS COLBERT

If We Must Die

Violence as History Lesson in
Seven Guitars and *King Hedley II*

August Wilson's *Seven Guitars* (1996) and *King Hedley II* (2001) each present a man: seductive guitarist Floyd "Schoolboy" Barton and headstrong ex-convict, King Hedley II, respectively, who negotiates for control of his environment. Floyd loses his struggle for control, dying at the hands of his friend, Hedley, who is King's father. Although King meets a similar fate, *King Hedley II* imbues the protagonist's death with a significant difference, one that challenges the social codes established in each play. Floyd's death creates a subtle sense of lawlessness in Pittsburgh's Hill District of 1948; however, the burgeoning cultural codes in *Seven Guitars* proliferate exponentially in *King Hedley II*, presenting a world governed by the mantra "blood for blood." The violence that permeates the 1985 Hill District of *King Hedley II* portends apocalyptic repercussions. Attempting to instate rules in a world seemingly governed by chaos, King and the other characters do not realize that, as Stool Pigeon, a soothsayer, forecasts in the prologue to the play, "the story's been written. All that's left now is the playing out" (7). Therefore, King's choice at the end of the play to enact his own law in order to end the cycle of violence creates a historical detour that ruptures the chronological relationship between *Seven Guitars* and *King Hedley II* and enables a diachronic one with *Joe Turner's Come and Gone* (1987) and *The Piano Lesson* (1990). *Seven Guitars*, in other words, establishes a causal relationship with regards to social violence driven by the aphorism "an eye for an eye." Initially, *King Hedley II*, which features some of the characters from *Seven Guitars* and children of those characters, depicts an intensified expression of reciprocal violence. Yet, like *Joe Turner's Come and Gone* and *The Piano Lesson, King Hedley II* disrupts the naturalized chain of escalated aggression by depicting King's refusal to enact vengeance. *King Hedley II* shows the redemptive power of sacrifice by hearkening back to the spilling of blood shown in *Joe Turner's Come and Gone*, Wilson's third play, which bends the trajectory of the plays as a whole. Through this detour, *King Hedley II* recoups the positive potential associated with the spilling of blood and specifies Wilson's historical model as the cycle.

Seven Guitars intertwines the circumstances of Floyd's death with the advancement of his musical career and corresponding financial independence. The structure of the play establishes death as a possible by-product of the tension between progression and regression. The play materializes this tension through the singing that opens and closes act 1, scene 1. The first act ends with the disembodied sound of Floyd singing, creating a transition into scene 2, which depicts Floyd coaxing his estranged girlfriend Vera to listen to his song emanating from a radio. The airplay encourages Floyd to try to continue recording, but before he can return to the studio in Chicago he must get his guitar from a pawnshop and procure an advance from his manager, Mr. T. L. Hall. Of course, Floyd's plans do not come to fruition; he experiences a number of setbacks culminating in Hall's arrest for selling fake insurance. Refusing to accept that Hall conned him, Floyd devises another plan to amass the money he needs and decides to rob a loan office with Williard Ray Tillery, a neighbor, who is also known as "Poochie." Although Floyd escapes with $1,200, the police shoot Poochie as he flees the scene. Later, when Canewell, one of Floyd's former bandmates, finds the money Floyd buried in Vera's yard, Floyd asserts, "Poochie took a chance. We both took a chance" (103), thus attempting to change the status as a wager Floyd knows he may lose. Canewell leaves Floyd with the money, and the young guitarist "begins to laugh. It is an odd mixture of laughter and tears. He has waited many years for this moment" (103). Just then, Hedley, a neighbor who suffers from delusions — in part induced by tuberculosis — enters, mistakes the guitarist for someone Hedley believes owes him money, and kills Floyd with a machete when Floyd refuses to surrender the money.

Picking up — in more ways than one — where *Seven Guitars* ends, *King Hedley II* demonstrates how death and depravity may emerge as the result of taking a chance, especially in a world in which chances are limited and rewards are unexpected. Floyd's notion of taking a chance draws attention to a philosophical worldview that dominates *King Hedley II*; aggressive action creates the possibility for positive outcomes but does not ensure them. *King Hedley II* depicts a world in which the characters recognize meritocracy as a myth that not only necessitates social relationships but also encourages certain kinds of psychic geographies. In both *Seven Guitars* and *King Hedley II*, the main characters die in the pursuit of opportunity made available through illegal means — by taking a chance.

By focusing on the role of chance in *King Hedley II*, I want to build on Harry J. Elam, Jr.'s analysis of the play and comment on the play's inclusion in the anthology *The Fire This Time: African American Plays for the 21st Century*, edited by Elam and Robert Alexander. I also engage Joan Herrington's theorization of violence in the play. Elam argues Wilson's plays continually produce the contemporary through historical return. Elam's reading of Wilson coincides with James Baldwin's assertion that "we cannot escape our origins, however hard we try, those origins which contain the key — could we but find it — to all that we later become" (Baldwin, 21). Although Elam's *The Past as Present in the Drama of August Wilson* focuses less on the relationship between the past and the future, one notable exception is the treatment of *King Hedley II*. In the analysis of the eighth play, Elam suggests that Wilson preempts apocalypse through the sacrificial death of King. Further solidifying the visionary nature of the play, Elam with Alexander demarcates the play as a meditation on apocalyptic history by including it in an anthology titled *The Fire This Time*. The anthology takes its title from another essay by Baldwin, *The Fire Next Time*, which predicts devastation as the result of America's inability to end its racial nightmare. The landscape presented in Wilson's play and examined by Herrington does not seem far from realizing Baldwin's description. Herrington argues that the play reconnects African Americans with "the cultural roots almost completely abandoned in the deadly 1980s" (*King Hedley* 170). She asserts a syncretism of Judeo-Christian and Yoruba imagery similar to that which scholars have found in *Joe Turner's Come and Gone*.[1]

I extend the *King Hedley II* scholarship in two ways. First, I offer a new way of understanding the shape of Wilson's cycle by furthering Elam and Herrington's assertions that King's death resonates with blood sacrifice in Wilson's other plays. Second, I argue that King's death revises the world-view expressed throughout the play and clarifies the destructive and productive, psychic and social facets of violence.

Unlike some psychoanalytic criticism, my approach does not ignore the historical and cultural specificity of the characters, but, instead, uses those codes to expand the language of psychoanalysis.[2] More than, as Wilson describes, "provid[ing] us with a mirror that forces us to face personal truths," *King Hedley II* uses the visual and acoustic dynamics of the stage to call attention to the function of identification (x). *King Hedley II* thus imagines a revision to Lacan's mirror stage by shifting the terms of identification from the selfsame image reflected on the surface of the mirror to a collective imago (2). According to Lacan the ego emerges through the infant's identification with what he or she sees in the mirror. David Eng explains, "According to the logic of the mirror stage, sense of self is introduced from the outside in, through an 'other' in the form of this external image. The I 'finds its unity in the image of the other'" (111). Eng further clarifies the "fictional quality of the mirror stage, and they [Lacan and his commentators] are quick to point out that the infant's infatuated love of its image is a tragic misrecognition — a self love compromised by '*méconnaissance*'" (112). Analogously using the imagery of a circle, King creates a sense of self by policing the other that results in a disidentification for King and potentially a moment of identification for the audience. In a conversation with Elmore, King's mother's lover, King explains, "I set me out a little circle and anything come inside my circle I say what happen and don't happen. God's in charge of some things. If I jump up and shoot you I ain't gonna blame it on God. That's where I'm the boss. . . . I can decide whether you live or die. I'm in charge of that" (36). But Elmore challenges King's premise: "Question: What if you in somebody else's circle and you don't know it? And all the time you thinking you in charge?" (36), to which King replies, "They got a name for that." King's friend, Mister, immediately glosses, "It's called a rude awakening" (36).

Elmore, King, and Mister's conversation theorizes the way social domains hinge on a perspective that results from and serves to solidify the ego. In the same way that Lacan's mirror serves to instantiate the ego of the child, Wilson's historically and culturally informed perception of what is before one's eyes serves to create King's sense of self. If somebody else forces King to realize the limitations of his terrestrial boundaries, the shift in perspective would result in a psychic break depicted here as a rude awakening marked by pain and the transformation of the ego.

At the same time, Wilson uses King's misperception — his belief that he has the ability to control his surroundings — to shift the perspective of the audience and offer a hopeful representation of urban black America in the 1980s. In order to change the game, *King Hedley II* depicts the impact of the death of Aunt Ester, the embodiment of history in the form of "a 366-year old conjure woman" whom Wilson describes as a maternal figure to all the characters in his plays by having the lights go down in the theater and whose resurrection he suggests through a cat's meow (x). The cat's meow creates an uncanny quality that ushers in ambiguity, distinguishing the spirituality in *King Hedley II* from the other plays as it links it to the spiritual practice represented by Aunt Ester. In Wilson's other plays, specifically *Two Trains Running* and *Gem of the Ocean*, Aunt Ester seems immortal (she is 349 years old in *Two Trains Running*) and acts as an intercessor in the healing process. In *King Hedley II* the cat's meow suggests Aunt Ester's resurrection but leaves that occurrence open to interpretation; the play also leaves ambiguous the impact of Aunt Ester's possible return. Moreover, even if one acknowledges she has been reborn, the elderly ancestor figure has also been reincarnated. As an established game changer, Aunt Ester's change in form signifies a more general shift in the order of things. Wilson's play emphasizes that, since "times ain't nothing like they used to be," outcomes vary as well (7). *King Hedley II* promises, nevertheless, conditional redemption from the incessant violence that plagued urban black communities in America in the late 1980s and early 1990s. Offering a device to understand this violence, the play connects black-on-black crime to a messianic history.

As with all of Wilson's plays, *King Hedley II* provides insights into the decade it represents — in this case the 1980s — by depicting not only urban violence but also the reasons for its proliferation. In so doing, the play presents the possibility — albeit ambiguous — of life (psychic, physical, and social) after death, as it suggests a way to understand violence and death as necessary historical conditions. Wilson's play filters the issues of urban violence and historicity through the personal narrative of King. Act 1 closes with King's affirmation, "I want everybody to know that King Hedley II is here. And I want everybody to know, just like my daddy, that you can't fuck with me" (58). These lines endorse the violence enacted by Hedley, the man King believes to be his father, in response to someone denying Hedley's psychic, historical, and social status. In act 1 of *Seven Guitars* the audience learns Hedley killed a man for refusing to call him King (67). Obviously, Hedley is physically present in the altercation; however, Hedley's assertion reveals his perception that he must battle for the social legibility due his familial and social lineage. Similarly, in *King Hedley II*, King claims, "Pernell made me kill him. Pernell called me 'champ'" (73). In the preface to *King Hedley II*, Wilson categorizes losing one's name as a tragedy particularly suffered by enslaved Africans in the United States and, therefore, calls attention to the social implications of misnaming black people. When Hedley's interlocutor refuses to call him King and Pernell calls King "champ," their antagonists participate in a discursive practice aimed, in part, to disallow black lineage and the corresponding social, cultural, and financial inheritances that lineage entails.

The title of Wilson's eighth play ties the theme of misrecognition to Hedley the Second, who persistently claims his familial lineage, demands his inheritance, and demonstrates his propensity for violence. Importantly, Floyd's death is also a case of mistaken identity, bolstering the claim that *Seven Guitars* presents the social precursors to the deaths depicted in *King Hedley II*, which map the psychic struggle for recognition as an additional cause for urban violence in the 1980s and early 1990s. This commingling of violence with recognition and redemption, through the management of familial histories, acts as an addendum to Sigmund Freud's depiction of the death drive. In 1915, in "Reflections on War and Death," as in *Civilization and Its Discontents* (1930), Freud claims that civilization suffers when aggression is turned outward. He maintains, however, that under certain circumstances — in war, for example — aggressiveness must be deployed and therefore persists in every stage of human development. In this context, I am suggesting that *King Hedley II* imagines how certain manifestations of violence informed by personal and social histories may have productive potential.

Nevertheless, the social landscape of *King Hedley II* seems ripe for the death of the eponymous protagonist. In the first act we learn that the main character lacks a financial support system, recently served a murder sentence, sells stolen refrigerators, carries a Glock 9mm pistol, and plans to commit armed robbery. The newspaper reports the escalation of violence marked by a stabbing and drive-by shooting, which, after hearing about, King laments, "It used to be you get killed over something. Now you get killed over nothing." Mister responds, "You might look at somebody wrong and get in a fight and get killed over that" (34). Moreover, King's mother, Ruby, and his girlfriend, Tonya, both warn him he's going to get killed. Ruby also warns Elmore that King is "liable to kill you [Elmore] if he [King] finds out" that Elmore killed Leroy, King's biological father (45).

As pervasive as the violence appears, the play resonates with life in urban America in the 1980s. Two of the leading studies of factors contributing to urban homicide in predominantly black neighborhoods, William Julius Wilson's *The Truly Disadvantaged: The Inner City, the Underclass, and Public Policy* (1987) and Douglas S. Massey and Nancy A. Denton's *American Apartheid: Segregation and the Making of the Underclass* (1993), establish that the alienation of black people in urban environments diminishes political power, access to public services, and police assistance. *King Hedley II* highlights this progressive lack of access. In *Seven Guitars*, the government denies Floyd the money he earned in the workhouse because he lacked the proper documentation, but by the 1980s King is unable to claim his photographs from Sears even with a receipt. *The Truly Disadvantaged* and *American Apartheid* concur that structural and cultural factors including the changes to the urban economy during the 1970s and 1980s "produced the disastrous social and economic outcomes observed in the inner cities during these decades" (Massey and Denton, 8). Like Massey and Denton, William Julius Wilson does not focus on the nature of the counterculture produced by the social and economic fallout of the 1970s and 1980s, but on an understanding of urban violence in black communities as a manifestation of the cultural and structural transformations.

Wilson's language in the Preface of *King Hedley II* also evokes Elijah Anderson's study, *Code of the Street: Decency, Violence, and the Moral Life of the Inner City*, which considers the development of inner-city violence in Philadelphia in the 1980s. Focusing on the lack of structural access for urban, working-class, black Americans, *Code of the Street* explains that "lack of police accountability has in fact been incorporated into the local status system: the person who is believed capable of 'taking care of himself' is accorded a certain deference and regard, which translated into a sense of physical and psychological control" (34). The logic of Anderson's statement is consistent with the act of preservation detailed in Wilson's depiction of codes of conduct: "I wanted to present the unique particulars of black American culture as the transformation of impulse and sensibility into codes of conduct and response, into cultural rituals that defined and celebrated ourselves as men and women of high purpose" (viii). Wilson is pointing out how cultural codes not only preserved black men and women but also celebrated them. Paradoxically, the particulars in *King Hedley II* seem to reflect survival instincts — the drive to take care of oneself and to exercise control — instead of celebration. In the play, Tonya, King's 35-year-old wife who is also a grandmother, refuses to have a baby that will be younger than her grandchild because of her fear of the effect the environment will have on a black child, and Ruby has lost her will to sing. Throughout his cycle, Wilson uses song as a particular device to communicate life and purpose. In *Joe Turner's Come and Gone*, the pursuit of the protagonist's song is synonymous to the act of claiming one's identity. In *King Hedley II*, as Elam explains, "Wilson uses music as personal memory, theatrical device, and force of history that promotes action and change" (53). As a former blues woman, Ruby refusing to sing further solidifies the wasteland that is the setting of Wilson's play for the 1980s. If song functions in Wilson's work as a device that promotes social change,

Ruby's unwillingness to sing points to a level of nihilism that emerges for the first time in Wilson's work dedicated to the 1980s.

Wilson's calling the cultural codes a celebration, therefore, may seem odd. *King Hedley II*, however, demonstrates the power of an imaginative work to participate in the cultivation of cultural codes. Wilson does not foreclose all possibilities for social change in *King Hedley II* by referencing the devastating violence of the 1980s, which by his own estimation "started somewhere around '84 or '85; you had this rash of these young kids with guns out there killing one another. I think of Washington, D.C., with 500-and-some murders in one particular year. That's more than one a day" (quoted in Elam, 120). Instead, Wilson contends with that violence by connecting cultural practice to a historiography that expands the potential of his cycle. In order to move beyond the survival mentality of the 1980s, the characters in *King Hedley II* must reconnect to black spirituality, despite the irreparable damage caused by Aunt Ester's death.

If her reincarnation — represented by a cat's meow — suggests some form of return to spiritual practice, the play emphasizes the costs of the return in psychic and social consequences. Elmore, the consummate hustler, for example, recalls killing Leroy over a gambling debt. After loaning Leroy some money to gamble with, Leroy refused to share his winnings with Elmore and eventually pulled a gun on Elmore for bad-mouthing him to other members of their community. "I'm supposed to be a dead man 'cause he was supposed to pull the trigger," Elmore explains. "That's the first thing you learn about carrying a pistol. When you pull it, you better use it" (93). Initially, Elmore planned to leave town, but when he saw Leroy in a barbershop laughing, he became infuriated: "Leroy tried to play a game he didn't know how to play. He didn't know the rules. He tried to lead with the ace and didn't know the rules. He tried to lead with the ace and didn't know I had the trump" (96). Elmore's interpretation is another example, in a play of chronic negotiation, of the need to establish control. Elmore regained his social position by killing Leroy, and he undermines King's position when he ends the story by telling King, "Leroy was you daddy" (97).

Confronted with the news that Elmore killed his father, that his mother lied to him about his paternity, and that he was named after a man to whom he has no biological relationship, King must decide how to maintain his social legibility. Ruby, Tonya, and Mister believe King will try to kill Elmore. Instead, King gives Elmore fifty dollars to pay Leroy's debt and then challenges Elmore to a game of craps, asserting, "My name ain't Leroy Slater, Jr. My name is King Hedley II and we got some unfinished business to take care of" (99). Evoking the language of his surrogate father, King reestablishes his name and enters into a game of chance. Echoing Floyd Barton, Elmore warns, "Somebody got to win. And somebody got to lose" (99). After Elmore has won sixty dollars, he cautions, "I'm gonna roll these dice again. I don't know what's gonna come out of them. I'm taking a chance. I'm willing to take it. You playing a man's game now. Just be sure you know how to play" (101). Rolling an eleven, Elmore wins the game and commits psychic murder for the second time that day.

King's sense of self is based in part on the belief that he is Hedley's son. He had, after all, justified killing Pernell on the basis that "I want everybody to know King Hedley II is here. And I want everybody to know, just like my daddy, that you can't fuck with me" (58). Similarly, King reminds Elmore before they begin to play craps that he is King Hedley II to ward against the paternal relationship Elmore reveals; Ruby solidifies Hedley's paternal power, claiming, "King just like Hedley" (78). Nevertheless, the inadequacy of King's discursive strategy is evident in his having, repeatedly, to assert his name. His constant reversion to the act of naming indicates that his reiterations are insufficient. Therefore, King, by challenging Elmore to a game, reshapes his approach into one that allows for revolutions and detours.

Comparably, Freud depicts the use of a game, "fort/da," to manage the symbolic force of the other. In *Beyond the Pleasure Principle* (1920), Freud describes fort/da as a strategy developed by a child, little Hans, in response to his mother leaving. Freud observed that Hans did not cry when his mother left the room but instead threw his toys under his bed. Perhaps most interestingly, as he threw his toys Hans uttered "fort," the German word for "gone." On another occasion Freud noticed Hans playing this game with a wooden reel on a string, a yo-yo–like apparatus with which he demonstrated the conceptual frame of "disappearance and return" (14).

By developing the game with the wooden reel, the boy was able to manage the return of his mother through a substitution solidified in language. The game enabled the boy to cope with the painful history of his mother's leaving and therefore suggests how individuals learn to manage psychic loss through creative behaviors that secure the individual but do not address the loss directly. Because the game, however, does not resolve the primary issue by recovering the lost mother the behavior must be repeated.

In *King Hedley II*, the fort/da game — compulsively repeated — is a violent game, and, in light of that violence, the need to manage the immediate environment proliferates a chaos that underscores the deficiency of violent repetition without a significant difference; of cyclical behavior without a detour. Notably, King's game of craps with Elmore also engages Freud's linking of compulsive repetition, in *Beyond the Pleasure Principle*, to the need to manage the death drive. In *Civilization and Its Discontents*, he further posits that civilizations tend toward joining into "ever larger units," but that a "contrary instinct seeking to dissolve those units and to bring them back to their primeval, inorganic state" exists: "That is to say, as well as Eros there was an instinct of death" (76). Like the game of fort/da, King plays a game in an attempt to control his circle, guard against chaos, and disqualify Elmore's control. Whereas Freud's depiction results in consolidation of negative, chaotic feelings, Wilson reasserts the pervasive force of chance. King loses the game, as well as his opportunity to evade yet another psychic death. Although King's challenge to Elmore fits into the predominant cultural codes of the time period, Wilson stresses that King "strives to live by his own moral codes" (5). Stool Pigeon, moreover, prophesies King's transformative potential, saying, "You got the Key to the Mountain. You can go sit on Top of the World" (100). Therefore, although it comes as a surprise to Ruby — and to Mister, who goads King by repeating "blood for blood" — King does not attempt to kill Elmore. Like the vacant lot between two buildings in the play's set, the gap between the general cultural mandate and Elmore's historically specific circumstances creates the space in which King may live up to his name by producing cultural and historical redemption. This redemption in effect means reshaping the circle of his domain so that it breaks the cycle of violence.

After Aunt Ester dies in act 1 of *King Hedley II*, Stool Pigeon buries her cat in Ruby's yard, claiming that if the cat has not used up its nine lives and a blood sacrifice is made within ten days, Aunt Ester will return. In the final scene of play, after King loses the craps game, Ruby enters her house, gets a gun, calls out Elmore's name, and shoots — but the bullet fired from Ruby's gun accidentally hits King in the neck. As he falls "near where the cat is buried," his blood flows onto the ground: "Stool Pigeon suddenly recognizes that the sacrifice has been made" and begins to celebrate what he perceives as a crucifixion (102). As the lights go down, "the sound of a cat's meow is heard" (104). Aunt Ester's implicit claim on King's death, therefore, suggests that King's death facilitates a redemptive history: "King's blood is the blood of a King, the purifying, sanctified blood of Shango's ram, the blood of human sacrifice that can bring about social, spiritual, and cultural resurrection" (Elam, 213). Therefore, just as in *Joe Turner's Come and Gone*, when Loomis finds redemption through the shedding of his own blood, and in *The Piano Lesson*, when Boy Willie and Berniece are able to exorcise a ghost by remembering the blood sacrifice made by Boy Willie and Berniece's ancestors, *King Hedley II* too calls for a ritual practice that will break the cycle of bloodletting.

When King's death is viewed in this way, *Radio Golf* becomes as much a sequel to *King Hedley II* as it is to *Gem of the Ocean*, in that it situates *King Hedley II* in direct relation to *Gem of the Ocean* as fulfilling the cycle of Aunt Ester's sacrificial life and death. If Wilson is in effect reworking the idea of history delineated in his previous plays, he is evoking what Walter Benjamin has called "a *weak* Messianic power, a power to which the past has a claim. That claim cannot be settled cheaply" (254). The high price of King's death — remember that Aristotle locates the death of a king at the heart of tragedy — thus becomes the price paid for Harmond Wilks's ascension, just as the price of Wilks's ambitions is the high price that must be paid in the next stage of Aunt Ester's resurrection, which itself is a stage in the redemption of her community.

By noting the ways *King Hedley II* engages, extends, and theorizes history, I draw attention to the creative and imaginative work of the play. In the way that *King Hedley II* shapes a history that borrows and departs from the idea of Messianic time, the play complements sociological and historical studies by offering a way to understand the psychic dynamics that inform human interaction. As the force of chance — seemingly random violence — continues to plague young people's lives in America, the play ponders the worth of considering this violence not as aberrant but as symptomatic. In so doing, it calls for a visionary future that valorizes sacrifice in urban settings in the same way that the City of Bones, in *Gem of the Ocean*, valorizes the sacrificial aspects of the Middle Passage.

Notes

1. See Sandra Richards's "Yoruba Gods on the American Stage: August Wilson's *Joe Turner's Come and Gone*," Kim Pereira's chapter "*Joe Turner's Come and Gone*: Seek and You Shall Find," in his book *August Wilson and the African-American Odyssey*, and Paul Carter Harrison's "August Wilson's Blues Poetics" for a further discussion of the syncretism of Judeo-Christian and Yoruba imagery in *Joe Turner's Come and Gone*.

2. Although many theorists have raised reservations about the applicability of psychoanalytic theories to ethnic studies, I find the language of psychoanalysis a useful starting point to consider the ways *King Hedley II* comments on the formation of perspective and identity. My turn to the language of psychoanalysis resists pathologizing the black community represented in the play and considers instead the ways Wilson's drama articulates a rich sense of humanity by commenting on and extending Freudian and Lacanian psychoanalytic models.

You Can't Make Life Happen without a Woman

Paternity and the Pitfalls of Structural Design in *King Hedley II* and *Seven Guitars*

> The people who look around to see what the society has cut
> out for them, who see the limits of their participation, and are
> willing to say, 'No, I refuse to accept this limitation that
> you're imposing on me; — that's the warrior spirit.
> — August Wilson

There is considerable evidence that August Wilson's *King Hedley II* (1999) is a sequel to *Seven Guitars* (1995). Together, they constitute the two works in August Wilson's ten-play cycle whose plots are most directly linked, with a number of the same characters appearing in both works. (In a somewhat looser way, *Radio Golf* can also be viewed as a sequel to *Gem of the Ocean*.) This nominal connection, however, is only one indication of the conceptual thread unifying the two plays. Of all the Wilson plays, with the exception of *Fences, Seven Guitars* and *King Hedley II* are the only plays that are set outdoors in Pittsburgh's Hill District. Thirty-seven years after Hedley severed Floyd "Schoolboy" Barton's windpipe with his machete in the backyard of the tenement, his son, King Hedley II, plants seeds in the same backyard. That is the backyard, first seen in *Seven Guitars*, of the tenement King shares with his mother, Ruby, also first seen in *Seven Guitars*, and his wife, Tonya.

This action outside the house symbolizes the outside of black men's American Dream, because instead of being centered on the achievement of "justice for all," that dream has crystallized around the notion of home ownership (preferably in the suburbs where few blacks can afford to live).

The open spaces of the suburban development thus suggest — perhaps deceptively — a sense of expansion, while the open spaces caused by "urban renewal" indicate decay. In this regard, Wilson uses these urban spaces to mean, in both the positive and negative sense, the exact opposite of suburban utopia. If the yards in his plays invoke community — shared benefits and shared responsibilities — suburban yards denote privacy. At the same time, the yards in Wilson's plays represent urban decline, whereas in suburbia they represent the dream of prosperity.

As urban dreamers, however, Floyd and King (and King's father, Hedley), in their respective positions in the liminal space of the backyard, call attention to the manner in which black men's struggle for visibility in the public sphere often has implications that reverberate into the community. Thus, if the house signifies the happy home, the omnipresence of the house — both the physical structure and the patriarchal logic that situates men's position at the apex of gender hierarchy — issues from the relationship between masculinity and the cultural imaginary. As Gaston Bachelard observes in *The Poetics of Space*, the house "shelters daydreaming, the house protects the dreamer, the house allows one to dream in peace" (6).

In his essay "Untitled: The Housing of Gender," architectural critic Mark Wigley notes that gender distinctions are actively produced within the space of architectural discourse[1] and indicate architecture's complicity in reproducing power inequities masked by the ubiquitous need to create "safe" and "beautiful" spaces where individuals can realize their full potential. Noting that "architectural discourse is clearly defined more by what it will not say than what it says," Wigley asserts that in the relationship between sexuality and space, "sexuality is privatized without being housed." Wigley's comments regarding the interrelatedness of marriage and the house are instructive:

Marriage is the reason for building a house. The house appears to make a space for the institution. But marriage is already spatial. It cannot be thought outside the house that is its condition of possibility before its space. The word *oikos* refers to the identity between the physical building and the family it houses. Equally it refers to their hierarchical division. The word for dweller of the house becomes "husband," such that the art of economy which orders the *oikos* is literally that of "husbandry." While the house protects the children from the elements, its primary role is to protect the father's genealogical claims by isolating women from other men. Reproduction is understood as the reproduction of the father. The law of the house is undoubtedly no more than the law of the father. The physical house is the possibility of the patriarchal order that appears to be applied to it. (336)

In relation to this idea of a sexuality simultaneously private and exposed, I want to suggest that these two plays offer a unique approach to the spatial issues informing human relationships, particularly when we consider the relationship between intimacy and inhabitation.

It is cohabitation, in the form of Floyd's attempt to reconcile with Vera, whom he left to pursue a recording career in Chicago, that conflicts with his desire to live a life of material comfort, and in *King Hedley II*, habitation turns on the strained relationship between King and his mother Ruby, who are engaged in a dispute over who owns the house. As a consequence, inhabitation signifies the manner in which occupants fill a dwelling with possessions accumulated over time, rendering the space rife with memories, secrets, and dreams. Although Floyd and King (and to a lesser degree, Hedley), try to imagine a future of prosperity and notoriety, when each attempts to put plans in motion that will solidify the future, he finds himself in the midst of violence and criminal transgression — such that the communal space registers the cost of ambition — because not only the individual but the whole community suffers.

Thus the fact that both dramas are staged in the "open" spaces behind tenement housing likewise calls attention to Floyd's and King's liminal status. When the plays begin both men are "betwixt and between" — either on the verge of a reversal of fortune or ready to tumble into a violent abyss. At the start of *Seven Guitars*, Floyd has just completed a ninety-day sentence in the workhouse for vagrancy; as *King Hedley II* begins, King has just returned from serving a seven-year prison sentence for manslaughter.

In both instances, the issue of personal value is evident and each character has come to locate his sense of value outside himself.

It is telling, then, that Floyd's jail sentence results from being charged with "worthlessness." As for King, his decision to murder Pernell arises out of the fact that the latter had referred to him as "champ" rather than by his name. "I told myself," King says, "'He don't know.' He don't know my daddy killed a man for calling him out of his name. He don't know he fucking with King Hedley II" (73). In what constitutes an ironic turn, King has murdered Pernell for using an honorific, as if Wilson means to suggest that black men are so alienated from the notion of self-value that they cannot distinguish friend from foe. Moreover, King locates himself in an ancestral line characterized by its propensity to assert identity through violent means.

Though they are not related by blood, Floyd and King are kin, in the sense that neither can separate his desire to escape the confines of life on the Hill from criminality, and neither possesses the ability to engage in self-critique of the sort that would lead him to reassess his behavior. Each problematically seeks, however, to establish (or, in Floyd's case, reestablish) intimate relationships with women that involve marriage. The houses, literally in the background in both plays, thus foreground the paternal aspirations of Floyd and both King Hedleys — indicative of the dynasticism synonymous with patriarchy. It is interesting, then, that both King and Floyd see marriage as inseparable from their desire for respectability and prosperity. But this returns us to the need to understand the manner in which masculine acts of design — insofar as they relate to negotiating public space — are so often fraught with violence.

The outdoor setting also de-emphasizes familial space occupied by one family in favor of communal space reminiscent of the common areas to be found in the African village. Both plays are populated by characters who revel in the oral tradition of storytelling and signifying, and who share — often without verbalizing it — a cognizance of common plight and the need to pool their resources in order to hold deprivation at bay.

In many ways, moreover, the outdoor settings call attention to the differences between a sacred design, where the characters — as Africans trying to find their way in America — struggle to recover a link to the spiritual life in the midst of an urban space's built environment. In that environment, real estate speculation has led — as it did in Harlem at the start of the twentieth century — to absentee landlords, dilapidated housing, and a gentrification that, by the end of the 1980s, attracts suburbanites back to the city to occupy factories and warehouses renovated as pricey condominiums or high-rent apartments that the current dwellers cannot afford. Wilson's use of shared space thus demonstrates how communal rituals remain important in the African American community.

In his book *The Myth of the Eternal Return*, Mircea Eliade identifies the relationship that inheres between ritual and social structure: "To assure the reality and the enduringness of a construction, there is a repetition of the divine act of perfect construction: the Creation of the worlds and of man. As the first step, the 'reality' of the site is secured through consecration of the ground, i.e., through its transformation into a center; then the validity of the act of construction is confirmed by repetition of the divine sacrifice" (20). Both Wilson plays enact, then, the dilemma of characters trying to locate the proper site to perform the act of consecration and to determine who should benefit from the act of renewal. The 1940s ushered in a society more driven by the need to consume and more prone to secular explanations for the individual's place in the universe. Along with this, then, as postwar prosperity makes owning a car and a home attainable, we see in the black community the growing impulse to seek personal, subordinate collective needs.

In the 1980s, deregulation of the banking industry created a growing class of millionaires who had risen from the managerial class. Endorsed by the specious notion that "a rising tide lifts all boats," a record number of white individuals attained millionaire status, while in the black community the violence and despair that accompanied the spread of crack cocaine proliferated. The 1980s also invented a new term to describe those left behind: the underclass. In light of those social changes, the very successful '80s television show *The Cosby Show* — depicting a black middle-class family with two parents, both professionals — served as an ironic contrast to the lives of African Americans who had been displaced from the workforce by the closing of steel mills and auto plants in cities in the Northeast and the Midwest, leaving many of them permanently alienated from the idea of holding a job or even of feeling connected to the nation's fortunes.

From this perspective, the 1940s and the 1980s were radically distinct time periods in African American history, particularly in terms of the amount of faith the black community invested in the idea of achieving an equitable society. While the former moment laid the seeds for the nascent civil rights movement that flowered in the next decade, the latter moment confronted black elected officials with decaying infrastructure, a decreasing population, and shrinking tax revenues that rendered black political influence of little consequence in the face of a conservative turn.

Wilson uses the thirty-seven years of social change that separate the action in the two plays to examine the vagaries of black masculinity, which displays markedly different features in some respects and powerful similarities in others. The most glaring similarity is the propensity of male characters in both plays to place futurity at the center of their identity. I want to examine, therefore, the manner in which paternity and violence relate to the act of imagining and achieving a black futurity in which the individual and the community can thrive spiritually without sacrificing material needs. In this context, moreover, I want to understand how both plays suggest that the warrior spirit, as Wilson has termed it, can only be reproduced at great cost.

Set alongside *Seven Guitars, King Hedley II* indicates the ways that masculine privilege in the black community has, in the wake of the civil rights and black power movements, damaged the community's prospects by setting black men and black women at odds. Putting the plays in conversation, then, points at the ideological imperatives of postwar masculinity. *King Hedley II* commences with King planting seeds in the soil behind his house, which can be seen as an act of faith as well as a symbol of King's paternal aspirations. Like his father, Hedley, King seeks to become a successful business owner, raising capital by selling stolen refrigerators and pulling off small robberies with his friend Mister in order to invest in a respectable business. Hence, Floyd's insistence that for black men to succeed, black women must demonstrate an unyielding belief in them can

be seen as the sign of black men's culpability in what will become, in the
1980s, the political scapegoating of black women. That scapegoating issues
from several sources. It can be found in the conservative rhetoric of the
Reagan administration, which made the "welfare queen" an icon of the
black community's failure, in the representation of black women in hip-
hop and R and B, and, as well, in the church, whose institutional power
was waning in the face of an increasingly secular middle class in which
black women's labor was essential to its sustenance but marginal to its decision making.[2]

Paternity is a central issue in *Seven Guitars*, in part because Hedley
speaks throughout the play about the jazz trumpeter Buddy Bolden, who
has promised him a large sum of money to build a plantation, and also because Floyd declares early in the play, "You can't make life happen without
a woman" (13). He is right, of course, because the act of fathering a child is,
by biological dictate, an act men cannot bring to closure; it falls to women
to bring the male seed to fruition. However, Floyd's preceding line reveals
that he has no interest in the woman's role in reproduction: "A man that
believe in himself still need a woman that believe in him" (13). Rather than
acknowledging the partnership (however tenuous) or the essential role
women play in the cycle of reproduction, Floyd articulates the ideological underpinnings of masculine hegemony and female subordination. He
believes that, irrespective of the amount men swagger, women nonetheless
should serve to transform black men's private potential into public status.
Floyd stresses women's wholesale acceptance of the black male aspiration,
leaving unsaid his expectation that black women will abandon their own
aspirations — step *outside* of history — in favor of those of black men.

It is also particularly ironic that the conflict between King and Tonya
turns on her unwillingness to have his child after she becomes pregnant,
because the conflict hearkens back — if only circumstantially — to King's
birth, when Ruby's desire to escape her tangled past in the South led her
to lie down with — and then name her child after — Hedley. Though we
eventually learn that Hedley is not King's father, he and King share an
investment in the patriarchal ideology that reproduces itself by offering
women a place at the "side" of men, where masculine attainment stands, as

well, for female dominion. In 1948 Hedley loudly asserts, "I am the man to father your children. I offer you a kingdom" (89), and in 1985 King is dismayed that Tonya asserts her right not to have another child, because she eschews the conservative and sexist logic that insists that childbearing legitimizes women. That logic does not apply in the black community, she suggests, because it is strongly linked to the rhetoric encouraging white middle-class reproduction as one strategy to counter the rising birthrates of black and immigrant children. But it is more likely a reflection of something more palpable — namely Tonya's decision to choose herself and thus to have a role beyond child rearer.

Tonya, demonstrating her ability to recognize her own limitations and failures as a parent, directly links issues of paternity to the materialism and violence of life in a faltering black community. Bemoaning the fact that her daughter, Natasha, is pregnant, she says, "She seventeen and got a baby, she don't even know who the father is. She moving so fast she can't stop and look in the mirror. She can't see herself. All anybody got to do is look at her good and she run off and lay down with them. She don't think no further than that. Ain't got no future 'cause she don't know how to make one. Don't nobody care about that. All they care about is getting a bigger TV" (*King Hedley*, 37–38).

In a moment when black women regularly appear in the music videos of black male R and B singers and hip-hop artists as little more than sex objects, Tonya is asserting that Natasha is so susceptible to the male gaze that she interprets all forms of male attention as a statement of sexual desire. Tonya further insists that her child — so often viewed in terms of the wellworn cliché that children represent the future — has removed her ability to move into the future. Tonya's resistance to having King's child, then, reflects the position that childbearing renders women incapable of self-determination. Tonya's comment that she "don't know what to do ... how to be a mother," moreover, shifts the terms of motherhood from the terrain of capability to that of emotion, where the "middle ground" between women who "love too much or don't love enough" (38) is impossible to discern in the face of random forms of violence.

Wilson is thus depicting both Floyd and King as men who, by choosing

violence and criminality, align themselves with the ideological imperatives
of the American century, which turns on their embrace of the berserker, the
black man; not as warrior, which implies functioning in a system characterized by discipline and an ability to see the larger picture, but as weapon.
After Elmore describes the events leading up to his murdering King's real
father, Leroy, King takes the opportunity to establish a bond with him by
describing his dispute with Pernell, and in the process, by placing himself
in a dynasty of violence: "He don't know my daddy killed a man for calling
him out of his name. He don't know he fucking with King Hedley II. *I got
the atomic bomb as far as he concerned. And I got to use it*" (73; emphasis
added).

King's reference to the atomic bomb is unusual in light of the fact that in
1985 it is not the most lethal weapon in the U.S. arsenal. But reading *King
Hedley II* alongside *Seven Guitars* clarifies King's posturing: Floyd states in
1948, at a time when the atomic bomb's potential as an instrument of total
annihilation had been realized by the attacks on Hiroshima and Nagasaki,
"I am going to Chicago. If I have to buy me a graveyard and kill everybody I
see. I am going to Chicago. I don't want to live my life without. Everybody
I know live without. I don't want to do that. I want to live with. I don't
know what you all think of yourself but I think I'm supposed to have.
Whatever it is" (81). In expressing his willingness to resort to mass violence
to acquire "the good life," Floyd anticipates King's moment thirty-seven
years later, when young boys murder each other over things as inchoate as
"turf" or "respect" or as insignificant as sneakers or, as Stool Pigeon notes,
a fish sandwich. These acts profoundly foreground black men's ability to
embody — irrespective of their economic status — the kinds of imperialism and hegemony characteristic of U.S. power. That power, established at
the end of World War II, in 1985 could maintain the idea of a "winnable"
nuclear conflict without admitting to any cognitive dissonance.

In this nuclear age, the meaning of which should be drastically distinct
for the black community from the dominant white culture, Floyd's and
King's identification with atomic power demonstrates their alienation
from their ancestral past — something highlighted by Floyd's attitude toward music. In a conversation with his sidemen, Canewell and Red Carter,

he declares that the key to having control over one's fortunes in the recording industry is to "get the record out there. Let the people hear it. Then come back and ask for more money. Then you can get double if it's any good" (46). Floyd, anxious to return to Chicago where he has been invited by the president of Savoy Records to record another song in the wake of his previous efforts,[3] fails to recognize that despite the letter asking him to provide his services to Savoy Records, he has opted to be a cog—an easily replaceable one at that—in the cultural machinery of entertainment.[4] The years following World War II ushered in new approaches to communication that were antithetical to humane forms of transaction.

This consideration is timely because it focuses the question of cultural power and influence and asks whether artists and entertainers wield influence of the sort that will translate into institutionalized force. For if the entertainment industry institutes legal and business models whose ultimate purpose is to render originality inconsequential in the face of profitability, then the desire to "leave evidence," as Gayl Jones would put it, must be understood in a completely different way. But in an age when "airplay" and the concept of the "hit" have become central to the criteria for evaluating what constitutes "good music," Floyd situates the measure of his influence as a musician—and the leverage that issues from it—outside his purview. He determines that the record serves as the best indicator—in a cycle consisting of production, marketing, and consumption—of value, and, as well, of the artist's ability to demand a greater portion of the spoils. Hence, he concludes, "You can't be good just 'cause you say you is. The people got to hear it and want to buy it. That's what make you good" (46).

A final important link between *Seven Guitars* and *King Hedley II* is that both Floyd and Ruby are performers. How strange, then, that when Ruby shoots the derringer, the bullet winds up hitting King in the throat—mirroring the site of injury in Hedley's murder of Floyd. This is significant for multiple reasons that give full testimony to the connections to be drawn between these plays. Perhaps most important is that the Floyd/Hedley and Ruth/King acts of violence constitute the rhetorical figuration of chiasmus. Hedley's use of the machete to sever Floyd's windpipe is symbolic of the ways that violence has silenced his voice. This is not a difficult conclusion to reach, but in a play where there are black men whose dreams are in jeopardy — Hedley's because he is dying of tuberculosis and Floyd's because he has perpetrated a robbery in which his coconspirator was killed — the significance of that connection is greatly heightened.

Moreover, Hedley mistakes Floyd — who is in the backyard digging up the money he has stolen — for Buddy Bolden. When Floyd refuses to give him the money, Hedley resorts to violence because he thinks that Bolden has arrived to give him the money his father prophesied. We can understand this, in part, simply as Wilson's use of Aristotelian tragic conventions, which turn on instances of misperception or omissions of information that set the play's final events into motion. But the tragedy is also one of dislocation, as indicated by the characters' failure to understand the communal value of the open spaces where they perform as much as they fail to understand the meaning of the musical space that frames their performance.

In his 1962 essay "Jazz," drummer Max Roach, echoing Wilson's understanding of the outdoor urban spaces that delimit the dramatic action in these plays, declares that jazz is "an extenuation of the African chants and songs.[5] He eschews the idea that jazz can be described simply in terms of its musical attributes and opts instead to argue that in performing the music, the musician is engaged in a historical act in which the music becomes

> an extension of the pain and suffering of those long, and too often, destinationless trips across the Atlantic Ocean, deep in the holes [sic] of those dark, damp, filthy, human slave ships, endured by chained, innocent, black men, women, and children. "Jazz" is an extension of the humiliations suffered by these same human beings while being sold as cattle or produce. It is an extension of the pain of the whip, the assaulter, the procurer, the "driva" man, the patrol wagons, the kidnapper, the sunup to sundown slave field and plantation. (113)

As far as Roach can discern, jazz is a metaphor for the African American experience in the New World. To perform the music, then, is to engage, as Albert Murray has suggested, in an act of elaboration, for, despite the fact that instruments such as the saxophone and the piano predate the existence of jazz, Roach's argument places "the black man's hell on earth" as the grist from which the music springs; to play jazz is an act of sublimation that yields beauty "that makes for the esthetic contribution" to American musical history.

Roach's observation, in part because it bears some resemblance to August Wilson's notion of a black theater, also serves to frame my conclusion. What can be discerned from Roach's comments is that African American artistic endeavors must by necessity partake of the historical on their way to making an aesthetic statement. It is likewise a political assertion in its insistence that art forms like jazz are both a testimony to the resistant postures assumed by our African forebears in the face of dehumanization and commodification, and as well an improvisation — what Albert Murray refers to as "the also and the also" of African American subjectivity — through which those aspects of African American humanity that slavery and racial segregation attempted to destroy are elaborated upon and renewed. To put it another way, jazz power, as distinct from the nuclear power that has seduced Floyd and King, is a productive rather than an annihilating form of violence — one that values the communal space rather than eschews it, that views conception in non-paternalistic terms, and that reveres ancestry without succumbing to the sins of the fathers.

Notes

1. Mark Wigley, "Untitled: The Housing of Gender," p. 330.

2. The 1990s will see the rise of theatrical productions that combine a Christian message with bawdy humor and songs by R and B singers who have been discarded by a recording industry in transition. These plays often make women's sexual escapades and immorality central to the plot, with salvation coming in the form of the love of a good Christian man. See Henry Louis Gates's description of these plays in an essay he titled "The New Chitlin' Circuit" in the *New Yorker*.

3. Those familiar with August Wilson's *Ma Rainey's Black Bottom* know that the letter inquiring as to Floyd's "status," though brief, is nothing if not a reason to exercise caution. As Ma Rainey observes, "They don't care nothing about me. All they want is my voice. . . . As soon as they get my voice down on them recording machines, then it's just like I'd be some whore and they roll over and pull their pants on. Ain't got no use for me then" (79). The point here, I would

suggest, is that there are countless moments in African American history and culture when athletes and entertainers have found themselves in circumstances when they recognized the necessity of accepting humiliating and inequitable terms.

4. Indeed, in act 1, scene 2, we find the radio playing his song, "That's All Right," which, if only by its title, is reminiscent of Elvis Presley's song of the same name (though in listening to the Presley version, it is clear it is not the same song). In what must be considered something beyond mere coincidence, Wilson's decision to give the same title to Floyd "Schoolboy" Barton's hit record suggests that any discussion about the relationship between the recording industry and posterity must begin with the fact that the recording industry has reinvented many of the mechanisms utilized by slave owners to maximize profit. Foremost among them is the act of stealing black musicians' labor by seizing music written by African American composers and rearranging it for white artists. One of the most famous instances of this, of course, is Pat Boone's 1956 cover of Little Richard's "Tutti Fruiti."

5. Max Roach, "Jazz."

Turn Your Lamp Down Low!

Aunt Ester Dies in *King Hedley II.* Now What?

Didn't he say Tuesday, baby? Go on I'll see you on Tuesday" (prologue, *Gem of the Ocean*). Thus began an unceremonious introduction to one of August Wilson's most enigmatic, most significant — and certainly one of the *oldest* — characters in his ten-play cycle: Aunt Ester Tyler. Audiences at the 2003 premiere of *Gem of the Ocean* at Chicago's Goodman Theatre were the first to witness the embodiment of this feisty elder who comes to the stage as no stranger to those who have followed Wilson's plays. Even before he accorded Aunt Ester an onstage presence, the reality of her existence had been established in *Two Trains Running*, where satisfied clients of this Pittsburgh community spiritual advisor give convincing testimonies about the spiritually endowed healer Ester: "Aunt Ester got a power cause she got an understanding," Holloway testifies. "Anybody live as long as she has is bound to have an understanding" (22).

Prior to Aunt Ester's physical debut, Wilson had carefully guarded this harbinger of the African American presence. Yet when she calmly enters the room in the opening scene of *Gem* to quell the ruckus, she needs no formal introduction. In the cycle of Wilson's plays, Aunt Ester is a trusted spiritual advisor and revered resident of Pittsburgh's Hill District community. While safely ensconced offstage at 1839 Wylie Avenue, this character, who serves as a metaphor for the African American experience, continually provokes bafflement and speculation not only from the audience but also from the characters in the four plays that involve her. They wonder out loud about the accuracy of her age (allegedly 366 at the time of her death in 1985) and the validity of her powers.

Although much has been written about Aunt Ester's significance to Wilson's cycle, relatively little light has been shed on the scenario that awaits the Pittsburgh community when she finally dies. In fact, when one looks back over the cycle, much evidence suggests that Wilson's grand design included moving the story steadily toward a day of reckoning for those who have lost contact with their ancestors, their spirituality, and their song. For that reason, the pivotal moment of Aunt Ester's death in *King Hedley II* serves as the decided climax of the entire cycle. Coming to grips with the denouement of the ten-play chronicle, then, is where our work begins. The 366-year-old Aunt Ester dies. Now what?

Prior to the cycle's completion in 2005, many scholars and theater critics posited wide-ranging—and not entirely flattering—views of the seemingly immortal Aunt Ester. Harry Elam, Jr. in *The Past as Present in the Drama of August Wilson* describes her as "a critical figure mediating between the African past and the African American present, between the practice of Christianity and the Africanist-based spirituality" (184) and as "the 'ancestor,' the connection to the African American past, that is both personal and collective, both material and metaphysical as within the limits of individual plays" (185). Joan Herrington regards Aunt Ester as "Wilson's ever-present reminder of the need for a connection to the past. For his characters, she is the conduit to the source" (*King Hedley II* 172). But not all could see past the physical and the literal implications of Aunt Ester. A baffled *New York Times* theater critic, Ben Brantley, withheld praise for Aunt Ester's character, alluding to her as "less a credible character than a walking metaphor" (*NYT* May 20, 2007).

Born during the year the first slaves arrived in America, Aunt Ester exists both as a symbol of the African American past and as a most formidable enabler in the present. For those distressed and dislocated souls in search of a cultural identity and for those in need of a spiritual healing, Aunt Ester is a supreme matriarch, "Earth Mother," and healer — one who skillfully creates the illusion that she possesses extraordinary powers. Wilson's characters want this, and they want to believe that she is their deliverer. In *Two Trains Running*, Prophet Samuel, Malcolm X, and Martin Luther King Jr. have died and left a vacuum among black leaders; the people need a hero. Aunt Ester fills that role. By significantly shaping African American cultural identity, she makes sense out of the absurdity of their situations and shows them how to realize their own agency.

Wilson not only suspends disbelief about Aunt Ester's more than three hundred years, but he also uses a chorus of staunch supporters to testify to the reality of her healing powers and the credibility of her age. Holloway, the most vocal among Aunt Ester's cheerleaders, frequently acts as her agent. In *Two Trains Running* he repeats to anyone who will listen,

> All he got to do is go see Aunt Ester. Aunt Ester could straighten him out. Don't care whatever your problem. She can straighten it out. (23)

> Go on up there and see her. I go up to see her every once in a while. Get my soul washed. She don't do nothing but lay her hands on your head. But it's a feeling like you ain't never had before. Then everything in your life get real calm and peaceful (24).

> I'm talking about getting your luck changed. (25)

Holloway's stories about Aunt Ester emanate from a belief system that runs counter to conventional thinking about the aging process, which is also the brunt of jokes and source of skepticism among some of Memphis Lee's patrons. Even Memphis, despite his insistence on Aunt Ester's special powers, asks, "How in the hell somebody gonna live to be three hundred and twenty-two years old, nigger? You talk like a fool" (24). Those who do accept her longevity do so in large part because of their shared belief in the power of the spoken word to simply create reality; what critic Paul Carter Harrison refers to, in his essay "Mother/word" as "Nommo force — a creative elixir that activates the dramatic mode (context of experience) and reveals the symbolic gesture of the Mask (characterization). Embedded in this mode are references to common experience, myths and significations that define the collective moral universe" (xii). Holloway demonstrates this so-called mother word as he speaks and thereby gives further credence to Aunt Ester's reality: "She look like she five hundred. You be surprised when she say she ain't but three hundred and twenty-two. Don't ask me how she lived that long. I don't know. Look like death scared of her. Every time he come around her he just get up and get on away. Ask West about her. He'll tell you. He done went up there to see her. He been waiting to bury her since he saw her. Even told people there in the house that he'd do it for free" (25).

While *Two Trains Running* establishes Aunt Ester's unquestionable capabilities as a healing force within the black community, *King Hedley II*, set in 1985, reflects her fatigue, her unusual orneriness, and her bodily deterioration as the world around her increasingly slips into chaos and, correspondingly, as Aunt Ester slips into the hereafter. Before doing so, she requires medicine for a lingering ailment and around-the-clock care as she tries to recuperate in her home. Aunt Ester's death not only confirms her mortality; her physical departure also signals the onset of complete collapse of the world around her.

The profound turn of events that occurs in *King Hedley II*, set in the ninth decade of the ten-decade cycle, is the appropriate departure point in assessing Aunt Ester's role. Deemed apocalyptic for its tragic and foreboding tone, *King Hedley II* contains the moment when Aunt Ester passes away, taking with her all the stories for which she was the sole surviving receptacle. Thus her death is the erasure of history and the removal of the medium that conveys that history. Fittingly, therefore, the news of her death comes from the compulsive newspaper hoarder and obsessive scripture-spouting neighborhood nuisance, Stool Pigeon, who rushes in announcing, "Turn your lamp down low! We in trouble now. Aunt Ester died! She died! She died! She died!" (19).

King Hedley II, often considered Wilson's "darkest" and "most depressing" play, reflects the chaotic homicide-ridden urban landscape of mid-1980s America. According to Gabriel Ajang's thirty-five-year-long study of Pittsburgh homicide rates, "The city of Pittsburgh, which serves as backdrop for *King Hedley II* was, during the 1980s, the largest municipality in Allegheny County and accounted for more than 50% of Allegheny County homicides" (1).

The play's 1985 setting is during what has been called the Reagan era — a time characterized in urban areas by guns, crime, family dysfunction, and neglect. For most African Americans, the Reagan years were hard. His eight years in office brought an attempt to cripple the New Deal and the

Great Society by cutting federal support for virtually every program important to African Americans. The industries which had, over the century, attracted immigrants to the cities closed their doors permanently. Finally, the price of cocaine dropped by fifty percent, making the one-time drug of choice among the 1970s elite available to the masses. With this came a new and corrosive industry that proved devastating to the inner cities. By 1985, many neighborhoods that had once been run-down but still thriving and vital became virtual ghost towns — or, worse, savage war zones. Gang culture, street justice, and lyrics to gangsta rap advocated new, antisocial codes of behavior.

In the 1985 of *King Hedley II*'s Pittsburgh, the baby boy that Ruby carried during *Seven Guitars* is grown-up, out of jail, and determined to settle several scores. Her thirty-seven-year-old son King — short for his assumed father's name — bears mental and physical scars that turn him into a walking time bomb. The Hill District community where King and his wife Tonya live continues to reel from the "Pittsburgh Renaissance" — the 1950s urban renewal project that displaced thousands of Hill residents and hundreds of businesses. The collapse of the steel mill industry had provoked a mass exodus from Pittsburgh resulting in a staggering population drop and an economy forced to shift from manufacturing to service, education, and technology. In a tragic series of events, King unravels the lie his mother had perpetuated to keep from him the identity of his biological father, Leroy Slater. King has basic life ambitions: to get enough money to please his woman, to father a child to carry his name, to honor the memory of his (assumed) father, and to settle a score against the man who dishonored and maimed him. There is constant turmoil in King's life — conflict that is fueled and sustained by a gang mentality that trades blood for honor. Believing his actions are entirely honorable, he hunts down and murders his nemesis who had earlier taunted him with the name "champ" and maliciously slashed his face. Upon learning the identity of his murdered biological father, King feels compelled, once again, to defend the honor of a father figure. This time, he vows to avenge the death of his biological father, Leroy Slater, even if it means killing his mother's suitor or risking his own life in the process. In his attempt to avenge Leroy's murder, King is fatally wounded when he steps into his mother's line of fire and takes a bullet intended for another.

Such is the environment in which Aunt Ester resides as spiritual healer. Despite all of the wisdom that she imparts to her clients, the most immediately recognized impact of her legacy is the devastating sense of abandonment that sets in after her death. Aunt Ester's importance thus comes into much sharper focus in the wake of her death. In this intensely apocalyptic moment, Wilson levels his most foreboding indictment of African Americans who have lost contact with their ancestors. As in William Shakespeare's *King Lear*, nature seems to confirm this indictment, producing on the day of Aunt Ester's death violent windstorms, massive power outages, and the unexplained death of Ester's cat.

To understand the meaning of Aunt Ester's death, we need to comprehend the Africanist worldview that informs Wilson's work. According to Wilson, "relating to the spirit worlds is very much a part of African and Afro-American culture" (quoted in Savran, 34) and "the metaphysical presence of the spirit world has become increasingly important in my work" ("American Histories" 1). Paul Carter Harrison underscores this need for an African-based thought alignment: "The study of African philosophical systems is crucial to an understanding of the aesthetics of black cultures" (*Totem Voices* xiii). Such an alignment abandons Western notions of time, aging, and death — adopting instead the complex African mythology that shapes Aunt Ester's character. When this alignment occurs, one is better able to understand how Aunt Ester's transition to the afterlife is not as much a cause for grieving as it is an opportunity to reconnect with the African ancestors.

Nevertheless, Aunt Ester is rendered in very mortal terms. King, after all, does cut her grass and run errands to the drugstore for her medicine. She, like most mothers, holds onto fond memories of her absent children. Black Mary fixes her food and tidies her house. Aunt Ester has had husbands and lovers, and, even at her advanced age, indulges in a bit of flirting. Certainly, therefore, we can assume legitimately that this 366-year-old woman died of natural causes. According to African scholar John Mbiti, however, many African societies believe that "every human death is thought to have external causes, making it both natural and unnatural. . . . Although death is acknowledged as having come into the world and remained there ever since, it is unnatural and preventable on the personal level because it is always caused by another agent. If that agent did not *cause* it, then the individual would not die. People must find and give immediate causes of death. . . . Natural death does not exist" (151). In *Myth, Literature and the African World*, Wole Soyinka indicts this tendency to think in a box, labeling it "a recognizable Western cast of mind, a compartmentalising habit of thought which periodically selects aspects of human emotion, phenomenal observations, metaphysical intuitions and even scientific deductions and turns them into separatist myths (or 'truths') sustained by a proliferating superstructure of presentation idioms, analogies and analytical modes" (37).

From the time Aunt Ester's name was first uttered onstage in *Two Trains Running* to her cataclysmic offstage death in *King Hedley II* to her ensuing legacy in *Radio Golf*, Aunt Esther's role as the spiritual center of August Wilson's dramatic universe has taken on increasing significance. *Gem of the Ocean*'s "re-introduction" of Aunt Ester has much to do with Wilson's manipulation of time in that he disrupts the order in which he reveals her story. His use of Aunt Ester throughout the cycle, moreover, subordinates the importance and boundaries of time in order to render Aunt Ester timeless, ageless, and possibly immortal. In the preface to *King Hedley II*, Wilson explains that "Aunt Ester has emerged for me as the most significant persona of the cycle. The characters, after all, are her children. The wisdom and tradition she embodies are valuable tools for the reconstruction of their personalities and for dealing with a society in which the contradictions, over the decades, have grown more fierce, and for exposing all the places it is lacking in virtue" (x). When pressed by those unwilling suspend their disbelief regarding this magical figure, Wilson explained,

Aunt Ester resembles any black woman in her early seventies — someone you wouldn't look at twice if she stepped outside. . . . Yet she is the embodiment of African wisdom and tradition — the person who has been alive since 1619 [when the first slaves were brought to Virginia] and has remained with us. . . . Of course no one is going to live to be 285 years old. She represents any old person in the community that keeps its traditions alive. She's not mystical or magical. She can't help you find your way to redemption. You have to find it. (quoted in Dezell, 255)

When read through the lens of an African worldview, Aunt Ester represents the crossroads between the spiritual world of the African ancestors and the temptations that both capitalism and popular culture present. Aunt Ester personifies African American historical reality that is — in the interest of sheer survival — spoken into being and kept alive in the testimonies from within the community. Soyinka further underscores this tendency toward collective agency and creativity, arguing that the audience "contributes spiritual strength to the protagonist through its choric reality which must first be conjured up and established. . . . The drama would be nonexistent except within . . . this communal compact whose choric essence supplies the collective energy" (39). As Joan Herrington notes, "Called forth and made present by their descendants, ancestors exist within the same world as those who succeed them. They exist in the here and now and one encounters them at the crossroads of life or invokes them in moments of crisis" (173).

Stool Pigeon was born with a veil that enabled him to see beyond objective reality. This sixth sense provides a degree of clairvoyance that puts him in touch with deceased ancestors who speak to the living through him. In this context, the complex ideological systems of Ogun — "one of many deities carried to the New World by Africans during the slave Diaspora which took place between the sixteenth and the mid-nineteenth centuries" (Barnes, *Africa's Ogun* 1) — proves particularly illuminating. According to Ogun philosophy, "the ancestral role of the deceased members of society is shown in an ability to live on in the spirit world and to direct, influence, and even control human activities from afar" (Barnes, 195).

Wilson emphasizes not only Aunt Ester's power while she lives, but he also suggests that a direct line of communication to her still exists even after her death — but only for those who believe in ancestral powers. Her death itself, in other words, finally establishes Aunt Ester as part of a culturally vital belief system, one born out of what Soyinka observes as "man's attempt to externalize and communicate his inner intuitions" (3) as they fuse with centuries of cultural memory. Focused by the century that Wilson has dramatized, Aunt Ester initiates and sustains the intertextual conversations that transcend those temporal limits. She not only ties the cycle together but also ties the cycle as a whole to the thousands of years and millions of individual histories that made the twentieth-century African American experience possible.

Situating *King Hedley II* within an African context yields a much clearer understanding of the far-reaching impact of Aunt Ester's character. To underscore the urgency of advice specifically for the African American community, Wilson adopts a "new spirituality" that, according to Elam, allows "a blending of African spiritualism and Christianity to produce allusions that conjoin the Christian and the African" and is "inflected with Christianity even as it critiques Christianity" (181).

The Christian inflections of that agency can be found in the apocalyptic qualities of *King Hedley II*. With *The Book of Revelation* as its master text, apocalyptic literature is written in times of catastrophic change as previously well-ordered worldviews collapse. Its messages are communicated in mysterious, enigmatic forms, using bizarre, oftentimes obscure symbols and images. It deals with secret or hidden information, which can only be disclosed by supernatural means, through dreams or visions from God or angelic intermediaries. Animals play a role in predicting the apocalypse, and its fantastic world of beasts, signs, colors, numbers, and angels seems to function as a code that effectively conceals the message from the uninitiated.

Because the storyline of *King Hedley II* shows a steady movement toward a catastrophic end, and because Stool Pigeon is obsessed with biblical babble about the last days, the play may also be read as Wilson's most apocalyptic text. Stool Pigeon's potentially misunderstood scripture-based apocalyptic warnings appear to trump all other competing stories within *King Hedley II* and portray him as the actual truth teller. Wilson facilitates the dual perspectives on Stool Pigeon by drawing upon the hybrid influences of African spiritualism and New Testament theology. This strategy turns *King Hedley II* into an apocalyptic narrative that moves strategically toward a day of reckoning, with Stool Pigeon serving as both his mad prophet and Greek chorus. His immediate reaction with the fervor of fire and brimstone suggests the intensity expressed by religious zealots of the First Great Awakening in America. Rushing in with the news, Stool Pigeon warns, "Aunt Ester died! She died! She died! She died! . . . We in trouble now. These niggers don't know but God got a plan. The Bible say, 'I will call the righteous out of the land. I will gather thee to thy grave in peace; and thine eyes shall not see all the evil that I will bring upon this place'" (*King Hedley II*, 20).

While apocalyptic literature is basically pessimistic about mankind's prospects — things are bad and they are only going to get worse — it nevertheless proceeds on the firm conviction that God, in good time, will intervene to end the evil of this world and proclaim his ultimate victory. This should be read as the context for Stool Pigeon's pessimism in his predictions of the doom that will beset the Pittsburgh neighborhood following Aunt Ester's death. Certain that the end is near, he makes it his duty to warn all who will listen, based upon the firm belief that "God got a plan" (21). He serves as the prophet of the apocalypse although his prophetic voice falls largely upon deaf ears. Like the biblical prophets, he is labeled a lunatic: "You old buzzard! Go on in the house! . . . This is my business. I'm going down to Pat's place and tell them to stop saving them papers for you. I don't know why they give them to you. That's a firetrap. I'm gonna tell your landlord you got all them papers stored in there" (27).

Yet, Stool Pigeon's seemingly inconsequential biblical passages and pseudo-scriptural recitations produce a prophetic warning to African Americans about imminent disintegration. "The scourge was upon the land," Stool Pigeon states, "and the wrath of the Lord God Jehovah was visited upon every house" (21). Although the play has an aura of inevitability, Stool Pigeon's recitations also contain a prescription to avert the dire outcome: "God got a plan. . . . Say, 'I will call the righteous out of the land and raise up in thy midst a Messiah from amongst my people to redeem thy iniquities and He shall by the remission of blood make whole that which is torn asunder even though it be scattered to the four winds, for Great is My Name and ye shall know by these signs the coming of a new day'" (21).

If one accepts this as a possible reading of Aunt Ester's death, then her demise may represent a new beginning rather than a destructive end. Although one must yield equally to black magic and Christian apocalyptic transformation — African ritual and American optimism — it is possible to see the play's end as hopeful. When the blood of King spills onto the grave of Aunt Ester's cat, Stool Pigeon "recognizes that the sacrifice has been made" and becomes "joyous" (102). One would be hard-pressed to imagine how this neighborhood could get beyond the death and moral decay that plague it. In the uncanny yelp of a cat, however, Wilson at least provides his characters with an opportunity to engage actively in finding an answer to the question framing Aunt Ester's death: "Now what?"

VIVIAN GIST SPENCER
AND YVONNE CHAMBERS

Ritual Death and Wilson's Female Christ

With the approach of his sixtieth birthday, August Wilson declared, "There's more life behind me than ahead. I think of dying every day.... At a certain age, you should be prepared to go at any time." Within months, when he was told that he would soon die as a result of inoperable liver cancer, his response was composed: "I've lived a blessed life. I'm ready" (quoted in Rawson).

Wilson's unruffled reaction to the news was not surprising, for in reviewing the corpus of his work it is reasonable to say that August Wilson was a playwright who worked very closely with death, although he firmly declared he did not purposely seek to write about death. Wilson was surprised, in fact, when he noticed the amount of death his plays contained. As he acknowledged in an interview with Sandra Shannon:

> There's death in all of the plays. When I wrote *Joe Turner*, I said, "Hey, good. Nobody died. No death!" Then I started looking back, and there was Mr. Seth's mother, and there's a ghost in *Joe Turner*. Miss Mabel comes back, and there were constant references to death. I didn't realize it — the two babies. And I thought I had gotten away and wrote [sic] a play in which it wasn't. (quoted in *Dramatic* 208)

Wilson has denied, however, conscious attempts to include death in his works:

> It's unconscious whatever it is. But it's no longer unconscious because I recognize it although I didn't purposefully decide. It just emerges. ... I didn't decide that death was going to be part of the play. Once you're in there and you're working, you're not even thinking. You're

working from another place. It's sort of like this stuff is given to you if you open yourself up for it, and half the time I just accept what I hear. (quoted in Shannon, *Dramatic* 223)

Possibly, what Wilson heard while in the process of chronicling the history of African Americans in twentieth century was the natural rhythm of humankind — the pulse of life and death. In the final analysis, however, Wilson staunchly insisted, "Death is such an integral part of life; you can't have one without the other" (Shannon, *Dramatic* 208).

Wilson's characters, as well, often exhibit the tolerance toward death that Wilson himself expressed, despite the emotional and social impact of death within the community. This is not surprising, for the indulgent outlook on death illustrated by Wilson's characters is similar to the attitude often found in traditional African and African American culture. In traditional African philosophy, people who die merely pass from a physical form to a spiritual one and continue to be active in the lives of their families and communities. According to African theologian John Mbiti, "Strictly speaking nothing is essentially dead or devoid of life (being) in the sight of African peoples" (119), and "Death is conceived of as a departure and not a complete annihilation of a person. He moves on to join the company of the departed, and the only major change is the decay of the physical body, but the spirit moves on to another state of existence" (205). Overall, death in African American culture has many faces: violent, sudden, and devastating yet also noble, intimate, rewarding, peaceful, and joyful. James Baldwin even suggests that often the only dignity or beauty a black man can find is in the arms of death (Kalish and Reynolds, 101).

If death is pervasive in Wilson's drama, equally so are rituals, but rarely in the purely ceremonial sense. Unlike earlier anthropologists who have studied ritual primarily in relation to religious practices of primitive cultures, Wilson's approach to ritual resembles that of contemporary scholars, who often explore "secular ritual" as an integral part of modern technological society. With the well-being of the society as its core, secular ritual can be considered "collective ceremony," which "states, reiterates or reinforces traditional social ties, or expresses social conflicts or delineates social roles" (Moore and Myerhoff, 5). Looking at ritual in this "secular" fashion makes apparent that collective ritual in modern society has the ability to authorize and legitimize the status of people, institutions, occasions, moral values, and worldview (3–4). As well as being an agent of legitimacy, ritual can also act as a means of social control (3).

Theater, a secular practice with its origins in sacred ritual, in many ways combines aspects of religious and everyday ritual. Ancient drama fulfilled the need to achieve minimal order within society by creating a controlled environment on the stage. The performance transformed the audience/ worshipers by arousing new perceptions, insights, and ways of thinking. The performer/priest, through his actions, was also changed by becoming something greater than himself. As a result, the ritual theater performance acted as a tool allowing the community of "performer-spectator, ensemble-audience to succumb to something larger and nobler than itself" (Sainer, 39). This is a potential that Wilson's drama exploits.

Wilson's drama, in other words, especially in the second half of the cycle, engages death in the redemptive action of theater, in the same way that Christianity engages death in its theology of redemption. Redemption effected through reconnection to a spiritual heritage is a recurrent theme in Wilson's plays, although Wilson's characters often reject traditional Christianity. While very much a product of an African American community steeped in the Christian tradition, Wilson did not consciously write Christian symbols into his plays. He said in a 1984 interview with Kim Powers that he writes what is there; whatever comes out of him (10). From his close association with the African American community, he found spiritual inspiration and language for the characters in his plays. Wilson has pointed out that although he was shaped by the forces of his cultural environment, the consciousness in the plays is not that of Wilson, but of the characters themselves (Feingold, 18). Of faith he said, "When you look in the mirror, you should see your God. If you don't, you have somebody else's God" (Moyers, video).

Although African Americans may not worship in the same manner as European Christians, Christianity has been an integral part of the African American community. "Blacks have relied on institutions," Wilson noted, "which are really foreign — except for the black church, which has been our saving grace. I have some problems with it but I recognize it as a central social organization and sometimes an economic organization for the black community" (quoted in Savran, 34). Christian symbols and concepts that often profoundly affect the lives of African Americans find their way, therefore, into many of Wilson's plays, especially in connection with the wise and historical persona of Aunt Ester. Ester's name alludes to the biblical Queen Ester, a woman who risked her life to save her people from genocide. Like Christ, moreover, Aunt Ester is both in the world and not of it. She exists, as Harry Elam notes, "in and of the flesh" (*Past as Present* 185). Both Christ and Aunt Ester also lead miraculous lives and embody spiritual knowledge, in part through symbols and metaphors.

Aunt Ester, moreover, lives in a world subsumed by Christian imagery. Water, significant throughout the Christian ritual, plays an important role in every aspect of Aunt Ester's life.[1] She sends Citizen Barlow across a symbolic ocean to seek redemption, and the people seeking Aunt Ester's advice are sent to the river to perform a ritual sacrifice. According to Phylicia Rashad, who played Aunt Ester, Wilson stressed Aunt Ester's relationship to water. When Wilson first heard Aunt Ester speak, "she said that she couldn't talk about the water, but the water was all she talked about" (Rashad, 43).

Barlow's journey to the City of Bones, moreover, bears striking resemblances to the African American Christian baptism ceremony. Barlow, wearing special clothing, entered the water, was lead by a minister (Aunt Ester), and was assisted by deacons (Black Mary and Solly Two Kings). The songs they sang resembled African American spirituals, and the description of the City of Bones — with twelve gates and twelve gatekeepers — alludes to the heavenly gates in the book of *Revelation*. Water also connects Aunt Ester to spiritual guidance in *Two Trains Running*, when she tells several characters to throw twenty dollars into the river.

Essential to Aunt Ester's story, as it is to that of Christ, is the idea that death is not the culmination but a necessary step on the path to resurrection. This similarity is suggested not only by the fact that her name echoes "Ester" but also that she died from grief over the state of the souls of African Americans in the 1980s. At the end of *King Hedley II*, after her death, the resurrection of Aunt Ester's spirit is suggested by the sound of a cat's meow. In that play, Stool Pigeon chronicles the Christian biblical story from Genesis through Revelation. As Joan Herrington points out, Stool Pigeon welcomes an end to the severance and tragedy; according to Wilson, "It's really a joyful play. We start a new tradition, we can reconnect" (Herrington, 68). Because the forces of God acknowledged by Stool Pigeon are connected to the black community, King's death, like Aunt Ester's, repeats and revises the sacrificial death of Christ (Elam, 87). King's death paves the way for the renewal, called for by Stool Pigeon, who has become Aunt Ester's disciple. He is one among Aunt Ester's many disciples — the list includes her housekeeper, Black Mary; her "gatekeeper," Eli; and Barlow. Sterling Johnson becomes a devoted follower over the thirty-year span between the 1960s of *Two Trains Running* and the 1990s of *Radio Golf*, and King, in *King Hedley II*, also seems to be redeeming his connection with Aunt Ester. In the beginning of the play, King only shows a superficial understanding of the golden key ring that she had given him, but in the last scene, Stool Pigeon explains that King found the "Key to the Mountain." King, who had gone to jail for taking another man's life, finds that he cannot carry out his plan to kill again. The change in King evidently also affects Elmore, who, after looking into King's eyes, cannot kill King.

Gem of the Ocean, in which the only onstage appearance of Aunt Ester converges with three significant ritual deaths, thus foregrounds the way Wilson forges redemption out of the interaction between Christian, African, and African American ritual sacrifice. The first death in *Gem of the Ocean* — reported in the first scene of the play — is that of Garret Brown, a worker at the local mill who had jumped into the river and drowned because he was falsely accused of stealing a bucket of nails (*Gem* 11). The second death is the symbolic death of Citizen Barlow when he reenacts the Middle Passage, and the third is the shooting of Solly Two Kings when he tries to escape Pittsburgh and the law of Caesar. These three deaths, we want to argue, structure the dramatic action of *Gem of the Ocean* so as to employ the ritualistic aspects of theater to transform the ritualized practices of everyday life that define a community into the ritual sacrifice that preserves it.

In *Violence and the Sacred*, René Girard contends that sacrifice is the ritual that "protects the entire community from its own violence by substituting its violence to a harmless victim who cannot reciprocate or retaliate" (7–8). Since one function of ritual is to curb violence within the community or to keep it entirely outside the community, a particular type of ritual often replaces a violent act — such as a murder — with "purified" violence that exhausts itself on victims whose injury or death provoke no reprisals. The society is able to unleash its pent-up aggression against a surrogate victim in a ritual of sacrifice, a performance of simulated violence enacted to offer substitute satisfaction. In addition, Girard considers sacrifice the most crucial, fundamental, and commonplace of rites (300), with elements of sacrifice being found in every ritual. Girard further argues, "Sacrifice has the ability to restore harmony and reinforce the social fabric of the community" (8). Because of its efficacy within the society, sacrifice is indispensable. It is only appropriate that Wilson's works display sacrifice, for it plays an important role in traditional African life and is considered one of the most common acts of worship among African people (Mbiti 75). Within African culture, sacrifice can take many forms and has personal as well as communal benefits.

The sacrificial quality of Brown's death is made clear by Aunt Ester, the embodiment of African culture and "spiritual advisor of the community," who supplies the most plausible response to the inquiry in a conversation with Citizen Barlow, the troubled young man who has come to her for counsel:

He died a lonely death. Wasn't nobody but him. All them people standing around watching and he was the only one who died. . . . That's the only way he had to say he was innocent. It must have meant an awful lot for him to say that. He was willing to die to say that. . . . Jesus Christ was falsely accused. He died a bitter death on the cross. This man was just like Jesus. He say he would rather die innocent than to live guilty. (*Gem* 21)

He didn't care if anybody else knew if he did it or not. He knew. He didn't do it for the people standing around watching. He did it for himself. He say I'd rather die in truth than to live a lie. That way he can say that his life is worth more than a bucket of nails. (*Gem* 45)

Brown's suicide makes the importance of truth clear to Citizen Barlow, whom Wilson describes as being "in spiritual turmoil" (*Gem* 5). Barlow, at the time of Brown's death, was unable to admit that he had stolen the bucket of nails.

Brown's death thus functions as a ritual sacrifice, an act of "purified" violence that provides no reprisals. According to descriptions by Barlow and by Wilks, conditions at the mill are deplorable. Barlow stole the bucket of nails because he was not being paid well, and Brown dies while other mill workers provide no assistance to the drowning man. Brown, in a ritual of sacrifice, offers the other workers "substitute satisfaction" for their anger over the hardships on the job.

Brown's death may have had the valuable ritual effect on Citizen Barlow of validating the importance of truth telling — creating awareness of the ethical act that should have been performed — but, paradoxically, rather than quell the "disruptive influences" within the community, Brown's death amplifies them as Wilks, the local constable, indicates:

These niggers gone crazy! . . . They was over at the mill rioting. Busting out the goddam windows. Talking about they ain't going to work. They had all kinds of chaos and confusion over there. Police had to arrest about two hundred people. I ain't never seen nothing like it. Want to bust out the goddam windows! Running around like a pack of animals. (*Gem* 30)

It becomes apparent from the chaos that occurs as a result of Brown's death that the sacrifice is inadequate, and the need for further ritual acts is imperative.

Certainly the most ritualized death in *Gem of the Ocean* is the symbolic death that Barlow undergoes in order to be washed of his sins. His journey to the City of Bones is the most exhaustive rite in the entire play. In true ritual fashion, Barlow's journey begins after he admits to Aunt Ester that he stole the bucket of nails and thus became responsible for the death of Garret Brown by keeping silent: "I told myself to tell them I did it but every time I started to tell them something got in the way. I thought he was gonna come out the water but he never did. I looked up and he had drowned. It's like I got a hole inside me. If I ain't careful seem like everything would leak out that hole. What to do, Miss Tyler?" (*Gem* 44). Aunt Ester offers Barlow the only possible redemption: a ritual journey to the City of Bones. Because Barlow's actions have separated him from the rest of society, he must strongly desire the acts of transformation that will return him to society. Aunt Ester explains that she can take Barlow to the City of Bones and then asks, "Do you want to go, Mr. Citizen? Do you want to get your soul washed?" Barlow replies, "I got to get this thing off me, Miss Tyler. Yeah, I want to go" (*Gem* 54). With his acceptance, Citizen Barlow begins the process.

The next phase of Barlow's journey includes his preparations for the journey by a ritual cleansing of bathing and prayer. Aunt Ester reminds Barlow that because prayer is particularly significant, he should try to pray — even if he does not know how. Following these preparations, he is ready for the trip; besides Aunt Ester he is joined by Black Mary, Eli, and Solly — all of whom have previously traveled to the City of Bones. Because the journey is symbolic — from a state of personal slavery in "spiritual turmoil" to one of personal freedom, relocating his moral center — Aunt Ester's Bill of Sale as a slave is made into a small paper boat called the "Gem of the Ocean," and Barlow must hold onto the boat at all costs.

The passage to the City of Bones is Barlow's reconnection to his African roots and culture, and to the values he has lost. The city itself and its significance is described by Aunt Ester:

It's only a half mile by a half mile but that's a city. It's made of bones. Pearly white bones. All the buildings and everything is made of bones. I seen it. I been there, Mr. Citizen. My mother lives there. I got an aunt and three uncles live down there in that city made of bones. ... That's the center of the world. In time it will all come to light. The people made a kingdom out of nothing. They were the people that didn't make it across the water. They sat down right there. They say, "Let's make a kingdom. Let's make a city of bones." (*Gem* 52)

In addition to Aunt Ester's Bill of Sale and the bones of those lost in the Middle Passage, Barlow receives other items intended to reconnect him with his roots. Solly gives Barlow a link of chain — symbolic of the chains of the African slaves — that has brought Solly luck throughout his life. Finally, Barlow is led down into the bottom of the boat where he sees people chained to the boat who all look like him and have his face (*Gem* 66).

When Barlow finally reaches the City of Bones — with its gates of pearl described in the book of Revelation — he is confronted by a gatekeeper in the guise of Garret Brown, who requires payment before he will allow Barlow to enter. However, Barlow is stopped from entering the City of Bones because of his sin. As Revelation 21:27 states, "And there shall in no wise enter into it any thing that defileth, neither whatsoever worketh abomination, or maketh a lie: but they which are written in the Lamb's book of life." The only payment Barlow can offer the gatekeeper is to tell the truth about his complicity in the death of Garret Brown. As Aunt Ester explains, "You got to tell him, Mr. Citizen. The truth has to stand in the light. You got to get your soul washed. . . . You got to tell him, Mr. Citizen. Otherwise you'll never be right with yourself." With that, Citizen confesses/admits, "It was me. I done it. My name is Citizen Barlow. I stole the bucket of nails" (*Gem* 69). As a result of Barlow's admission, the gates of the city open. At this point Wilson's stage directions indicate the effect of the ritual: "Overwhelmed by the sheer beauty of the city and the people with their tongues on fire, Citizen Barlow, now *reborn* as a man of the people, sits down and begins to cry (*Gem* 69–70, emphasis added).

Although Barlow has died and been resurrected, his transformation is not complete. The final portion of Barlow's renewal requires the last ritual in the play: the death of Solly Two Kings. Solly is another character well suited as a ritual victim, for he has spent the better part of his years risking his life to lead people to freedom. In Solly, Wilson creates another character who represents the strength and courage of African Americans who can be viewed as role models for contemporary African Americans.

When Solly is killed by Wilks, Solly's death becomes the sacrifice that finalizes the process by transforming Barlow into the man who takes on Solly's role of saving others. Earlier in the play, Solly had made the connection between slaves who lost their lives during the Middle Passage and the condition of his sister and other blacks in Alabama during the first decade of the twentieth century: "I told myself I can't just sit around and collect dog shit while the people drowning. The people drowning in sorrow and grief. That's a mighty big ocean. They got the law tied to their toe. Every time they try and swim the law pull them under" (*Gem* 60). Although the time of actual slavery is past, the segregation of the Jim Crow South is just as harmful. The letter from Solly's sister, which recounts the troubles that blacks were having in Alabama, reflects a pattern of chaos that needs to be transformed. As Solly explains to Aunt Ester, "I just got a letter from my sister today. I got to go! She say she can't hold on no more. Say the white people have gone crazy. I got to go back down there to get her. . . . This my last trip. I'm getting old. I can't do more than one more. I don't know what I'm gonna do then. I was thinking of living my life for you. But I got to go back down there and get my sister" (*Gem* 19).

As the "funeral" for Solly begins with Aunt Ester, Black Mary, and Eli singing over Solly's body, Barlow is transformed. Again Wilson's stage directions clarify the significance of the moment: "Citizen takes off his coat. He puts on Solly's coat and hat and takes Solly's stick. He discovers the letter from Solly's sister in the hat. Eli pours a drink and raises it in a toast." Eli then states, "So live." The stage directions continue, "Without a word Citizen turns and exits" (*Gem* 85). Barlow is now willing to take over Solly's role as a "conductor" on what was once the Underground Railroad.

Gem of the Ocean's ritual deaths show that death, despite its destructive qualities, can be a positive force in order to create new life. Garret Brown, Solly Two Kings, and Citizen Barlow each in his own way confronts death — literally or figuratively — to improve himself or others around him. These characters thus represent death as transforming, validating, and reaffirming the members and the standards of the community by providing outlets for unsettling forces within the society. Through death, the new replaces the old, and society is regenerated. By undergoing the ritual process, the characters from *Gem of the Ocean* — as well as the audience — are reminded of the importance of reclaiming the culture, regaining the values, and rebuilding the "moral personality" of the African American past.

In *Radio Golf,* set at the end of the cycle, Aunt Ester's house, like the Church of Christ, extends the spiritual legacy past death to bind and support the community of followers. In this play, her spiritual influence — as represented by the houses of Aunt Ester — continues through the lives and work of others. As a method of survival, Caesar Wilks has developed an affinity with whites and an adversarial position toward the interests of the African American community. In *Radio Golf,* Caesar's son is described as a tough but fair businessman. We find out that for years he had paid the taxes on Aunt Ester's house anonymously. Harmond Wilks, Caesar's grandson, already identifies strongly with the African American community. However, he is a mayoral candidate for the city of Pittsburgh and also has strong individual business and political interests. That house connects Harmond not only to Aunt Ester, but through her to the lost branches of his family and his African American spiritual roots.

Old Joe, he learns, is the son of Barlow and Black Mary, who, he discovers, is his aunt. But Black Mary had also followed directly in the footsteps of Aunt Ester, assuming Ester's name, garb, and role. Old Joe has also named his daughter Black Mary. If in the Christian tradition a succession of spiritual leaders assumes the mantle of Christ, so too in Wilson's cycle a series of Black Mary/Ester Tyler characters portend the continuance of the African American spiritual memory embodied in Aunt Ester. As the church binds Christians together through common spiritual ground, the spiritual influence of Aunt Esters and Black Marys continues to bind the African American Hill District community.

Note

1. Wilson himself stated that before he writes, he washes his hands: "I always want to say I approached it with clean hands — you know, a symbolic cleansing" (quoted in Lahr, 32).

Miss Tyler's Two Bodies
Aunt Ester and the Legacy of Time

em of the Ocean, the penultimate play in August Wilson's dramatic cycle, gives Aunt Ester a body, a substance, a materiality, and a future as it establishes a history that identifies her genesis. In three other Wilson plays she is talked about, but remains out of view. The first play to speak her name, *Two Trains Running*, is set in the pivotal 1960s, when African Americans were redefining themselves and pushing hard for justice. Extracting Aunt Ester from that effort is impossible, in that she had survived every challenge African Americans have faced. In *King Hedley II*, set in 1985, her body gives out at the age of 366 not from old age, Stool Pigeon explains, but from disappointment over the forgetfulness of her children. In *Radio Golf*, set twelve years later, Aunt Ester's house at 1839 Wylie is slated for demolition.

Already 285 years old in 1904, when the events in *Gem* occur, Aunt Ester opens her red door to converse with others, to remember her mother, and to recall her four marriages (and one husband in particular). She mourns her favorite son, finds fault with the woman who will eventually take her place, conducts an excursion to the sacred City of Bones, and proposes to a sixty-something freedom fighter who returns her affection. We see her foibles, tenderness, and also her loneliness as she befriends a troubled worker named Citizen Barlow, who becomes for her not only the son she lost to a noose but a representative of the working community she, in the tradition of the tribal healers of the first continent, is committed to healing. In *Gem*, Aunt Ester also reveals that she is neither the first nor only woman to submerge her previous identity and emerge as Aunt Ester: "Miss Tyler gave me her name. Ester Tyler. I don't tell nobody what I was called before that" (45). Who she was before no longer matters because her personal past has died so that she can take on the collective past of all the prior Aunt Esters.

Aunt Ester's story thus comprises a cycle within the Wilson cycle, starting with *Two Trains Running*, the fifth play, and ending with the closing trinity, *King Hedley II, Gem of the Ocean,* and *Radio Golf.* In this context, this essay considers the double bodies of Aunt Ester — her duality — which *Gem* highlights with two living incarnations of Ester Tyler: the formerly renamed Aunt Ester and the yet-to-be-renamed Black Mary, who live together at 1839 Wylie. As a lineal role, revivified in each generation, Aunt Ester sustains threads of collective memory, replicating the principle of royal and papal succession: the head does not die, but rather regenerates with a new face. Just as sovereignty legislates who belongs within the zone of protection and who does not,[1] Aunt Ester, thanks to her double cultural perspective — Eastern, as derived from Africa, and Western, as produced by slavery and emancipation — can reverse the givens, transforming outsiders as America defines them into insiders. As a daughter of Africa, Aunt Ester mediates between those gone before, those here now, and those waiting to join the living — being conversant with each and holding each in tandem so that the entirety can be strengthened by the interstitial flow. As a child of America, Aunt Ester merges what she knows with what she needs to survive. Her duality — a double duality, *recto-verso* — hinges cultures by connecting present and future with past and present in the successive bodies. As such, it opposes W. E. B. Du Bois's notion of double consciousness, which understands blackness as at odds with itself and judged negatively by the external eye. Double consciousness cuts the other down to procrustean dimensions in service to a constantly disapproving audience that is satisfied thereby with a spectacle of its own greater merit and standing.[2] While Du Bois's twoness, which relies on the body as owned — not owning — is disjunctive, Aunt Ester's twoness, which claims and accumulates component histories, is conjunctive.

From 1839 Wylie Avenue, Aunt Ester functions as spiritual purifier and mistress of ritual, mediating between past, present, and future to provide good fortune to the laboring community of African Americans in the Hill

District of Pittsburgh. When she started her apprenticeship, the Aunt Ester of *Gem* was a child of nine and Ester Tyler was her guardian and mentor, preparing her as she was prepared by the previous Ester Tyler. By the time she stepped into her role, the Aunt Ester of *Gem* was well trained to push forward the tradition, which is dispersed like water throughout the African diaspora, particularly in areas and circumstances that privilege the syncretic, which is improvisatory and additive, incorporating older traditions within the new.

As successive realities emanating from a point of origin, such that collectively she is Mother Genesis, Ester Tyler stands inside a continuum spanning centuries. Two incarnations of Aunt Ester — one born before and the other after emancipation — preside over the twentieth century, encompassing the transition from plantation to manufacturing and processing plant and mill, from the agricultural plain to the corners of industry, from rural to urban. At the dawn of the twentieth century, African Americans, like searching waters after the breakup of an old order predicated on bondage, entered the century as ostensibly free people looking for a new home. Many settled in Pittsburgh's Hill District with its diversity of jobs, though few offering more than basic subsistence. Aunt Ester fed their hungry spirits, letting them know that — despite the dispossession of their bodies — they had options outside the official flow, through which to unify body and spirit.

In 1904, as the beneficiary of a tradition that had transcended almost three hundred years of the slave ships and auction blocks — of the lash, the field, and the house — Aunt Ester understood the adaptability and fluidity that the new century demanded. She understood the imperative of flowing with and also against the times. In shifting circumstances, she knew how to stay balanced; how to improvise and let rituals lighten the load of time, particularly for men and women barely able to stop the roof from leaking on their lives. For these people, Aunt Ester signifies immortality.

Like Aunt Ester, Wilson rejected a system that failed him and turned into memory the history of hard times in the city, under the hand of men who counseled him and women with the wisdom and spirituality Aunt Ester embodied. In finding a way to ease difficulties in *Gem* as well as in

Two Trains Running and *King Hedley II* — and in bringing neighborhood people together to fight against the eradication of her memory from the Hill in *Radio Golf* — Aunt Ester connotes resistance.[3] As she tells Caesar in *Gem*, she must not respect the laws and practices that made her and her kin objects. She is thus not beholden to capitalism, which turns the body of the worker into a cog ground down in the acquisition of money. Instead of accepting cash from the men and women whom she helps, which would subordinate them to the usual rules of business, she asks them to throw twenty dollars into the river. She then waits for the good she has produced to flow back to her as a gift, so that she avoids a mercenary transaction that entails no bond and no reciprocity.

Aunt Ester's world is inclusive; focused on the many. This is also reflected in the personalities of the two Aunt Esters living together on Wylie Avenue in 1904. The prospective Aunt Ester is Black Mary, whose name suggests the Black Madonna inherited through medieval European Catholicism. In 1901, two years before Du Bois published his view that blacks were condemned never to pull their combative selves into wholeness (Du Bois, 2–5), Black Mary knocked on Aunt Ester's door looking for work and shelter. Fitting in at Aunt Ester's house was not easy. Aunt Ester was particular, and Black Mary was a grown woman in her late twenties. Near the end of *Gem*, Black Mary insists that she has to be free to pursue her own preferences. When she cooks, for example, she wants her fire high and hot; not low. "I got my own way," Black Mary asserts, "and that's the way I'm doing it" (77). Aunt Ester's response, "What took you so long" (77), suggests that she was just testing Black Mary's limits and forging her mettle.

Understanding the importance of passing on her legacy, Aunt Ester had dreamed that Black Mary was coming, anticipating the moment in 1925 when Black Mary fulfilled that vision by recording the deed to 1839 Wylie. From the nineteenth century through the twenty-first century, Aunt Ester changes from ward to housekeeper to heredity. In the twenty-first century Aunt Ester moves into dynastic legitimacy, gaining her status not by labor but by birthright. This change might also reflect the reconfiguration of black family structure since slavery. If before emancipation parents did not own the bodies of their offspring, and afterward families were still frayed, blacks — as people set adrift — sought whatever connections they could find. By the late twentieth century, however, many family relations became more secure; in some instances a foundation for stability and the intergenerational accumulation of resources was produced. In this context, Aunt Ester's lineage of women as community custodians provides the perpetuity out of which a black milieu is strengthened and reproduced.

Bearing kinship to the female water divinities of Africa — such as the androgynous Mammy Wata — and having learned through long training the lore and healing power of the ancient continent, Aunt Ester is attuned to the forces of nature represented by the rivers. Mammy Wata is the Goddess Mother of Waters[4] — amphibious, at home on land and sea, able to navigate long distances and disappear to the bottom of the water when necessary — and has access to an alternate kingdom and other sources of power. In Haiti, Mammy Wata is kin to LaSiren; in Trinidad, to Maman Dlo — and she goes by other names in Cuba and Jamaica. In Brazil, she is known as Yemanja or Queen Mother of the Rivers. Under different names, Mammy Wata is honored throughout the diaspora and in eastern and western Africa — especially among the Yoruba of Nigeria, where she remains a strong influence in the writings of authors such as Chinua Achebe, Buchi Emecheta, Flora Nwapa, and Ben Okri. Like Mammy Wata, Aunt Ester is partial to water — she requires that any money meant for her be deposited first in the river, which is the current she honors — and is a sensuous woman. Even at an advanced age, she can still draw to her side a prospective husband. The sexual energy between Aunt Ester and Solly, in fact, is thick, because they are kindred spirits — they both see black life as worthy rather than unworthy and as deserving of autonomy. Mammy Wata has her rules that must be followed, and so does Aunt Ester, who will only see her clients on Tuesdays, and not every Tuesday. Prosperity is part of Mammy Wata's blessing, and the same is true of Aunt Ester. Although she makes clear that she does not intend to bestow material wealth, but rather to point the seeker the way to peace, she has turned the monetary tide for many including Prophet Samuel and Memphis Green in *Two Trains*. Lady Luck may be her closest North American analogue, even if in *King Hedley II* she seems associated with ill fortune: a black cat, the death of that cat, the death of

King, and her own death. Nevertheless, the meow heard at the end of the play suggests the promise of Aunt Ester's spirit finding new incarnations in the life of the Pittsburgh community.

The promise with which *King Hedley II* ends — that the line of Aunt Ester has not passed away without succession — is taken a step further in *Radio Golf.* The only woman to become Ester Tyler in the twentieth century breathes still in the body of her second, who is also her granddaughter and namesake, Black Mary. If chronologically the cycle begins with Ester Tyler's two bodies, one of whom bears the name Black Mary, it ends that way as well. At the end, however, one of the twain is not flesh but hull and wood — a structure enclosing life in much the same way that the body is the shell of the spirit. The twenty-first-century Ester Tyler stands in abeyance, an unseen presence who replicates the way Aunt Ester began her career in *Two Trains Running.* But her invisibility renders her more — not less — powerful. Through her invisibility, as Harry Elam notes, Aunt Ester channels the force of the eternal (185). In employing drama that stands equidistant between an African and a Western understanding, Wilson reweaves the divisive dualities that impinge upon African Americans' residence inside a system postured on their exploitation and suppression, positioning Aunt Ester as the countervailing and accumulated force of resistance. Her house remembers, renews, and revitalizes the past. As the demolition trucks roll toward 1839 Wylie, Wilson's dramatic project culminates with the red door of Aunt Ester's refurbished home, which the community has readied for her imminent return, so that Wilson's decennium cycle concludes with the specter of the dispossessed reclaiming their inheritance.

Notes

1. See Agamben, 4.
2. Double consciousness is an inherently theatrical term much written about in the eighteenth century. In *The Paradox of the Actor*, Diderot posits that genius actors have greater impact if they create emotion in others but remain separate from the feelings they generate. Joseph Roach links a discussion of eighteenth-century acting theory and Du Bois's double consciousness, which he describes as

emergent out of "bifurcating pressures" (Roach, 83). That bifurcation, I believe, comes from the subsidiary status of the limbo body that does not own the self.

3. Her house number, 1839, corresponds to the year when the black neighborhood in Pittsburgh was attacked and many homes were destroyed (Elam, *The Past As Present* 186).

4. Mami Wata is another frequent spelling; see Drewel, 161.

NATHAN GRANT

August Wilson and the
Demands of Capital

The plays in the second half of August Wilson's cycle emphasize more deeply than the first the idea of coming to terms with the realities of capital. While the earlier plays assume conditions of economic inequality, in the second half of the cycle characters must confront the advantages and complications of capital, such that thematic continuity throughout the cycle — upon closer scrutiny — actually reveals Wilson's skill at blending new themes with older ones. Wilson's varied metaphoric and rhetorical patterns reveal the components of these blends. While capital or its absence always comprises a given in Wilson's plays, its treatment in the second half-cycle suggests its increased influence in the development both of civil rights and of modernity.

In *Two Trains Running*, for example, the trope of the railroad and the South-to-North theme of African American migration assist the demands of capital that assert themselves in concrete ways in the drama between the character Memphis and the city of Pittsburgh over the property he wishes to sell. In this connection, some of the deadliest aspects of the alliance between capital and race announce themselves at the end of the line in the figure of Jim Stovall, the white Mississippi antagonist whose theft of Memphis's land and the murder and mutilation of his mule drove Memphis to seek refuge in Pittsburgh. In the same play, the scarred and obsessive Hambone, who ten years earlier had painted a fence for the butcher Lutz, had never received the ham he was due as payment. In this light, *Two Trains Running*, which presumably ends the first half of the cycle, can be viewed as a transitional work. In his analysis of the first half of the cycle, Kim Pereira omits treating *Two Trains*, a play set in 1969, noting that the themes of separation, migration, and reunion — so much a part of the inner matter of the four earlier plays — "are not integral to its structure." "Only faint traces of the old themes," Pereira writes, "linger as new ones emerge" (*Odyssey* 5). This thematic difference reflects, I think, not only the influence of capital in the lives of African Americans, but urges blacks to pay greater attention to that influence. Memphis, dismissing the younger Sterling's reverence for Malcolm X, declares that few things are more absurd than black folk "talking about black power with their hands and pockets empty" (41). For Memphis, fiscal soundness is the only real power. Similarly, as Wilson has noted, "Hambone dies not getting his ham because he never took it. That's the premise for life in American society. It's the American way."

While Memphis's and even Wilson's perspectives on life in America may seem rather harsh — they generally oppose the master narrative of the dignified struggle for social justice rooted in the history of the African in the West — these perspectives should be understood in terms of the de-volving material conditions of the people of Pittsburgh's Hill District. Stu-art Hall suggests that fixed ideological categories do not shape proletarian, or bourgeois, or entrepreneurial perspectives. Rather they are informed by one's fundamental relations — the "facts on the ground," as it were — to materialism. Nor do those economic relations prescribe a "single, fixed and unalterable" way of conceptualizing materialism. Materialism, Hall writes, "can be 'expressed' within different ideological discourses" (Mor-ley and Chen, 39). Our various perspectives, in other words, on what we understand to be capitalism arise from our location in its system: "Each [discourse] thus *situates us* as social actors or as a member of a social group in a particular process to the relation and prescribes certain social identi-ties for us" (40; emphasis in original). Factors of race and racism crucially underwrite and intensify Memphis's place in the economy and lend it its uniqueness. If the vitality of the collective has depended on the mutually beneficial acts, large and small, of black community, Memphis's family and community — the victims of racial terror — have been lost in the urban wilderness. In this connection Malcolm's rhetoric falls as dismally short as Martin Luther King's passive resistance, essentially divorced, as it is, from a discussion of acquisition. Wilson captures in this disturbing mo-

ment the fact that the deferred success of both men's words has often given
way in the black community, either to despair or a more aggressive brand
of American Dreaming. Memphis's eventual monetary triumph over the
Pittsburgh city government not only allows him to return to Mississippi
to settle his score, but also to revive his business and resituate capital once
removed from the South through the ethnic cleansing perpetrated by men
like Stovall. Either of the two trains leaving daily for Jackson now reverses
for Memphis the South-to-North migration theme, and returns to him the
pride once lost through violence.

There is no such fortunate resolution for the men of *Seven Guitars*,
the play that was written five years after *Two Trains* but depicts the Hill
District of the 1940s. This play may be Wilson's most enigmatic regarding the larger issues of capital and community, but the drama also deftly
involves elements of masculinity and native skill that are at once endur-
ing, and through fantasies of capital, defamiliarized. The principal action
takes place between Floyd Barton, a talented guitarist who rarely gets his
due, and Hedley, who fiercely advocates black advancement in the public
sphere, but whose delusions are at war with black possibility, fueled as they
are by his heavy drinking and his insistence on things as he dreams them.

The life of Charles "Buddy" Bolden, the great cornetist known vari-
ously as "King" Bolden and the putative "father" of jazz, is mirrored in
Hedley's character. Born in 1877, Bolden developed a style of playing that
made him famous at outdoor fairs and in clubs located in the often tough
streets of New Orleans. Bolden was a musician with a style so distinctive
that people, drawn to the sound of Bolden's horn, would flock from almost
any of the neighborhood's popular outdoor music venues. Bolden referred
to this phenomenon as "calling my children home" (Marquis, 62). Unlike
other musicians of this period, who usually took additional jobs to support themselves, Bolden's unique style enabled him to list "musician" as his
sole occupation after 1900 (46–47). But by 1907, plagued by alcoholism-
induced insanity, Bolden was institutionalized for the remaining twenty-
four years of his life. Not a musician himself, the fifty-nine-year-old Hedley
(four years older than Bolden was at his death) shows considerable musi-
cianship with a diddley bow, using this most basic of blues instruments

to craft a tune that makes the others recall their dead parents and their prayerful pasts. This ability to reach others in the depths of their emotions was a characteristic of Bolden's native talent: "That his sound was unique," Marquis writes, "and affected people deeply despite any reservations they might have had about his technical abilities comes through in any number of interviews" (Marquis, 99).

The tune best identified with Bolden is "Funky Butt" or "Buddy Bolden's Blues," a vehicle for sheer raucous entertainment. It became so immensely popular that it spread to towns up the Mississippi from New Orleans. It had varying, often extemporaneous and unrepeatable lyrics and was Bolden's "crowd pleaser, the one that broke things up" (Marquis, 109). The basic chorus was:

> I thought I heard Buddy Bolden say,
> Funky butt, funky butt, take it away.

Hedley and the other men, particularly Floyd, communicate most deeply through this basis for Buddy's blues, but without any of the wild, risqué times usually associated with the lyric. Hedley is always the respondent:

Floyd: (*begins to sing*) "I thought I heard Buddy Bolden say . . . "
Hedley: What he say?
Floyd: He said, "Wake up and give me the money."
Hedley: Naw. Naw. He say, "Come here, here go the money."
Floyd: What he give you?
Hedley: He didn't give me nothing. (*Guitars* 39)

"Buddy Bolden's Blues" thus devolves from the relaxed, communitarian setting of the New Orleans jook to describe both men's most closely held aspirations (and fears) regarding capital. The re-release of a past hit and Floyd's anticipating a trip to Chicago, a bigger payday, and a full career evince a measured, practical, and focused entrepreneurial spirit consistent with capitalism's iron logic. When Canewell complains that it was less the matter of being cheated by a manager than the indifference he was shown, Floyd interjects to insist that it really *is* all about the money: "He don't have to care nothing about you. You all doing business. He ain't got to like you. . . .

You got to take advantage of the opportunity. It don't matter if he like you or not. You got to take the opportunity while it's there" (*Guitars* 47).

The eccentric and delusional Hedley, on the other hand, has the recurrent dream that an inheritance he thinks is due from his father will allow him to buy a plantation. Hedley believes that the money will be passed from his father's hands to his by Bolden, the leader of Hedley's father's band and thus Hedley's namesake, as his real first name is King. Desperate both to be — and to beget — someone who "would not bow down to the white man," Hedley seems to want to reverse the long-unequal power struggle between blacks and whites, although he does not make clear whether, on his imaginary plantation, whites would be his slaves, or whether he would be as cruel a master as the white slaveowners of past ages. When Canewell suggests that Hedley should plant sugarcane on his plantation, Hedley says, "No sugar. I hate the sugar. Sugar beat many a man" (25), calling attention to the backbreaking work of harvesting cane as well as his sense of superiority over Canewell, who was named for his ability to chop sugar cane. Hedley's fixation on the greatness of Toussaint L'Ouverture, however, recalls the Haitian Revolution, which was successful in reconstituting the labor of the Spanish half of the island so that laborers would be paid proportionately for their cultivation of sugar. What appears to be a curious gesture on Hedley's part may be an attempt to reach his departed father, who in Hedley's eyes is diminished for not trying to be as great a man as was Toussaint. The reorganization of capital, as instituted by Toussaint and perhaps envisioned by Hedley, is an attempt to humanize and give meaning to labor.

The tragedy of seeing Buddy Bolden as an agent of Hedley's inheritance is that while both Bolden and Toussaint could make labor and capital work for communitarian good, this is only briefly suggested by Hedley's playing his one-string guitar to bring the group even closer together. The ruminations of those summoned by Hedley's guitar playing morph into the possibility of a similar goal being served by the radio broadcast of Joe Louis's fight with Billy Conn. (This fight should actually fix action in the play as taking place on the night of June 19, 1946, though in the preface Wilson officially sets the play in 1948.) It was the second fight between the two boxers, with Louis defeating Conn by a knockout in the eighth round, as the ring announcer intones. Conn nearly beat Louis in the first fight in June of 1941, and a rematch would not successfully be rescheduled until after World War II. Though both men's strength had been attenuated by their long years of service, Louis — remaining at the height of his fame after his second fight with Max Schmeling in 1938 — somewhat maintained his skill with exhibition fights during the war, thus having the physical reserve to best Conn on this night (*My Life* 193–195). The euphoria experienced by the listeners in *Seven Guitars* was typical of black communities all across America. Hedley hails not only Louis's reserve of physical power but also the labor necessary to maintain it: "The black man hit hard, you know" (*Guitars* 52). Later, during a post-fight card game, Floyd and Red Carter chat briefly about Louis's labor and its broad public sanctioning:

> Floyd: Now here's what I don't understand. If I go out there and punch a white man in the mouth, they give me five years even if there ain't no witnesses. Joe Louis beat up a white man in front of a hundred thousand people and they give him a million dollars. Now you explain that to me.
>
> Red Carter: He got a license and you don't. He's registered with the government and you ain't. (58)

The fight testifies not only to black success, skill, labor, and — with these — the accumulation of capital, but the cost at which these things are preserved in the crucible of war, which, as Randolph Bourne once warned, is the health of the state. Louis being "registered with the government" — that is, achieving fame by becoming a tool of American propaganda — shifts Floyd's ordinary ideas about the character of American racial justice. In both the eras of slavery and Jim Crow, the black body was always desired for its labor power, however the labor was construed. The later, tragic inversion of Louis's fortunes, as with that of Buddy Bolden's, converts this power into despair. If Buddy Bolden "didn't give me nothing," as a frustrated Hedley complains, his dream is similarly frustrated by the legend of Joe Louis's labor. His mind mystified, as was Bolden's, Hedley can only dimly see in Bolden the anxiety surrounding his dream of an inheritance.

Hedley's answers to Floyd's final question, when they sing Buddy's blues, are: "He give me ashes" or "He didn't give me nothing." Both answers foreshadow the bottoming out of Hedley's soul after he kills Floyd, replete with his treating the remaining cash as if it *were* ashes. Hedley soon discovers that far worse than the zeal produced by his dream is the pain and fragmentation his action has rendered to his community.

But the complex roles of labor and of the father as threatened or ironic testator link *King Hedley II* intriguingly to *Seven Guitars*, in that the nuances of pride in both plays rest on the falsehood of patrimony in the one play, and the falsehood of the father in the other. Just as patrimony as the route to capital is established, it dissolves: as Hedley's inheritance is lost to his dream, so is Hedley falsely construed as father to King. Hedley's stake in *Seven Guitars* is replaced by the need for the hustle in *King Hedley II*, as life in the Hill District in the 1980s again undergoes rapid downward change. Undone by a distorted sense of his patrimony that is inextricable from his relationship with capital, King does whatever he must in order to be a husband and father in the economically hostile circumstances of the Hill. Youngblood in *Jitney* is similarly challenged, believing more expressively that racism is his chief impediment despite being counseled otherwise by Doub. It seems at first that Youngblood is unlike his brothers in poverty, as racism curiously has him refuse some of that to which he is entitled — such as all of the benefits due him under the G.I. Bill — but it is necessary to return to Stuart Hall's reading of Marx, wherein regardless of one's station in the economic hierarchy, the expression of materialism is significantly influenced by the particularities of one's social reality. While racism is not an immediate cause of Youngblood's economic circumstance, as it was with Memphis, his having been "registered by the government" — as was Joe Louis — suggests his life as a man of color as being overdetermined by the power of that government, having witnessed as he surely must have the nameless slaughter of the Vietnamese.

The younger Sterling of *Two Trains Running*, who embraces the ideas of black consciousness and also tries in vain to transmit this idea to Hambone, reappears as an older and hard-bitten man in Wilson's last play, *Radio Golf*. Sterling's new perspective has acquired something of Memphis's sense of economic justice. As Sterling ends *Two Trains* by breaking into Lutz's store and taking the ham to be put into Hambone's casket, he returns later in *Radio Golf* with a cool rationality that admits as much of capitalism as communitarianism. As he informs Harmond Wilks in response to a newspaper article,

> The wealth of a city is not its two new stadiums. The wealth of a city is its people. People who need job opportunities that last longer than nine months of stadium building. People who need a city willing to invest in them with long-term jobs, enabling them to invest back in Pittsburgh the wealth of their work. . . . We need them stadiums. Don't they hold big crowds of people? You're gonna need them. That's where you're gonna have to put the unemployment office. You're gonna need both of them. (42)

This older Sterling now knows that the problems that have plagued black Pittsburgh for generations will not be solved either by simple aggression or by massive, glossy public works projects. At least as important as a sense of pride for African Americans is a concomitant economic empowerment that in turn further powers their humanity.

Gem of the Ocean and *Radio Golf* not only stand as bookends to the twentieth-century cycle of plays, but also they speak across the cycle to issues of capital and its abuse of characters in each play. In *Gem*, Caesar Wilks, landlord and local sheriff, seems the very king of capital, as everyone in his sight — especially newcomers to Pittsburgh such as Citizen Barlow — is an object of suspicion. Forty years beyond slavery, the men of Caesar's generation are now free, but Caesar feels himself to be beyond freedom; as his sister, Black Mary, observes, he overcharges for the rooms he rents and puts others in the street. The obdurate Caesar complains loudly, however, about rioting black mill workers: "I'll tell you whose fault it is. It's Abraham Lincoln's fault. He didn't know like I know. Some of these niggers was better off in slavery. They don't know how to act otherwise. . . . You try to and give them an opportunity by giving them a job and they take and throw it away" (35–36). But as Laurie Graham points out, only by 1974 were there sanctions against racial discrimination in the U.S. steel industry; through most of the twentieth century, the black worker was either dangerously cast as the strikebreaker or, even after the 1940s, had the lowest, dirtiest, and most demeaning jobs — referred to by many in the industry as "nigger jobs." Caesar's "niggers" are being used as strikebreakers, and they are likely refusing to work because of the overwhelming violence unleashed against them by striking white workers; he cannot fathom why "some damn fool took it upon himself to steal a bucket of nails and run and jump in the goddamn river" (34), thus misconstruing the plight of black workers and the objectives of capitalists. The irony surrounding Becker's accidental death in *Jitney*, set in the mid-1970s, is compounded by *Gem*'s glimpses at earlier phases of American labor injustice. It is this obduracy of his grandfather and this legacy of injustice that Harmond Wilks confronts as part of his inheritance at the century's end.

At stake for Harmond, real-estate developer and Pittsburgh mayoral candidate in *Radio Golf*, is the razing of the legendary house at 1839 Wylie Avenue — originally the home Aunt Ester shared with Harmond's forebears — which will mean the "modernization" of the Hill District and the launching of the younger Wilks into prominence. Aunt Ester unites the cycle as the ancestral anchor of all the characters and the bulwark against a return to any form to subaltern status. Slaves, as Orlando Patterson points out,

> were not allowed freely to integrate the experience of their ancestors into their lives, to inform their understanding of social reality with the inherited meanings of their natural forebears, or to anchor the living present in any conscious community of memory. . . . That they reached back for the past, as they reached out for the related living, there can be no doubt. Unlike other persons, doing so meant struggling with and penetrating the iron curtain of the master, his community, his laws, his policemen or patrollers, and his heritage. (5)

The "iron curtain" of the master included inexorably his impulse toward capital, which included ensuring that his slaves would never be valued for anything beyond their ability to produce.

For Harmond the choice becomes clear. He takes the burden of materialism upon himself in order to save his kin, his heritage, and the Hill

District community he had vowed in his political life to improve. His role as community organizer at the end of both the play and the Wilson cycle is inimical to the demands of capital, which are forever shackled to the severe human cost of acquiring and securing it. As community organizer rather than community developer, he honors each of Aunt Ester, Buddy Bolden, Martin, and Malcolm — as well as the others who struggle across the cycle of the Wilson century with the unresolved conflict between human duty and the vagaries of fortune.

DAVID LACROIX

Finite and Final Interruptions

Using Time in *Radio Golf*

In an interview with Suzan-Lori Parks shortly before August Wilson's death, Wilson noted that he had consciously included characters from the African American middle class in his play *Radio Golf* (2005) — figures mostly absent from his Pittsburgh cycle. The earlier plays had focused on the working class and the poor, often illustrating these characters' struggle with what Wilson saw as the long-term effects of the Great Migration. Rather than an interruption — a hiatus between two fields that does not permanently break their relationship — Wilson spoke of this change as an irreversible rupture; a disaster for the continuity of black traditions. It was "a transplant that did not take," as he once put it: "We were land-based agrarian people from Africa. We were uprooted from Africa, and we spent two hundred years developing our culture as black Americans. And then we left the South. We uprooted ourselves and attempted to transplant this culture to the pavements of the industrialized North" (quoted in Rothstein, 8). Expanding on this theme in his conversation with Parks, Wilson argued that many African Americans who have since entered the tax brackets and ideological headspace of the privileged have continued this process: they have "adopted the values of the dominant society and have in the process given up some of their cultural values." "There are ways to live life on this planet without being a consumer, without being concerned about acquiring hundreds of millions of dollars," Wilson noted (Parks, 22). "These people that stack it up, man," he declared. Parks laughed in response to this bluesy provocation and asked ironically, "What's he going to do with it?" Wilson replied with no small vehemence: "He's going to die!" (24). Even if one's available resources multiply the possibilities for acquisition, the ability to use that which one has acquired eventually ends, punctuated with mortal finality.

Among the injunctions that Wilson's oeuvre lays upon its audiences is a call to fulfill two sets of demands illustrated in his talk with Parks: those created by the finitude of an individual human life and those necessitated by the continuity of that life with the finite lives of others. *Radio Golf* dramatizes the relationship of its black middle-class protagonist to these issues, ultimately suggesting that it is at least possible to conceive a world in which such a figure no longer acts only from self-interest. In addition to reinvigorating familiar tropes from African American literature — most notably a younger figure's intellectual encounter with a range of black worldviews — *Radio Golf* makes the implicit claim that individuals' use of their finite time both grounds and reveals their deeper ethical and political commitments. Attending to the use of time in the play not only foregrounds the choices made by characters, but also sheds light on how time is implicated in larger structures of privilege, access, and exploitation. One's finite time may be multiplied by access to the time of others, or divided and subdivided at the command of others. For Wilson, recognition of the finitude of time is the only viable counterclaim to privilege. Moments that interrupt that privilege can make alternatives visible.

In African American literature, questions of time are rarely framed from a standpoint of plenitude and privilege. As seen though Toni Morrison's spectral and ancestral figures, the boomerang of history in Ralph Ellison's *Invisible Man*, Booker T. Washington's admonishments to productivity and frugality, and the laments of ex-slaves like Equiano, Douglass, and Jacobs about their exclusion from Western measures of temporality, the control of one's own time is always a hard-won accomplishment. Characters who take time for granted are rare, no matter how one conceives it. This condition characterizes most of the Pittsburgh cycle as well, and prior considerations of time in Wilson's oeuvre have drawn out the implications of his characters' frequent inability to use their time as they see fit, or only to use it with some freedom after negotiating conflicting claims on it.[1] But by 1997 — the time of *Radio Golf* — much of this has changed, at least for some.

The action of the play revolves around the house at 1839 Wylie Avenue,

which has lain empty since Aunt Ester's death in 1985. Taken for an abandoned property, the house is seized by the city of Pittsburgh and then sold
to a black real-estate developer, Harmond Wilks, who then bundles the
property with others surrounding it to create the space for a multimillion-
dollar urban development in the Hill District. Harmond thinks of himself
as a native son of Pittsburgh's Hill District, and displays a social conscience
heavily inflected by the mercantile desire mocked by Wilson in his interview with Parks. Upon learning that he is related to descendents of 1839
Wylie's former residents, who have returned to claim it, Harmond comes
to understand that his personal connection to the house requires him to
redesign the development. Temporarily halting the demolition through
legal action, he ultimately chooses solidarity over privilege, his efforts to
save the house effectively ruining his political aspirations and many of his
personal ties.

By this time, the black middle class has risen to levels of material comfort and privilege previously unimagined. They have considerable control
over their time and considerable access to the time of less-privileged others.
They can access not only this time, but also the time available through
powerful social and political networks. Where before Wilson's characters
were most often made the object of others' constructions of time, in *Radio
Golf* the black characters have others waiting on them or, when made to
wait, either they have much to occupy their time or the wait is not long. For
example, Harmond and his friend and business partner Roosevelt Hicks
wait through most of act 1 for the city government to declare the Hill District "blighted," which will allow their development project to go forward
with the assistance of federal funds (11–12). Immediately before the two
receive news of this declaration by phone, Hicks is unwinding his anger at
the demands of his white boss at Mellon Bank, where he is vice president.
His boss's secretary "says [he] needs to see me in his office immediately. I
felt like I was being called into the principal's office. So I get there and then
the motherfucker makes me wait" (49). While the form of these situations
recalls characters' experience of waiting in earlier plays, in both cases the
experience occurs against a background of heightened privilege that the
earlier characters did not have.

Harmond's evolving awareness of the finite nature of time creates an index to his changing choices with regard to his understanding of that condition. While Harmond spends much of the play in the position of the "big man," as another character says (20), once he begins to realize the finite nature of the time available to any one person, he moves rapidly away from multiplying his own time by dividing that of others. This is not to suggest that Wilson sends Wilks on a nostalgically motivated quest for lost time, as if such a quest might succeed. Wilks already has such aspirations, as would-be agent of renewal. "We're going to bring the Hill back," he notes at one point: "We're going to rename it Bedford Hills" (15). Wilks comes to see such anachronistic desires as options generated by his own privilege. Sterling Johnson, who first appeared in Wilson's *Two Trains Running*, checks these commercial aspirations: "How you gonna bring it back? It's dead. . . . What you mean is you gonna put something else in its place. Say that. But don't talk about bringing the Hill back. The Hill District's dead" (15). Recalling the laughter of Wilson and Parks over the hubris of the wealthy millionaire who nonetheless dies the same death as anyone, here Sterling introduces *Radio Golf*'s central claim about the finite nature of time.[2]

Even if we do not take Harmond literally, his words still have godlike connotations: he wants to bring the Hill back despite its death. Johnson suggests, moreover, that renewing this once lively neighborhood under the gentrifying signs of Starbucks, Whole Foods, and Barnes & Noble entails something else entirely. Sterling is not very persuasive at this point in the play. "We're going to bring back the whole area" (16), Harmond responds, unaffected by Sterling's demand for clarity. Such moments not only highlight the differences between Harmond and the Hill's residents but also demonstrate Harmond's ability to assimilate their desires to his own plans. Here, Harmond's idea of the continuity of his plans resists interruption. This should come as no surprise given the generally high level of privilege in his life. In the course of *Radio Golf*, we learn that he has casually traveled to Puerto Rico, bringing back expensive Cohiba cigars (11). Harmond's privilege and position descends from his father, the prior owner of Wilks Realty and son of *Gem of the Ocean*'s policeman and slumlord Caesar Wilks. Another character, Elder Joseph Barlow, offers this snapshot of Harmond as a boy: "Used to see you riding in the car eating ice cream. Everybody else was walking" (26).

Moreover, Harmond takes for granted one of the signal indicators of privilege: the ability instantly to command the use of others' time. As Sterling points out, "If you even *whisper* everybody sit up and stop to listen" (60). Harmond instructs his assistant Dena to set up his access to the board of the health center planned for Bedford Hills in order to change the name of the center from the "Model Cities Health Center" to the "Sarah Degree Health Center" (10). He demands that the Pittsburgh *Post-Gazette* modify a transcript of one of his speeches, despite their deadlines (32). When Barlow — who was arrested for painting the house at 1839 Wylie — comes to Harmond for assistance, Harmond tells Barlow to use his name at the local Hill House assistance center. When Barlow indicates that he plans to have his daughter move into the house, Harmond says: "Have her go up to Wilks Realty on Centre and Herron and tell them I sent her" (26). Harmond's phone is always his ally in using others' time, calling not only Dena but also a police sergeant for a favor (25) and the police commissioner to extend an invitation to the Bedford Hills groundbreaking (33). The city's declaration of "blight" that will free the millions of federal dollars required to start Bedford Hills comes over the phone (49), and, of course, the phone inflects even Harmond's use of the time proper to his wife, Mame. She affirms the agreement and plan between them, saying, "I'm not wasting my time on your campaign if you're not committed to winning this. I'm sacrificing my business. Giving up my clients. Harmond, we've worked too hard" (29).

The older solidarity and shared time, as Elder Joseph Barlow demonstrates, have not disappeared entirely. Born in 1918, Barlow has firsthand knowledge about local and national history, the Hill District, and the lines of force and family that unite its residents in temporal continuity. Barlow is among those who are, as Harry Elam has written, "culturally organizing figures" who, in Wilson's plays, can "convey the significance of history and reinforce the impact of the past upon the present" (*Past as Present* 64). Elam counts Stool Pigeon (in *King Hedley II*) and Hedley (in *Seven Guitars*) as examples of this character type. Broadening the definition to those characters who, as Bonnie Barthold put it, are the "Keepers of Time" — people who endure "chaos with a clear, though largely impotent, vision of order and continuity" (50) — we can also include others, especially Aunt Ester herself. Most often these keepers — through memory, recitation of experience, or access to some unofficial archive — attempt to keep the knowledge of the past in play. In the movement from *King Hedley II* to *Radio Golf* and from Stool Pigeon to Old Joe (as he is called in the play), Wilson changes this figure. Where Stool Pigeon's connections between past and present are often derived from his oracular use of newspaper headlines drawn from the piles of papers he has accumulated in his apartment, Old Joe has no print archive. When Stool Pigeon's papers are lost in 1985, destroyed by robbers in a moment of black-on-black crime, nothing takes their place. Old Joe's temporal contributions, however, are based on his memory of events and their calendar dates. Although these references suggest Old Joe's eccentricity within *Radio Golf* — Harmond's business partner and friend Roosevelt Hicks cannot stand them — their cumulative effect is formally similar to that of the Pittsburgh cycle's other figures of continuity over time.

Old Joe's references remind his black middle-class listeners of some of the classic tropes and themes of the African American tradition, such as the black male hero and migration, irregular access to economic networks, and failures of equal opportunity in access to public services. On March 5, 1978, after leaving Pittsburgh for points west and southwest, Old Joe saw Muhammad Ali in Louisville (20); on January 22, 1970, he pawned his guitar (21); in 1952, the Pittsburgh city government "say they ran out of electricity" and were thus unable to install lights to allow nighttime use of an athletic field in the black Hill District (22). Barthold's suggestion that such characters have little effect is perhaps overly simplistic, but in *Radio Golf* the four other characters split evenly in their reactions to Barlow. While Harmond appreciates Barlow's living memory, for most of the play he remains convinced that such a figure cannot accurately describe the current moment: "This is 1997," Harmond says at one point in response to Barlow's skepticism that he, a black man, might win election as mayor of Pittsburgh: "Things have changed. This is America. This is the land of opportunity. I can be mayor. I can be anything I want" (21).

Mame Wilks and Roosevelt Hicks generally display contempt for Barlow's outlook on time and value. Roosevelt, who has Barlow arrested for
painting the house at 1839 Wylie, views the older man's claims about time
as laughable in an era in which the black middle class is taking advantage
of its increased need to move away from past forms of intra-racial solidarity among African Americans. If Hicks's attacks leave Barlow more or less
unfazed, Mame's response shows the effects of middle-class privilege both
on her manners and on her ability to conceive other approaches to time.
Barlow tells how on the "fourteenth day of November 1937" (31) he "seen
the people call God down" (30), whereupon God demonstrated his divinity by making it boil without fire. When Barlow concludes, "You can't bet
against God and win" (31), Mame's comment breaks Old Joe's pattern:
"You say the people put up their money? They were betting against God?
Well, tell me, did God walk out the door with the money? If God walked
out the door with the money he wasn't nothing but a Negro from Mississippi with some dry ice" (31). As Wilson's stage directions wryly note, *"For
the first time, Old Joe is speechless"* (31). While apparently willing to allow
Old Joe some of her time, Mame is unwilling to give it to him without
taking her due. While she does not interrupt him factually, conceptually
speaking she temporarily ruptures his force in the play.

This moment is consistent with the views about time Mame expresses
elsewhere in the play. By no means an unsympathetic character, she has
invested much in her husband's plans. Yet the use of time from Mame's
point of view is highly instrumental, even objectified:

Harmond: How about: "Now is the Time"?
Mame: No, we don't need the "Now." Let's try "It's Time." That
     works better. But my favorite's still: "Wilks Works for You."
     That will let the people know where you stand. (40)

The final slogan, in which the political campaign offers to concentrate
all of the voters' time in that of Mayor Wilks, suggests that Harmond's
time will be used to work for the voters. This idea — that Harmond will
continuously occupy the role of a leader who shares a temporal outlook
with the electorate — runs contrary to the ways power, access, and privilege
actually work in the play. Mame's startling elision of the "Now" deletes

the possibility of locating a moment at which to effect some other kind of change. Possibly "we don't need the 'Now'" because such a moment would only endanger all of the needs and desires that the privileged do sustain throughout the play, or possibly we don't need "now" because "now" presumes a "then" — a past with a relationship between time, labor, and community that Mame wants to escape.

Systems of privilege, whether economic, ideological, or cognitive, demand loyalty. This loyalty is maintained most insidiously by soliciting those with privilege to misrecognize it and themselves. In Harmond's case this misrecognition is his desire to revitalize the Hill, become mayor of Pittsburgh, and to do so in a United States that no longer demands that its black citizens go through life in a state of double consciousness. In short, he wants to be an exception. In order for Wilks to understand the competing claims dramatized by the other characters, he will ultimately require a new way of understanding the meaning and use of time. This process begins once he finally visits 1839 Wylie, where he gains access not to the time of others but to a scene bearing evidence of an approach to the use of time in which it is not merely a multiplier for the will of those with privilege. After visiting the house, he returns to the office with a description for Roosevelt: "It's a Federalist brick house with a good double-base foundation. . . . It has beveled glass on every floor. There's a huge stained-glass window leading up to the landing. And the staircase is made of Brazilian wood with a hand-carved balustrade" (61). He further notes, "If you run your hand slow over some of the wood you can make out these carvings. There's faces. Lines making letters. An old language" (62). These details exist for Harmond's inspection because of the time spent by all the craftspeople, residents, and visitors to 1839 Wylie. While they may well have labored under constraint, the effects of their time last beyond their finite use of it. Because Harmond benefits conceptually rather than materially, this use of his time to engage the time spent by others — and the time span over which their time has endured — allows him to step outside of time in the same manner that Ralph Ellison's Invisible Man steps outside of time.

This engagement with the time of those who have reached the end of their finite measure is reflected in Harmond's reassessment of his place within his family. The broadest framework within which his life has oper-

ated is what he calls "the plan" — the set of paths scripted for him and his
dead twin brother by their father: "He planned for Raymond and me to
go to Cornell, then take over Wilks Realty" (65). Raymond's decision to
instead attend historically black Grambling College[3] in Louisiana to play
football and his subsequent death in Vietnam leaves Harmond without
a strong alternative claim with which to articulate the shape of his life.[4]
In classic dramatic fashion, as twins the brothers double each other; their
being twin sons multiplies the distinction of the male firstborn in a way
that successive birth of two sons separately conceived could not. Everything that a single firstborn son can do in the symbolic order created by the
father, twin sons can do in tandem. If from the standpoint of household
economy this doubling creates more expense, it also generally allows the
father to demonstrate his status. Scripting the sons' lives multiplies this
status by repeating it, as their physical identity further suggests identities of
value, belief, and time. Once out of college — ostensibly unaffected by the
loss of Raymond — Harmond is rapidly ensconced in this world, and in its
temporality: "My father set Wilks Realty out before me when I got out of
school. All I had to do was follow the plan. It was a Monday. I got up that
morning and went into work with him. We walked in Wilks Realty and
there on one of the doors was my name: 'Harmond Wilks.' That looked
good. I thought, 'Yeah, this is what I'm supposed to do'.... Then the phone
rang and I answered it"[5] (71–72). As if repeating a temporal trajectory that
had always already existed, this typical day creates the pattern for all those
that follow — even down to Harmond's first moment as privileged black
businessman on the phone.

Harmond and Raymond are heirs to privilege acquired by their father
and grandfather, but Raymond's choice is an indictment of the plan that
Harmond must disavow. Within the world Mr. Wilks created for his sons,
if Harmond represents the choice Raymond refused then Harmond's time
opposes Raymond's. But Harmond is both double *and* survivor. As the
living twin, Harmond employs the time meant for both brothers, making his time incomplete without Raymond's. While Harmond cannot
recover the absolute loss of Raymond, he can reinterpret it and rearticu-
late it.

Radio Golf ultimately suggests that the most ethical approach to the use of time is not to divide and appropriate the finite time of others, but to organize and articulate time in relation to a conscious understanding of choices. The party to repaint the house at 1839 Wylie, organized by Sterling, is an example (54, 71). The flyer advertising it reads: "Come one, come all. Paint party; 1839 Wylie Avenue. Thursday, ten A.M. Music, dancing, refreshments" (54). The time for the party coincides with the scheduled demolition of Aunt Ester's house, for Sterling has chosen to take his stand in space and time at the same coordinates as the forces that desire removal of the house and access to the space and time that it occupies. Here Harmond can learn, if he so chooses, the conceptual version of a known physical law: at such a moment of confrontation two opposing frameworks of value cannot occupy the same space and time. One must not simply *use* time at such a "now"; one must *choose* it. Harmond's earlier plan to redesign the development so that 1839 Wylie may be kept intact while the development is built around it cannot work. It is a well-meaning factual compromise, but a compromise that has no place in the ethics of this "now." The play thus moves toward a new version of a haunted and historicized "now" — one circumscribed by but also embracing death.

Early in the play Sterling asks Harmond, "How you gonna bring [the Hill District] back? It's dead. . . . What you mean is you gonna put something else in its place. Say that. But don't talk about bringing the Hill back. The Hill District's dead." This question can only be answered with a "now" very different from Mame's sense of the contemporary, Sterling's sense of living in the moment, or the simultaneity of time in Barlow's oral history. Nor can it be the period that commemorates Raymond's death, or Aunt Ester's death, or the death of the Hill. In Wilson's broader, more productive understanding of "now," something else will likely end up in place of the Hill. Wilson himself imagined that the destruction of the house was a likely outcome, given all that is set in motion in the final scenes of the play. The changes in Harmond's sense of time, and with them his emerging understanding of his relationship to Aunt Ester, must produce something other than a nostalgic simulacrum of the Hill, or a commercial monstrosity that is more zombie than Lazarus. What comes next must be a synthesis, perhaps a hybrid twenty-first-century form that can redress the failure of transplantation that so vexed Wilson.

Notes

1. See Adell, Elam, Nadel, and Shannon.

2. Johnson also updates the Einsteinian claim about the dependence of time on the relative position of multiple observers as he riffs on the effects of his failure to live up to imposed constructions of time. Recounting his early life in an orphanage, he tells Harmond how his intelligence was always underrated. He seemed slow, he seemed lazy, he seemed dumb. But he explains that, in fact, "I was so fast it made me look slow. I was waiting for them to catch up . . . [and] that made it look like I was standing around doing nothing" (42).

3. The school became Grambling State University in 1974.

4. The scenario echoes the situation of Cory Maxson in *Fences*, who instead of playing football joins the army in 1965, at a time when his next tour of duty would most likely have been in Vietnam.

5. Answering the phone at the end of *Jitney* is also the way Booster signifies his assuming his role in the world his father had created.

An Exercise in Peripheral Vision

Loyalties, Ironies, and Sports in *Radio Golf*

> We literary people should always keep a sharp eye on what's happening
> in the unintellectualized areas of our experience. Our peripheral vision
> had better be damned good. Because while baseball, basketball, and
> football players cannot really tell us how to write our books, they do
> demonstrate where much of the significant action is taking place. Often
> they are themselves cultural heroes who work powerful modification in
> American social attitudes. And they tell us in nonliterary terms much
> about the nature of possibility. They tell us about the cost of success,
> and much about the nonpolitical aspects of racial and national identity,
> about the changing nature of social hierarchy, and about the role which
> individual skill and excellence can play in creating social change.
> — Ralph Ellison, "Remembering Richard Wright"

Sports have played an important symbolic role in the twentieth-century history of African Americans. From Jack Johnson becoming the first black holder of the world heavyweight boxing championship in 1908, to Joe Louis winning the title in 1937, to Jackie Robinson's first Major League baseball game in 1947, to the epic symbolic gesture of Tommie Smith and John Carlos at the 1968 Mexico City Olympics, sports have carried the weight of promising a fair shake for a section of the American population otherwise relentlessly denied fairness. The undertone played by the game of golf in the final play of August Wilson's Pittsburgh cycle is not necessarily all that satisfactory in terms of drama. The play is not about golf, as such; instead it enables this game to resonate symbolically. Because of the changing role that class plays for sections of the African American population at the end of the twentieth century, it is especially appropriate not only that the culminating expression of Wilson's cycle uses as its central metaphor a game, but that the game is golf.

One of the attractions of sports in general is that they provide an idealistic respite from the much more practical realities of daily life. Perhaps one of the reasons many naïvely insist on the separation of sport and politics is to fortify the borders of this idealistic state from real-world incursion. Within sports, this idealistic narrative goes, the playing field is level, the rules are clearly defined, known by all, and enforced by disinterested arbiters — umpires, referees, judges — so that the best participant wins. Perhaps this sense of the ideal also explains why people (and sometimes even the legislative branches of governments of sovereign nations) get so exercised in the face of cheating.

Even the ideal world of the game, of course, has at least one structural acknowledgment of real-world temptations: those arbiters whose role it is to help participants do the right thing, despite occasional impulses to the contrary. While he wasn't talking about the presence of the rules official in his 1983 introduction to C. L. R. James's classic, *Beyond a Boundary*, Robert Lipsyte might as well have been, when he resolved the relationship between the ideal and real worlds of sport this way: "Lurking beyond the boundaries of every game are the controlling interests, the forces of oppression: the economics of the owners, the politics of the government, even the passions of the fans. Sport is no sanctuary from the real world because sport is part of the real world, and the liberation and the oppression are inextricably bound" (xii).

Another double-edged aspect of sport arising from this relationship between the real and the ideal is the notion of loyalty. On the one hand, loyalty to one's team as a player and the commensurate stimulus of one's own teammates, in the right circumstances, can inspire levels of performance unattainable alone. On the other hand, such loyalty as a supporter in the wrong circumstances can justify behaving unacceptably toward individuals or groups whose loyalties reside with another club. This sense of competing loyalties makes *Radio Golf* so compelling, as the play reflects the ambivalent and, at times, ironic nature of the progress made by African Americans over the century chronicled by Wilson's plays. In the America of 1997, Harmond Wilks can run for mayor of Pittsburgh, a city that could not stomach the thought of a black quarterback leading their beloved Steelers less than a quarter century earlier. But Harmond must also wrestle with the burdens attendant to this relatively newfound privilege, the most pressing of which is a division of loyalties between the history from which he emerges and the future to which he aspires. Wilks himself may be thought of as the fulcrum on which the relative weights of competing loyalties are precariously balanced. Approaching *Radio Golf* on these terms does not suggest that the interests of those in the black middle class and those of the black working class must necessarily diverge, or that the black middle class must see themselves as the exceptions that prove some other unfortunate rules. Rather, this approach highlights how the ethical interests of these sub-groups of the American population converge.

In his 1998 essay, "Justice as a Larger Loyalty," Richard Rorty theorizes conflicting senses of loyalty by first presenting the conventional opposition between loyalty and justice:

> All of us would expect help if, pursued by the police, we asked a family member to hide us. Most of us would extend such help even if we knew the child, sibling, or parent asking for help to be guilty of a sordid crime. Many of us would be willing to perjure ourselves in order to supply this family member with a false alibi. But if an innocent person were wrongly convicted as a result of our perjury, most of us would be torn by a conflict between loyalty and justice. (45)

Rorty goes on to clarify his central position by redescribing this conflict in terms of one between "loyalty to our family and loyalty to a group large enough to include the victim of our perjury — rather than between loyalty and justice" (45). The philosophical problem he is attempting to resolve is the common one borne of expediency, in which "the tougher things get, the more ties of loyalty to those near at hand tighten, and the more those to everyone else slacken" (45). This basic eventuality explains, for instance, why we might be willing to horde food only for close family members in times of scarcity while being able to share generously in times of plenty, since a theoretical commitment to justice per se would insist upon sharing resources no matter the economic circumstances.

Rorty's principal redescription in his essay is to think about justice and loyalty not as conflicting motivations based on rationality and sentiment, respectively (he cites Kant for this formulation), but as points on a continuum: "Should we describe such moral dilemmas as conflicts between loyalty and justice, or rather, as I have suggested we might, as conflicts between loyalties to smaller groups and loyalties to larger groups?" (47). Rorty's redescription is engaging and encouraging on a philosophical but also on a practical level, since, he writes, "The opposition between rational argument and fellow feeling thus begins to dissolve, for fellow feeling may, and often does, arise from the realizations that the people whom one thought one might have to go to war with, use force on, are . . . 'reasonable.' They are, it turns out, enough like us to see the point of compromising differences in order to live in peace, and of abiding by the agreement that has been hammered out. They are, to some degree at least, trustworthy" (54–55).

Of course, such practical resolutions in the face of more theoretical problems are not come by easily, but this, I will argue, is the resolution to which Harmond Wilks arrives by the end of *Radio Golf.*

Stephen L. Carter's discussion of integrity, in his 1996 book of that name, demonstrates how the sporting arena serves as a useful condensation of the sorts of smaller group/larger group loyalties that Rorty theorizes and Wilson dramatizes. Carter describes the inspiration for his book as a moment during the telecast of a football game, when a receiver who had *not* caught a pass thrown to him jumped up and celebrated as though he had in fact caught the ball: "The referee was standing in a position that did not give him a good view of what had happened, was fooled by the player's pretense, and so moved the ball down the field" (4). One of the announcers broadcasting the game refers to the player as having made a "heads-up play" (5). Carter's illustration throws into sharp relief the problem of competing loyalties, as he suggests to "suppose that the player had instead gone to the referee and said, 'I'm sorry, sir, but I did not make the catch.

Your call is wrong.' Probably his coach and teammates and most of his team's fans would have been furious: he would not have been a good team player" (5). This player faces the same problem illuminated by Rorty; he feels a loyalty to the smaller, immediate group — his team — but should at least also feel some loyalty to the larger group — those who have, do, and will play, watch, or care about the game. He chooses the smaller group because of the sorts of expediencies with which one cannot help but sympathize, if not totally agree, with. The team pays his salary; the team's win-loss record will determine whether or not it gets into the playoffs (more money for everyone); the team might actually sever its ties with the player if it feels that he has chosen his loyalty to this larger, more theoretical "game" over the smaller, more immediate group. This is Harmond Wilks's problem in *Radio Golf*.

Sport and loyalty are equated in the set design of *Radio Golf*, as Harmond's friend and partner Roosevelt Hicks puts up a Tiger Woods poster on the office wall of Bedford Hills Redevelopment, Inc., at the beginning of the play. Harmond returns the poster to Roosevelt at the end of the play, indicating the dissolution of their partnership. In addition to being emblematic of the partnership's status, the poster stands in for a momentous occasion in a very specific sport at a very specific time. *Radio Golf* is set in 1997 — the year in which Woods won The Masters golf tournament for the first time, with a record-breaking, color barrier–breaking performance. (The tournament is, of course, mentioned in the play, if only in passing.) As the only prominent African American golfer, both then and now, Woods also stands for a potential change in American country club sports culture (moved further along by the Williams sisters in tennis) — the country club being the venue held together by traditions of handshakes and gentlemen's agreements; a site of privilege long established to exclude the presence of people like Woods himself, not to mention Harmond and Roosevelt.

In the play, golf stands for the newfound privilege to which some African Americans at the end of the twentieth century have access. Roosevelt makes this historical association plain when he celebrates his promotion to vice president of Mellon Bank: "I have to run down the bank and pick up my new business cards. . . . I don't have no cards to pass out on the golf course. Without them cards they'll think I'm the caddie" (18). This acknowledgment by Roosevelt resonates with the immortal words of Clifford Roberts, one of the co-founders of The Masters golf tournament, who notoriously once said: "As long as I'm alive, golfers will be white, and caddies will be black" (Lee). Roosevelt's anxieties about being mistaken for a caddie also revive memories of the Professional Golfers Association's infamous "Caucasians-only" clause, which until 1961 stated that only "professional golfers of the Caucasian race" (Glenn) were allowed to participate in its events. The clause serves as a vivid vestigial reminder of the unique status golf maintains among sports as a pastime that symbolizes the leisure, privilege, and status of its participants. As John Lahr puts it: "Golf — with its lavish disregard for time and money — is a symbol of the two men's bourgeois achievement (and of their burden, which is to assume the attitudes and the leisure activities of the white man)" (*New Yorker*). Lahr's description actually draws attention to the important differences that emerge between Roosevelt and Harmond as the play progresses.

That Roosevelt and Harmond both play golf, and that Harmond after discovering his golf clubs have been stolen from the trunk of his car says of them, "You can't replace them. They're a part of me" (31) situate this sport as fundamental to who these two men have become. Wilson connects this game of privilege to the specifically African American history of the two businessmen, though through an ingenious updating of the myth of flight used by many African American writers as a metaphor for the freedom historically denied African Americans. Roosevelt describes his first experience hitting a golf ball in terms that make the experience less physical than spiritual and confrontational:

> I hit my first golf ball I asked myself where have I been? How'd I miss this? I couldn't believe it. I felt free. Truly free. For the first time. I watched the ball soar down the driving range. I didn't think it could go so high. It just kept going higher and higher. I felt something lift off of me. Some weight I was carrying around and didn't know it. I felt like the world was open to me. . . . I felt like I had my dick in my

hand and was waving it around like a club. "I'm a man! Anybody want some of this come and get it!" That was the best feeling of my life. (13)

The position of the game of golf in the play is underwritten by the irony that a game historically associated with exclusion is — for Roosevelt — one that symbolizes freedom; not to mention the affirmation of his manhood. The affirmation of African American masculinity has conventionally been associated with baseball, basketball, football, and boxing; never, until Wilson's play, with golf.

The version of masculinity that Roosevelt describes is relatively new to the experience of African American men and is distinguishable from that of the more conventionally physical sports mentioned above. The sports more commonly associated with black masculinity tend to be inexpensive to play and typically do not require much by way of specialized equipment beyond a flat plot of ground (a concrete playground will do in most cases), a few basic implements, and a willingness to compete. Access to country club sports like golf, tennis, and swimming, by contrast, demonstrates less a physical prowess taking place on the vaunted "level playing field" and instead makes a display of the attainment of sufficient financial resources to be able to afford membership in the rarefied environs in which such pastimes tend to take place. In other words, whereas the masculinity that is confirmed by baseball, basketball, football, and boxing takes on a physical and — in the case of boxing — a sometimes quite brutal form, the perception of masculinity that accrues to Roosevelt through his golf club membership registers his attainment of sufficient disposable income and privilege to partake in the "lavish disregard for time and money" of which Lahr speaks. In effect, the masculinity of conventional sports says to the black man, "you can do this." The masculinity enacted by Roosevelt and Harmond through their association with golf instead says, "you can afford this."

You may want to consider that golf has not been associated with white masculinity, either, at least not in a direct manner. Rather, golf has always functioned in a secondary way — the same way that wealth and political power do: there's much more "masculinity" to be acquired from the status of the club to which one belongs than from the size of one's handicap. The act of playing golf, therefore, functions not so much as a sign of masculine prowess as it does a form of capital. Golf, as a signifier, marks masculinity associated not with labor — playing power forward or linebacker; boxing — but with cultural capital, in that one need not be a good golfer to accrue the benefits of investing in the game as long as one has access to a specific course.

The smaller group to which Harmond feels loyal is the group of investors, partners, and his wife, Mame, who are his immediate circle of friends and common interest in the play. The larger group that eventually enlists his loyalty comprises the people of the city of Pittsburgh, whom he wishes to represent as mayor. This larger group includes, of course, Sterling Johnson and Elder Joe Barlow — two other black men who, for various reasons, do not travel in the circles in which Roosevelt and Harmond now find themselves. Harmond foreshadows his eventual affinity for this larger group early in the play when he insists that the new health center that his company is building be named after Sarah Degree, "the first black registered nurse in the city" (10); his loyalty to the larger group seems assured and intact here. Because it comprises no conflict with his loyalty to the smaller group, his decision is tolerated by Mame and Roosevelt. However, his later decision to spare Old Joe's house from demolition is met with anger and confusion by the members of his smaller group. At this point, Harmond embodies the role of the football receiver from Carter's illustration, if that receiver had — somewhat unimaginably — admitted to the referee that he did not actually catch the pass. The nature of Harmond's decision also clarifies Rorty's point about the size of the group to which one feels a sense of loyalty and why Harmond's decision should productively be seen as a gesture of loyalty, enabling Harmond to commit to a modus vivendi with Old Joe — someone otherwise dismissed as standing outside the group to which Harmond's loyalty is owed. Sterling points out, after Harmond realizes that the company has illegally purchased the house at 1839 Wylie Avenue, that Harmond could still push through with the demolition of the house if he so chose: "Everybody thinks you bought it. That's why [Old Joe] can't call the police. Won't nobody listen to him. He trying to get them to listen. He shouting and nobody paying attention. If you even *whisper* everybody sit up and stop to listen" (60; emphasis in original). This is the position of prestige that Harmond has attained. Because things are going well for Harmond, he can afford, as Rorty explains, to conceive of his loyalties more broadly. The irony here, of course, is that capitalist logic conventionally works in the reverse, wherein the larger a company gets, the easier it is to concentrate its interests solely on its shareholders — often at the expense of those larger groups gathered under the economic euphemism of "externalities": the surrounding natural ecosystem, the population living downstream from a plant, or the employees whose jobs are replaced when cheaper labor is found elsewhere.

Sterling's observation about the relative influence Old Joe and Harmond might be able to exert on the controversy over 1839 Wylie makes clear that the play is not about justice at all, but about loyalties. The constructs of the law that move through the background of the play make clear that the law is characterized — by Roosevelt, at least — as a structure to be adhered to in the letter though not in the spirit. Roosevelt merely wants Old Joe paid off — an expediency Harmond attempts, although Old Joe turns down the offer of ten thousand dollars for the house. Old Joe's refusal of the money catalyzes Harmond's conflict of loyalties. Harmond does not interact with the abstract idea of justice; none of us does. He must come to terms with the old man standing in front of him and refusing to be bribed. It must be said that a concern about justice would similarly have rendered bribery incompatible with Harmond's point of view. What we get from Harmond instead is pragmatism: first the bribery attempt, and then the active reconfiguring of his sense of loyalties.

Bribery is, however, more in line with Roosevelt's point of view. Roosevelt's sense of loyalties initially appears to comprise Bedford Hills Redevelopment, Inc., his Lexus, his golf course membership, and Bernie Smith. Roosevelt works hard to prove his loyalties to this smaller group. When Harmond describes Roosevelt as "the black face" for Bernie Smith's proposed purchase of WBTZ radio, Roosevelt proclaims his loyalty loud and clear: "This is the game! I'm at the table! There was a time they didn't let any blacks at the table. You opened the door. You shined the shoes. You served the drinks. And they went in the room and made the deal. . . . This is not going to come along again. The window of opportunity is already starting to close. If I don't do this Bernie will get somebody else" (37). Of course, Roosevelt means that Smith will find another black businessman to be the face of the deal. Ultimately, Roosevelt's loyalty is to the smallest group possible — that comprising himself alone — as he announces when thinking about the financial repercussions of blight potentially not being declared on the Hill: "If the blight don't come through in six months the bank will have the keys to my house and Arleen's new Saab. I'll have to drive Arleen to work and rent a house from you. They'll have to fight me over my Lexus" (12). Roosevelt's sense of his loyalties is further fragmented by the difference between his class position and Harmond's. If blight were not declared, Harmond's financial prospects would not be devastated in nearly the way that Roosevelt's would be. Roosevelt pictures himself having to rent a house from Wilks Realty, the successful company left Harmond by his father. Roosevelt's financial anxieties complicate the perception of the two men as equivalently representing the "black middle class." Roosevelt appears even to distance himself from his wife's interests if it means keeping his Lexus. Like his golf course membership, the car is an external status symbol, while Arleen — unfortunately for her — is not. Roosevelt even quits his job at Mellon Bank (and quite enthusiastically, it must be said) when his deal with Bernie Smith comes through. His loyalties are indeed only to himself.

The conflict of loyalties demonstrated in *Radio Golf* succeeds in characterizing the mixed blessing that is progress for African Americans in the late twentieth century. This is the principal success of Wilson's play. Roosevelt and Harmond occupy a place of vulnerability within American society and their choices of loyalties express — and attempt to resolve — this vulnerability. A useful description of this peculiar type of vulnerability emerges from the sociology of Pierre Bourdieu, who describes the conflicted social position of intellectuals as "dominant, in so far as they hold the power and privileges conferred by the possession of cultural capital and even, at least as far as certain of them are concerned, the possession of a volume of cultural capital great enough to exercise power over cultural capital; but writers and artists are dominated in their relations with those who hold political and economic power" (144).

Bourdieu does not apply this description of being simultaneously dominant but also dominated to captains of industry, who hold the political and economic power to which he refers. And one would not think to describe Bernie Smith as Bourdieu does, either. Because they are black, however, Harmond and Roosevelt occupy their positions as businessmen differently than the way Smith does his. In fact, Smith bears a notable resemblance to the spectral Joe Turner in *Joe Turner's Come and Gone*, principally since neither appears onstage — nor has to in order to exert his influence over the action. Cigdem Usekes has described Joe Turner as "the most prominent symbol, in August Wilson's twentieth-century cycle of plays, of the economic exploitation and abuse African Americans have experienced at the hands of whites" (118). Smith is not quite a latter-day Joe Turner, but his absent-presence in the play demonstrates a certainty of power that neither Harmond nor Roosevelt possesses. Their ability to exercise political and economic power (represented by Harmond's and Roosevelt's aspirations, respectively) remains contingent upon the authorization of people like Bernie Smith. Their vulnerability as members of a class both dominant and dominated means that their loyalties are pulled in different and telling ways.

Another irony of *Radio Golf* highlights the relationship between politics and the relative responsibility of the newly privileged in the context of the peculiar pragmatism embodied in Rorty's theory of loyalties to smaller and larger groups. We must remember that during his first appearance onstage, Old Joe says to Harmond, "They ain't gonna let no black man be the mayor. Got too many keys. The mayor got more keys than the janitor. They ain't gonna let you have that many keys" (20). He then reiterates his points, stressing his disbelief in Wilks's political prospects: "Is you really running for mayor? They ain't gonna let you be mayor" (21). The combination of Harmond's dominant but also dominated position and his emerging sense of loyalty to the larger group that finally includes his elder makes Old Joe's prophecy come true by the end of the play. Harmond will not be mayor; not because of the white "them" but because of Old Joe. If Old Joe would simply accept the money for the house, Harmond could move on with his career. It is Old Joe — a wise but marginal black man — and Harmond's willingness to conceive of Old Joe as part of his larger group that brings down the mayoral candidate.

This irony is particularly interesting in what it adds to an understanding of Rorty's argument and Wilks's position. After all, in refusing the money for 1839 Wiley, Old Joe identifies himself as another agent also announcing his loyalty to a larger group. His larger group includes his daughter (who plans to move into the house), the Hill District, the historic neighborhood in which the house is located, and all of the past, present, and future residents of "the Hill." Overarching this larger group is the spirit of Aunt Ester, the "very old, yet vital spiritual advisor for the community" (*Gem* 5), who is most specifically identified with this address. Had Old Joe merely behaved like Roosevelt Hicks, he would have accepted the bribe. Both Harmond and Old Joe pass the ethical tests with which they are presented, and this mutual success ends Harmond's political career.

In his 1989 book, *Contingency, Irony, and Solidarity*, Rorty describes what he calls the "final vocabulary": "All human beings carry about a set of words which they employ to justify their actions, their beliefs, and their lives. These are the words in which we formulate praise of our friends and contempt for our enemies, our long-term projects, our deepest self-doubts and our highest hopes. They are the words in which we tell, sometimes prospectively and sometimes retrospectively, the story of our lives. I shall call these words a person's 'final vocabulary'" (73). Both Harmond's and Old Joe's final vocabularies may ultimately be voiced in the same expression: a loyalty to the larger group. One person's final vocabulary, the play makes clear, however, may run counter to that of another, and the competition between vocabularies may be resolved by force (bulldozers), bribery (ten thousand dollars), or disenfranchisement (Sterling's comment about the relative importance of Harmond and Old Joe). The possibility of such resolutions encourages each competing agent to conceive of his or her antagonist in terms of a larger loyalty that includes that other. As it turns out, this is what happens at the end of *Radio Golf*, although it may not look like it at first. The play does not end with Harmond Wilks articulating some empty platitude like "there is more to life than personal ambition." Nor does it end with Harmond bearing more social responsibility than Old Joe because of Harmond's perceived privilege. Instead, he and Old Joe both embody individual agency working autonomously but within the same social system. As a result, their individual conceptions of their larger loyalties are both cooperative and competitive — cooperative in that they both ultimately work toward the community's better interest, and competitive because Old Joe's decision results in Harmond's short-term political loss.

Rorty's theory of justice as a larger loyalty is fraught with conflict and ironies. But it is nevertheless suggestive of the possibility of practical solutions to the problems of developing ways of coexisting with people whose immediate interests differ from our own. *Radio Golf* thematizes this point by presenting the end of the twentieth century as a time of both opportunity and new problems for African Americans. By privileging larger group loyalties over parochial ones based on racial or financial common interest, Harmond Wilks provides a complex and forward-looking ethical model.

Radio Golf in the Age of Obama

O n first viewing, *Radio Golf* raises some unique challenges seemingly separating it from the rest of August Wilson's cannon. We enter into analysis of this work knowing that unlike Wilson's other plays, this last play did not have the benefit of his nurturing guidance over time. *Radio Golf* made its way to Broadway and to publication without the advantage of Wilson's well-tuned process of playmaking, without his careful stewardship, without his molding and remolding of this play as it navigated the regional theater circuit byways; without Wilson in attendance at every production and rehearsal, rigorously writing and rewriting. After a successful run in Seattle, *Radio Golf* arrived in New York at the Cort Theatre on West 48th Street on May 8, 2007, instead of — more appropriately — at the August Wilson Theatre on West 52nd, named in his honor on October 16, 2005, some fourteen days after his death. The Wilson Theatre was then home to the long-running Broadway hit *Jersey Boys*, and even Wilson's own final work *Radio Golf* — which would go on to win the New York Drama Critics' Circle Award for Best Play of 2007, as did eight of his previous plays — could not supplant it.

Set in 1997, *Radio Golf* is of much closer proximity to the current moment and to recent events and circumstances than the other plays of Wilson's cycle. While it has immediacy, however, as historic subject matter it lacks, perhaps, that critical distance of time. But for Wilson there was another pressing matter of time and distance that infused this final work: the knowledge that Death was not far away, that he had months to live. Perhaps, like Troy Maxson in *Fences*, Wilson fought Death by hand and kept it at bay while he could. Perhaps he too shouted at Death, "Come on! Anytime you want! Come on! I be ready for you . . . but it ain't gonna be easy" (*Fences* 89). Given this urgent context, it is no wonder that this play in its structure might seem, as *Chicago Tribune* critic Chris Jones notes, "understandably, a little rushed" as Wilson hurried to complete his cycle; to tell this final story before his inevitable end.

Yet, even as we understand that the particular circumstance of *Radio Golf* differentiates it from the other works, we must also recognize that this work purposefully draws on all the previous plays. As he worked on *Gem of the Ocean* and *Radio Golf,* Wilson stated in an interview with Chris Jones that with these plays he hoped to build an "umbrella under which the rest of the plays can sit" (Homeward Bound 16). *Radio Golf* directly reaches back to *Gem*, connecting the characters past and present and providing more threads to the genealogy uniting the cycle as a whole. Moreover, I would now argue that reading *Radio Golf* in relation to the rest of the cycle clarifies meanings within this cycle as a whole and reaffirms the power of Wilson's intertextuality. *Radio Golf* revisits and reinforces earlier arguments as Wilson repeats and revises critical ideas from his earlier works: namely, the still-unfinished quest for freedom for African Americans and a pragmatic plan for African American ethical self-determination. In this play and throughout his cannon, Wilson asks that the question of freedom's utility and viability continually be reconsidered. Early in *Gem*, Solly, a former conductor on the Underground Railroad, asks, "What good is freedom if you can't do nothing with it?" (*Gem* 25). Within the decade of the 1990s — at a time when African Americans purportedly have more access to power; more resources at their disposal — Wilson argues in *Radio Golf* that the need for community, unity, connection to the past, and freedom are all the more urgent. Moreover, as I will argue in this essay, Wilson's strategy in *Radio Golf* is in line with what philosophy and religious studies scholar Eddie Glaude outlines as a politics of "African American pragmatism," within which the choices and strategies of action one takes are understood as critical to the structuring and formation of African American identity (3). At the end of the play, Harmond Wilks, the protagonist of *Radio Golf,* acts definitively in ways that torpedo his nascent political career and threaten his economic prosperity but that also provide him with a sense of liberty and a renewed spirit of commitment — and provide the audience with new hope in the communion of blackness.

The black politics proposed by *Radio Golf* speaks loudly to this watershed moment in the new millennium, which we might call the "Age of Obama." For in the current moment, when we have a black president, race supposedly is of less meaning and value within American life. Some scholars and critics have declared that we live in a time that is post race, or beyond race. In such a time — as evidenced by the prominence of Obama (or, for that matter, Condoleezza Rice or Oprah Winfrey or Bob Johnson) — the restrictions on black access to power no longer have the same resonance: we have arrived. And yet, I think both the particular and the peculiar politics in the Age of Obama and in Wilson's *Radio Golf* point to the fact that in America race very much still matters. Obama and Wilson, both sons of interracial unions, have publicly declared that they are black. Their self-designation — when juxtaposed with the exponential growth of mixed-race groups on college campuses and with the 2000 census, which marked the first occasion in American history in which respondents could check more than one ethnic category — underscores the constructedness of race. Obama and Wilson by their choice of blackness reinforce the notion that racial ascriptions are always political. Obama's racial designation and its meanings have become all the more contested as black conservatives such as Alan Keyes and Stanley Crouch — as well as Debra Dickerson, author of *The End of Blackness* — have proclaimed that Obama's blackness is suspect because he is the offspring of a Kenyan father and a white American mother; his blood quantum does not link him with the West African roots of North American slavery. Consequently, these critics — in a perverted invocation of racial biology and racial gatekeeping — argue that Obama is not black and cannot claim any connection to the legacy of African American struggle and survival. At the same time, conservative critics on such shamelessly biased national media platforms as FOX News — prodded by the incendiary racial claims made by the Reverend Jeremiah Wright, the African American pastor of Obama's Chicago church — have proclaimed that Obama is too black; too partisan to be America's president.

Here, the dynamics of Wilson's *Radio Golf* are instructive. This play argues that black identity is not simply a biological trait nor the result of prescribed agendas, but an active choice — an engagement, a doing in a historically specific moment. Like Obama, Harmond Wilks is running for public office. In his case, he wants to be the first black mayor of Pittsburgh. Harmond believes at first that politics is "about symbolism. Black people don't vote but they have symbolic weight" (*Radio Golf* 88). The trajectory of the play moves Harmond beyond settling for the symbolic capital of blackness to a journey of self-discovery and reawakens a collective racial consciousness arising from his own determination to act.

If our current moment in the year 2009 is the Age of Obama, the decade of the 1990s might be construed as the Age of August Wilson, who at that time was the most produced playwright in the United States. Like Obama's support and surprising victory with overwhelmingly white voters in the 2008 Iowa caucuses, Wilson's cycle in the 1990s was not simply a black thing but a crossover hit: his non–African American audiences identified and empathized cross culturally with the trials and tribulations of his black characters. White spectators have come out in large numbers to see Wilson's reflections on the black experience. Wilson, however, never imagined himself as a proprietary force in the American commercial theater; only as a visitor. In fact, Wilson felt compelled to resist and even speak out against the white patriarchal powers that controlled the theater industry. This position was not without contradiction and compromise. As I have written elsewhere, Wilson, as "a member of the bourgeoisie and as a recipient of two Tony Awards, is also committed if only unconsciously, to the continuation of the system that has granted him no small measure of success" (*Past as Present* 228).

The question for Wilson — one he poses for Harmond Wilks in *Radio Golf*— is whether one can remain committed to a liberal paradigm of black empowerment and at the same time achieve economic or political success within the more conservative, white-dominated American mainstream. Obama may have found himself in a similar position of needing to compromise, perhaps, as he sought to win over a portion of the all-too-valuable white male voting block and to gain funding from powerfully rich and predominantly white donors, while at the same time maintaining his overwhelming support within the black voting public. Conscious of her husband's need to appeal to white voters, Mame, Harmond's wife and campaign manager, wants him to open his campaign office in the predominantly white Shadyside area rather than the all-black, impoverished Hill District: "You don't want to start out your campaign excluding people" (*Radio Golf*, 8).

Mame voices an argument echoed by critics and pundits observing the campaign strategies of Obama and other black politicians: that an overabundance of blackness — even the appearance of endorsing black positions — threatens white voters and their potential for allegiance. On April 4, 2008, the fortieth anniversary of Martin Luther King Jr.'s assassination, white presidential candidates John McCain (who once apologized for voting against the King Holiday bill) and Hillary Rodham Clinton both spoke about King from the site of his assassination in Memphis, Tennessee. Obama, however — perhaps out of concern of being perceived as being too black — chose to commemorate King from a distance, campaigning in Indiana. In his now-historic acceptance speech at the 2008 Democratic National Convention — delivered on the forty-fifth anniversary of Martin Luther King Jr.'s "I have a dream" speech, Obama did not refer to King by name even as he quoted directly from his speech and referenced the King legacy. Mame Wilks, out of fear of alienating the support of powerful city labor forces such as the police, begs her husband to remove a segment of a soon-to-be published speech that condemns a particular incident of police brutality and racial profiling (reminiscent of the 1999 killing of Amadou Diallo by New York police officers and the much-publicized trial that followed). Ultimately, Harmond does not capitulate to Mame's request, and the speech goes to print with the offending passages included. Harmond's stance serves as an early example in the play of Wilson's assertion of black pragmatism, or the belief that an ethical commitment to act against conditions of injustice and oppression should always trump political expediency.

Yet, the history of white racism and black exclusion from mainstream American politics might lead some to conclude that the pursuit of a city-wide office (in Obama's case a national office) by a black candidate is inherently doomed. Elder Joseph Barlow — the wizened old Hill District resident who comes to Harmond's Bedford Hills Redevelopment Office (the site of the play) seeking legal counsel — balks at Harmond's candidacy, maintaining that the white hegemonic order has stacked the odds against any black candidate. He tells Harmond, "They ain't gonna let no black man be mayor. Got too many keys. The mayor got more keys than the janitor. They ain't gonna let you have that many keys" (*Radio Golf* 20). Old Joe equates "having keys" with the ability to open doors and move resources, and believes that they can never be wrested from white authority.

Yet Harmond's aborted mayoral campaign — or, for that matter, Obama's run for the presidency — challenges such pessimism and, if not disrupting white political authority, lays claims to the need for a more pluralistic system. Allowing for the possibility that Harmond could — as Obama did — actually win the election, Sterling Johnson, the wayward black utility man who also frequents the Bedford Hills Redevelopment Office, asks Harmond, "You get to be mayor is you gonna be mayor of the black folks or the white folks?" (*Radio Golf* 56). Sounding not unlike Obama's — or any other politician's, from Hillary Clinton's to John McCain's — rhetorical claims to represent not any one interest group but the American people as a whole, Harmond responds, "If I win I'm going to be mayor of the City of Pittsburgh. I'm gonna be mayor of all the people" (*Radio Golf* 56). Yet Sterling's question does not come out of a belief in the antithetical nature of black-and-white politics; rather, Sterling seeks to critique the overwhelming power and privilege embedded in normative whiteness. He continues:

> The mayor be the mayor for white folks. As soon as black folks start a club or something the first thing they say is it just ain't gonna be for blacks. Why not? They got five hundred thousand things that be just for white folks. It they have fourteen hundred students out at Pitt eating lunch in the cafeteria and they have five black people eating lunch together they say "Look, see, they segregate themselves." They ain't said nothing about them thirteen hundred and ninety-five white folks eating lunch by themselves. What's wrong with being the mayor for black folks? (*Radio Golf* 156)

Sterling is questioning why blackness can't be normative and therefore understood as central rather than tangential to American political strategies. His critique of the whiteness here echoes the spirited defense of black theater in his now-famous 1996 TCG speech, "The Ground on which I Stand." In this speech — in the face of the white paternalism that limits the cultural capital of black arts — Wilson demands the separate and distinct development of black theater: "We are not separatists. . . . We are artists who seek to develop our talents and give expression to our personalities. We bring advantage to the common ground that is American theater" (*Ground* 41–42). Like his character Sterling, Wilson identifies championing blackness as a strategy for fulfilling the ideals of the American Dream, rather than an act of separatism.

Sterling also decries — for Harmond as well as for the viewing audience — the pervasive authority and concomitant invisibility of whiteness within the American social system. Sterling's humorous challenge for Harmond to be the mayor of the black folks raises racial awareness by *racing* whiteness. As Richard Dyer points out in *White*, "As long as race is something only applied to non-white peoples, as long as white people are not racially seen and named, they/we function as a human norm. Other people are raced, we are just people" (1). Sterling prods Harmond to think not only about what it means to construct whites as a race, but also what it could mean for a black politician to make blackness an issue in an election where, as in Pittsburgh, African Americans are not the majority. Sterling argues that what is good for black people should not be antithetical to what is in America's best interests.

In his now-famous talk on race delivered in Philadelphia, the "Cradle of Liberty," on March 18, 2008, Obama — who throughout much of the campaign sought to minimize race — spoke out, attempting through the process of racing whiteness to make the country aware that the fight against racism must be a united American effort. He called on whites to recognize the unmarked issues of economics and class that construct the racial divide. Adapting or perhaps inverting the overused and problematic racial axiom of "the black community," Obama asked the "white community" to acknowledge that "what ails the African American community does not just exist in the minds of black people; that the legacy of discrimination — and current incidents of discrimination, while less overt than in the past — are real and must be addressed" (*NY Times* 6).

Obama asked Americans to recognize the real consequences in the present of racial histories, just as Wilson's project as a whole, and *Radio Golf* most specifically, probes what the past means to contemporary African American identity. From the outset of *Radio Golf,* Harmond finds his sense of self — his fundamental beliefs and principles — tested by the resurfacing of history. Harmond's challenge is to give them meaning. Elder Joseph Barlow, who claims he is the rightful owner of Aunt Ester's house — a house that Harmond at first intends to destroy in the name of progress — frequently enters Harmond's office and interrupts his plans in ways that compel Harmond to reconsider his redevelopment strategy. Barlow is literally the presence of the past: he is the descendant of Citizen Barlow, the troubled traveler in *Gem of the Ocean.* As the play unfolds, Old Joe and Harmond discover that they are related, as Harmond is the descendant of Caesar Wilks and Caesar's half sister Black Mary eventually married Citizen Barlow. Thus, both Harmond Wilks and Joe Barlow are the living consequences of this history.

The Elder Joseph Barlow, however, is not simply the consequence of the intersection of history and memory. Barlow repeats history and memories from Wilson's earlier plays. In his first visit to the redevelopment office, Barlow humorously recounts to Harmond his arrest for being a "fake blind man": "They tried to put me in jail for being a fake blind man. I didn't do nothing but walk the dog" (*Radio Golf* 21). In *Gem,* Caesar Wilks — Harmond's great grandfather — reminds his sister and Joe Barlow's mother, Black Mary, of their Uncle Jack, who deceived people by pretending to be a blind man. Caesar complains that Black Mary's mother would not visit Uncle Jack on his deathbed: "When Uncle Jack was dying she wouldn't even go see him. Say he was fooling people being a fake blind man. She was right. But that's her brother!" (*Gem* 38). Caesar Wilks in *Gem* foregrounds the value of family, and Joseph Barlow in *Radio Golf* both symbolically and materially reinforces the importance of family through his discovered familial ties to Harmond as well as his legal claim of ownership of Aunt Ester's house at 1839 Wylie Avenue.

Old Joe is obsessed with dates. In the list of characters, Wilson describes Barlow as "recently returned to the Hill District where he was born in

1918" (*Radio Golf* 6). While no dates are supplied in the descriptions for the other four characters in the play, Wilson foregrounds 1918 for Joe Barlow: the year of armistice in World War I, a year that witnessed racial riots in Philadelphia and sixty lynchings of African Americans in the South, and the year preceding the "Red Summer" of 1919, when racial conflagration lit up the country. The year 1918 was also when the flu pandemic reached Pittsburgh. More important for our purposes than these historic events, however, is what 1918 signifies within Wilson's own canon and within this play. With his birth in 1918, Old Joe is seventy-nine years old, his life therefore spanning the decades of the cycle (save for *Gem*, set in 1904, in which the meeting between Citizen Barlow and Black Mary is shown; their child, Joseph, is born fourteen years later.) Old Joe's memories of black life over the decades and his understanding of the past consolidate the passage of time that informs the cycle as a whole.

The particularity of the dates that Old Joe remembers organizes each memory for Barlow and situates it within a chronology. Old Joe recalls: "I seen Muhammad Ali in Louisville March 5, 1978" (*Radio Golf* 20). "They tore that down. June 28, 1974" (*Radio Golf* 43). "He got shot in the head on the second of November 1942. . . . December 4, 1945. The day I got out the Army and went and saw Joe Mott's mother" (*Radio Golf* 44–45). Barlow may believe that his recollection of dates fixes these events in history, but, as we know, memories are situational and change over time. Rather, the retellings are moments of embodied cultural practice, for Barlow shares not simply the dates but the events of that time that shaped his black consciousness. Meeting Muhammad Ali in 1978, for example, marked a "perfect day" for Barlow — a day when somehow his forty-six dollars and eighty-four cents became a hundred-and-sixty-eight dollars: "I ain't gonna tell you how that happened," he tells Harmond (*Radio Golf* 20).

Barlow's tale of the black soldier Joe Mott's commitment to the American flag and of his unfortunate death in battle in 1942 — as well as Barlow's own encounter with a white man, who ripped the flag lapel off of his uniform on his way to visit Mott's mother — recalls the bitter and ironic encounter with racism that black soldiers found upon their return to the United States at the end of World War II — after their valiant participation in the struggle to protect American democracy abroad. It also reflects on the charges made against Obama by conservative factions who questioned his patriotism and accused him of never wearing a flag pin. Eddie Glaude argues that "what we have done and are doing, and stories we weave about these experiences are absolutely critical for a pragmatic view of black identity" (55).

With Old Joe's stories of wariness about white racism and with his faith in black possibility, Wilson is thus crafting his vision of black pragmatism. Through Old Joe's recollection of dates and recitation of cultural memory, Wilson fuses the personal and political, the real and the figurative. 1945, the year Old Joe "got out the Army," was the year that August Wilson was born. 1978, when Old Joe saw living history (the iconic Muhammad Ali), was the year Wilson's first daughter, Sakina Ansari, was born.

In *Radio Golf,* the function of these dates and the recalling of history are also subject to interpretation. When he finds Harmond willing to back Old Joe and save the house at 1839 Wylie Avenue, Roosevelt Hicks — Harmond's erstwhile business partner and former college roommate — uses the dates he finds on Old Joe's police rap sheet to discredit Joe:

> He has a record that go all the way back to 1937. Stole a crate of chickens in 1938. Burglary. First-degree assault. Born 1918. . . . Discharged from the Army 1945. Two years for assault of a police officer, 1948. Three years Western State Penitentiary for hijacking, 1952.
>
> Thirty days loitering 1957, sixty days vagrancy 1958. Spent four months in Mayview State Hospital. Sent for ninety-day observation. Was kept an additional thirty days for further observation. It wouldn't take me thirty seconds to tell he's not all there." (*Radio Golf* 69)

This litany could lead one to conclude, as Hicks does, that Joe is "not all there." Yet what Hicks's recounting cannot record is the relationship between the dates, the histories found in the time between Joe's arrests, and his interactions that provide the rationale for his purportedly crazy behavior. Wilson's cycle is particularly attuned to the gaps and fissures in history into which the ordinary and idiosyncratic everyday lives of African Americans have too often fallen, consequently being left out of recorded history.

Barlow's rap sheet comprises an incomplete history, and the dates on it are subject to what in politics is known as "spin." Accordingly, politicians from Obama to Clinton and McCain must approach the dates within their personal histories — the written text — with a willingness to give them spin that will appeal to voters.

With Hicks, Wilson comparably gives black capitalists a specific spin. At first, Hicks, a vice president of Mellon Bank, appears to represent a justifiable race-based strategy for wealth accumulation. Dissatisfied with his treatment as the only black vice president at Mellon, he dreams of business opportunities previously restricted to white men. In the course of the first act of the play, he signs a deal with the rapacious white power broker Bernie Smith that enables Hicks to acquire a stake in the black urban radio station, WBTZ. With excitement, Hicks explains this deal to Harmond: "We're talking about an eight-million-dollar radio station! This is the game! I'm at the table! There was a time they didn't let any blacks at the table. You opened the door. You shined the shoes. You served the drinks. And they went in the room and made the deal. I'm in the room" (*Radio Golf* 36). In presenting his new partnership with Bernie, Hicks uses the rhetoric of black uplift that represents him as breaking the racial glass ceiling and his financial victory as collectively benefiting the race. Yet Wilson uses Hicks — as he does West in *Two Trains Running* — to argue that black empowerment and economic advancement are not necessarily synonymous. Like West, Hicks is interested in individual gain far more than any trickle-down impact on the rest of the black community. Eventually Hicks will use Bernie's money in the name of business to edge out his longtime friend, Harmond, and terminate their partnership in the Bedford Hills Redevelopment Project.

Hicks's victory, however, is pyrrhic in that Hicks is exploited even as he willingly exploits. Significantly, Hicks's proclamation of racial inclusion — that he is "in the room" and "at the table" — echoes, repeats, and revises that of Lorraine Hansberry's naïve Walter Lee in *A Raisin in the Sun*, who complains to his mother about his own exclusion from the world of high finance: "White boys are sitting back and talking 'bout things . . . sitting there turning deals worth millions of dollars. . . . Sometimes I see guys don't look much older than me" (60). Walter Lee, like Hicks, senses the racism of economic disparity and desires a place at the table. After he learns that the conniving Willy has absconded with the bulk of the family's fortune because of Walter's foolish miscalculation, Walter, in an ill-conceived attempt to recover the money, intends to make a self-denigrating deal with Mr. Linder of the Clybourne Park Improvement Association. Prior to so doing, he lashes out at his mother, sister, and wife in his own defense: "What's the matter with you all! I didn't make this world! It was give to me this way! Hell, yes, I want me some yachts someday! Yes, I want to hang some real pearls 'round my wife's neck. Ain't she supposed to wear no pearls? Somebody tell me — tell me, who decides which women is supposed to wear pearls in this world" (126). Walter seems to interrogate the American Dream and it racial limits, questioning whether there is in fact an inalienable right to economic prosperity. But Hansberry asks at what costs — ultimately, Walter Lee decides he can go through with the deal by selling his family's soul; he cannot sacrifice family pride and collective history for money.

Hicks, on the other hand, pushes and eventually pushes Harmond out, even as Harmond berates him for prostituting himself: "The shuffling nigger in the woodpile: how much [Bernie Smith] pay you for something like that? After he rolls over and puts his pants back on, what you got?"[1] (*Radio Golf* 80) Hicks turning away Harmond's attacks bolsters his own position: "My name is Roosevelt Hicks. I am part owner of WBTZ radio and I am not anybody's whore" (*Radio Golf* 80). What is unremarked or remarkable in his recitation of his part ownership is the diminished capacity of this participation. Hicks's business partner enlists him only because he needs a black face to take advantage of: in order to issue an FCC Minority Tax Certificate the federal government requires minority participation in radio ownership, so, by enlisting Hicks for truly a minority share, Smith can purchase and control the majority of the WBTZ revenues. For Hicks, however, his part ownership does not denigrate his identity but rather constitutes his new identity, since materialism trounces social reasonability and eschews racial disparities. Ironically, Hicks, despite economic advancement, remains caught up within American racial hierarchies that necessitate his running home to get his new business cards, lest — without the cards that announce his identity — the white businessmen at the country club mistake him for the caddie.

Golf in *Radio Golf* is critical to how Wilson differentiates between collective politics and the bankruptcy he finds in black individualism. Hicks imagines playing golf as a key to black mobility and possibility: "I wish somebody had come along and taught me how to play golf when I was ten. That'll set you on a path where everything is open to you. You don't have to hide under a rock 'cause you're black" (*Radio Golf* 13). Omitting the legacy of racial segregation in golf, Hicks maintains that golf skills can grant social and economic access. In fact, Smith offers Roosevelt the partnership on the golf course, as golf courses are the sites where such business deals are made daily. On the wall behind Hicks's desk in the Bedford Hills Redevelopment office — not far from the poster of Martin Luther King Jr. hung up by Harmond — Hicks places a poster of Tiger Woods. With his wealth, status, and achievement, Woods in some eyes functions as the primary embodiment of post race possibilities. Like Wilson and Obama, Woods — another biracial son — has made a different choice in terms of identity politics. After his much-discussed public declaration of his racial identity as "cablinasian," Woods now stands as an icon of mixed race. Certainly Woods has opened up the world of golf to a new, younger generation, and in so doing has broken age-old racial barriers. And yet, as symbolized by the two posters on the wall, his refusal to take positions publicly against racial injustices stands in stark contrast to Martin Luther King's engagement of the public sphere in the fight against oppression. *Radio Golf* militates against emulating Woods or adopting — like Hicks — an individualist posture that facilitates forgetting the past and forging destructive alliances in the name of self-interest. At the end of the play, Harmond returns the Woods poster to Hicks and kicks Hicks out of their business office.

As part owner of WBTZ, Hicks airs an instructional golf show called "Radio Golf." The very notion of radio golf is incongruous. Golf is not a game about the collective; it does not require teamwork but focuses on the virtuosity of the individual, like that of Tiger Woods — it furthermore lacks sustenance, as well as the ability to satisfy the community needs. Moreover, golf is not a game that lends itself to radio. It requires the visibility of the backswing; the flight of the ball. Golf is so much about visibility that the very conjoining of the words "radio" and "golf" seems incongruous.

Wilson plays on and with incongruity in how he positions not only his play's title (originally suggested by his youngest daughter, Azula Carmen) but the entire redevelopment project at the center of the play. Ironically, the financing for the Bedford Hills Redevelopment Project managed by Hicks and Wilks depends on the Hill District being declared blighted. In order for them to build up the area (and to prosper personally), they must tear down what is there — such that their financial success depends on the community's economic collapse. And so, when the city ultimately declares blight, Harmond and Hicks joyously sing, "Blight! Blight! The Gangs all here. Blight! Blight! The gangs all here" (*Radio Golf* 101). The notion that blight is not simply a material condition of urban poverty and neglect but something that city leaders can declare turns blight from a social reality into a political construction: behind such a veneer, blight does not appear to have an impact on real people. From our historic distance of the new millennium we have seen the actual blight that has hit urban centers like Pittsburgh and have experienced the failure of redevelopment efforts to improve the community and institute change, rather than just to fatten the pockets of developers.

The construction of Barack Obama as a political juggernaut has also been dependent on manipulations of reality and the play of incongruity. Politically Obama came of age in the old-style machine politics of Chicago. Despite these roots, his campaign slogans did not dwell much on this background and experience; rather, they played up his inexperience in Washington and argued that he was a fresh face — free of the bureaucratic beltway baggage that comes with a long Washington career. Moreover, even as Obama identified with blackness, others perhaps saw in his biraciality the ability to transcend race. He was able to capitalize on the perceptions that were simultaneously inside and outside of conventional racial paradigms and definitions. His opponents — first Clinton and then

McCain — sought to brand the Harvard-educated Democrat as an elitist removed from the masses, a strange designation, perhaps, for the son of a single mother raised in a lower-middle-class home.

In this play, more than any of the previous ones, Wilson explores the intersections of race and class. Like black scholar E. Franklin Frazier's classic, *The Black Bourgeoisie* (1962), *Radio Golf* questions the allegiance of the black middle class to the black masses. Sounding not unlike Bill Cosby in his much-publicized rant against self-destructive behavior amongst the black masses — a theme taken up with gusto by conservatives of all colors in this Age of Obama — Hicks rails against Sterling and what he views as black victimization: "Roosevelt Hicks is not part of any us. It's not my fault if your daddy's in jail, your mama's on drugs, your little sister's pregnant and the kids don't have any food 'cause the welfare cut the money off. Roosevelt Hicks ain't holding nobody back. Roosevelt Hicks got money. Hicks got a job because Roosevelt Hicks wanted one. You niggers kill me blaming somebody else for your troubles. Get off your ass . . . quit stealing . . . quit using drugs . . . go to school . . . get a job . . . pay your taxes" (*Radio Golf* 107). Separating himself from the masses, Hicks is "not part of any us." Speaking in the third person, Hicks expresses himself not only as individual but also as representative: the Roosevelt Hicks–type of the black middle class who has money. Hicks compliments his self-presentation by addressing Sterling not as a black individual but as part of a collective blight — the embodiment of the black poor. Hicks further charges the black urban enclaves with complicity in the problems of drugs, crime, and high school dropout rates that have plagued them.

Hicks's pointing, like Cosby's, to the need for black self-help and for blacks to divorce themselves from the victim status has some legitimacy. Hicks provides no policy, however, aside from self-help for helping black people move beyond this position. More importantly, his attack on the black poor obscures the historic conditions of neglect, job loss, and racism that contributed to the current crises' conditions. Between 1974 and 1992, with a shift in the U.S. economy, manufacturing jobs in the inner city declined severely, and, as a result, black unemployment never dipped below ten percent during the period (Glaude, 146). The poverty gap and racial stratification widened as the Reagan/Bush administration consistently cut funding to programs aimed at supporting inner cities.

Hicks pays no attention to this history, for he has lost his connection to the force of collective history—a force Wilson represents in his cycle through the figure of Aunt Ester, the ancestor who is as old as the black presence in America. Hicks is even ready to tear down Aunt Ester's house as part of his supposed urban-renewal project, a project that will enrich him and potentially Smith. As Wilson wrote *King Hedley II*, he talked about how the metaphysical was becoming increasingly important to him and how prominently Aunt Ester figured for this direction in his work. According to Wilson, "Aunt Ester has emerged for me as the most significant person of the cycle. The characters after all, are her children" (*American Histories* 1). The idea of the characters all being children of Aunt Ester speaks to the inherent interconnectedness of black people and black lives which Wilson underscores with the genealogical connections he ties together in *Radio Golf*.

This idea, however, is seemingly eroded by the fact that Aunt Ester's house sits in ruins and is about to be destroyed by the Bedford Hills Redevelopment Project. In *King Hedley II*, Aunt Ester dies; in *Radio Golf*, her house is evacuated and demolished. Harmond tells Hicks early in the first act, "That house has been abandoned for the past twelve years" (*Radio Golf* 18). Counting twelve years back from 1997 brings us to the 1985 of *King Hedley II*, the play that recounts Aunt Ester's death from grief at the senseless devaluation of black life, the disconnection of the African American present to the past, and the epidemic of black-on-black violence. If the condition of black life is desperate in the 1985 of *King Hedley II*, the situation is even more severe in 1997 when Aunt Ester's house—the last vestige of any symbolic link to the African American legacy—is scheduled to be destroyed in the name of progress.

Hicks's indifference to this dire situation stands in sharp distinction with the attitudes of Sterling and Harmond. While Hicks refuses to enter the house he describes as "raggedy-ass" for fear that it might collapse, Harmond finds himself transfixed by its magic and majesty: "I couldn't believe it. It has beveled glass on every floor. There's a huge stained-glass window leading up to the landing. And the staircase is made of Brazilian wood with a hand carved balustrade. . . . If you run your hand slow over some of the wood you can make out these carvings. There's faces. Lines making letters. An old language. And there's this smell in the air" (*Radio Golf* 61–62). Even without the presence of Aunt Ester, the house embodies history. It has faces and stories etched into its wood. It speaks old language and has its own smell. Hicks sarcastically retorts that the smell is mothballs: "People used to throw mothballs all through their old shit." Harmond, on the other hand, describes the smell as "sweet like a new day" (*Radio Golf* 61–62). If the past is literally present in the house, the house also holds — significantly — the possibility of the future: a rebirth, a new day.

Wilson's dramaturgical past is also present in the description of the house and of Aunt Ester. The carvings of faces in the wood that Harmond details are reminiscent of those carved by Willie Boy into the piano that lies at the center of the conflict in Wilson's *The Piano Lesson*, the piano that serves as an altar and memorial to the struggles of the Charles family, and synecdoche for the African American history. The house at 1839 Wylie Avenue, with its stained glass and wood carvings is both cathedral and sepulcher. Sterling urges Harmond to go and see Aunt Ester's house, just as Holloway some twenty-eight years earlier, in *Two Trains Running*, had encouraged him to visit with Aunt Ester. In fact, when Sterling recounts the visit, his words come directly from the earlier play when Sterling describes his time with Aunt Ester to Risa: "Aunt Ester told me I got good understanding. She just looked at me and said that. I talked to her a long while. Told her my life story" (*Radio Golf* 54). Although Wilson changes the order of the sentences, he uses the same phrasing. Old Joe too revisits images seen earlier in Wilson's cycle, not simply through his familial connection to Citizen Barlow of *Gem* but through his correlation to figures such as Gabriel in *Fences* or Hambone in *Two Trains Running*. He is the last in the line of Wilson's "fools" — characters that share unique connection to the African American past as well as a singular bond with God. Barlow's rap sheet states that he not only wants to bring charges against the United States for kidnapping — his own form of legal reparations for slavery — but also that he claims to be a descendant of a lost tribe said to

have migrated from the Arabian peninsula (*Radio Golf* 69). Like Gabriel
before him who believes he is the Archangel Gabriel, or Hambone whose
body literally bears the deep scars of slavery, there is a heap of signifiyin' in
Old Joe's assertion that he is tied to the lost tribes of Israel, which links the
notion of being chosen people to blackness and to Africa.

Wilson's willingness to repeat and revise his own dramatic opus foregrounds the cycle of history within his history cycle, such that Wilson's
dramaturgical history and his reliance on our memories of the earlier plays
and characters — including Hambone, Sterling Johnson, Citizen Barlow,
and Aunt Ester — significantly inform our reading of *Radio Golf.* In fact,
artifacts from his earlier plays in the cycle and their productions function
as what Pierre Nora terms *lieux de memoire*, or sites of memory. Within
lieux de memoire, according to Nora, history and memory intersect in "moments of history torn away from the moment of history." Nora explains
that *lieux de memoire* are "created by a play of memory and history, an interaction of two factors that results in their reciprocal overdetermination."
Consequently *lieux de memoire* are "material, symbolic and functional." In
Radio Golf, the *lieux de memoire* — such as Aunt Ester's house, Harmond
and Old Joe's shared lineage, and Sterling Johnson's repetition without reproduction — function as collective cultural memory. They symbolically
link Harmond to forces beyond the immediate context of *Radio Golf* but
contained within the cycle as a whole. As a result Harmond now determines
a new course of action that is at once cultural, spiritual, and political.

Harmond's decision to fight the demolition of Aunt Ester's house is both
pragmatic and spiritual. Notably, in *Radio Golf* — written as Wilson himself was feeling perhaps closer to God as his cancer progressed — the idea of
spiritual and the metaphysical that we saw in earlier plays is not as immediately visible. On first glance, it is the most secular of the later plays. Where
is Aunt Ester, after all? This is the question that, I think, this play wants
us to demand in the Age of Obama. Where is the space of spirituality? A
significant aspect of presidential politics in the Age of Obama — brought
home by the rhetoric around the Reverend Jeremiah Wright and the fear
that Obama might be a Muslim — is the place and space of religion and
spirituality. The separation of church and state is mere hyperbole. Contem-

porary American presidential politics depend on the visibility of religion: Obama must go to church and appear to be a God-fearing man. Old Joe first enters the Bedford Hills Redevelopment Office in search of Christian people: "You know where I can find any Christian people," he inquires of Harmond (*Radio Golf* 19). He then reports that he found none at the Mission. Given the history of unholy actions — even white supremacist endorsements of slavery and Jim Crow undertaken in the name of Christianity — Old Joe's finding no Christians in the Mission is humorous but not strange. That he asks this question of Harmond, however, is telling. As a result of his continuing interaction with Old Joe, his discovery of his own family's investment in surreptitiously paying the mortgage on 1839 Wylie, and his visit to Aunt Ester's house, Harmond undergoes a spiritual awakening. Harmond's attempt to rearrange the design of Bedford Hills around Aunt Ester's house, to give up his chance at running for mayor, and to forego wealth for his redevelopment project in the name of principle all might be read as acts of "Christian charity" as well as an active assertion of renewed faith. Discussing slave Christianity, Eddie Glaude argues, "The conversion experience equipped the slaves with the resources to imagine themselves as agents in the world. That is to say, the reordering presence of God in the lives of Christian slaves made possible a sense of individual and communal value that rejected the dehumanizing effects of slavery" (109). Harmond undergoes a conversion of sorts — a reordering — and he finds new agency. "I can't follow the plan this time, Mame," he explains (*Radio Golf* 72). Wilson presents not only the collective politics of Harmond's decision but also its spiritual implications.

Harmond's reinvestment in the past also helps him to formulate a stance of ethical black pragmatism grounded in this new course of action. For Harmond, defending Aunt Ester's house is a matter of right and wrong. When Hicks tells him that the Pittsburgh legal system would not uphold his injunction that would prevent Aunt Ester's house from being torn down, Harmond replies, "Common sense says that ain't right" (*Radio Golf* 74). Harmond bases his sense of right not merely on the fact that neither he nor the Bedford Hills Redevelopment Company legally own the house, but on the significance of the house to the community, to the legacy of Aunt Ester, and to perpetuating the spirit of the African and African American past in the present.

Wilson invokes his own dramaturgical history as he critiques the social efficacy of legal codes and the rule of law. Purposefully, Wilson has Harmond's discourse on the power of law replicate with a difference that of his ancestor, Caesar Wilks in *Gem*. When Caesar comes to arrest Aunt Ester for harboring the fugitive Solly after his crime of burning down the mill, Caesar justifies his actions by saying: "Now you know Miss Tyler, you got to have rule of law otherwise there'd be chaos. Nobody wants to live in chaos" (*Gem of the Ocean* 79). Correspondingly, when Harmond is determined to defend Aunt Ester's house from demolition by appealing to the courts, he explains to Mame and Hicks that "You got to have rule of law. Otherwise it would be chaos. Nobody wants to live in chaos" (*Radio Golf* 70). Caesar upholds the law as a rationale for seizing Aunt Ester, while Harmond appeals to the law to stop the city from seizing Aunt Ester's house to destroy it. In both plays, Wilson shows that the law is not the final arbiter of justice, for the law fails to prevent the demolition in *Radio Golf* and contributes to the subjugation of blacks in *Gem*. The law serves white economic interests and not those of African American advancement. As Harmond comes to finally understand, moreover, the system is rigged against black subjects: "They keep changing the rules as you go along. They keep changing the maps" (*Radio Golf* 78).

Rather than relying on shifting legal codes or abstract moralities, Harmond's ethics in *Radio Golf* are ultimately grounded within this history. Glaude argues that a pragmatic understanding of black identity "shifts the way we think about our moral obligation to the race" (55). Harmond's moral obligations have shifted. Harmond has come to read the small incremental changes in racial hierarchy witnessed in this Age of Obama — "Look we got a black astronaut. I just love Oprah" — not as significant developments but as maddening diversions. As he explains to Hicks in his climactic speech, the idea of change is mere illusion: "It's all a house of cards. Everything resting on a slim edge. Looking back you can see it all. Wasn't nothing solid about it. Everything was an *if* and a *when* and a *maybe*" (*Radio Golf* 79). Wilson presents this, however, not as fatalism but as a pragmatic cue for problem solving. Harmond now responds to a world that exacts new choices from him, understanding that his previous plan for redevelopment — naïvely aimed at revitalizing the destitute Hill community — will further damage the community by destroying its history as symbolized by Aunt Ester's house. At the end of the play, after saying goodbye to his old lifestyle and to Hicks, Harmond grabs a paintbrush and puts on war paint — symbols of his new identity and course of action — and then goes off to defend Aunt Ester's house by joining the paint party at 1839 Wylie Avenue. And in so doing, Harmond links himself with Wilson's other warrior spirits: Solly and Citizen Barlow of *Gem*, Levee of *Ma Rainey*, Boy Willie of *The Piano Lesson*, Floyd of *Seven Guitars*, Troy of *Fences*, Sterling of *Two Trains Running*, and King of *King Hedley II*.

Wilson's last play thus offers a prescient view of black politics as well as a retrospective review of his dramaturgy as a mobius strip, or, as he writes in *Fences*, "a song turning back on itself." Of President Obama and others working to define a new inclusive American politics for the new millennium, Wilson asks that they not lose sight of history; that they address the specific needs of the black urban masses without excuse and with moral obligation; that they understand how serving this constituency is not partisan politics but speaks to a greater good. August Wilson's ending of the cycle represents a new beginning, and with every performance or reading of *Radio Golf*, 1839 Wylie continues to stand as a *lieux de memoire* — as the address he feels should be as important in our consciousness as 1600 Pennsylvania Avenue.

Notes

1. The line "After he rolls over and puts his pants on" is very similar to an earlier line of a Wilson character, Ma Rainey in *Ma Rainey's Black Bottom*, where Ma explains to her guitar player, Cutler: "As soon as they get my voice down on them recording machines, then it's just like if I'd be some whore and they roll over and put their pants on." Ma herself recognizes her value and utility within the economics of exploitation of race in the music industry and determines to find a way to negotiate this situation to her own advantage, given its restrictions.

Appendix

Discography for *Seven Guitars*

The following discography lists recordings of language or subjects referenced in August Wilson's *Seven Guitars* (New York: Plume, 1997). The songs are listed in the order in which the related material first appears in that text, with the initial page number included last in the entry in parentheses. Readers are encouraged to consult the reissue CDs of these recordings for context of Wilson's work.

Anybody Here Want to Try My Cabbage. Maggie Jones 1924 (1) *Complete Recorded Works in Chronological Order Vol. 1*. Document 5348.

Anybody Want to Buy My Cabbage. Lil Johnson 1935 (1) *Complete Recorded Works in Chronological Order Vol. 1*. Document 5307.

You've Been a Good Old Wagon. Bessie Smith 1925 (4) *The Complete Recordings Vol. 3*. Frog 42.

Death Don't Have No Mercy. Gary Davis 1960 (5).

Ora Nelle Blues. Othum Brown 1947 (6) *Chicago Boogie!* P-Vine PCD 1888.

That's All Right. Jimmy Rogers 1950 (6) *The Complete Chess Recordings*. MCA Chess CHD2 9372.

Walking Blues. Son House 1942 (7).

No Job Blues. Ramblin' Thomas 1928 (9) *Ramblin' Thomas and the Dallas Blues Singers*. Document 5107.

Kind Hearted Woman. Muddy Waters 1948 (11) *The Real Folk Blues/More Real Folk Blues*. Chess.

Empty Bed Blues Pt. 1. Bessie Smith 1928 (13) *The Complete Recordings Vol. 4*. Columbia C2K 52838.

Ice Man Blues. Blind Blake 1929 (17) *Complete Recorded Works in Chronological Order Vol. 3*. Document 5026.

Ice Man. Memphis Minnie 1936 (17) *Complete Recorded Works in Chronological Order Vol. 2*. Document 6009.

Red Rooster Blues. Sonny Scott 1933 (20) *Alabama and the East Coast*. Document 5450.

Rooster Blues. Casey Bill Weldon 1937 (20) *Complete Recorded Works in Chronological Order Vol. 3.* Document 5219.

Buddy Bolden's Blues. Jelly Roll Morton 1938 (23) *Jelly Roll Morton: The Complete Library of Congress Recordings by Alan Lomax.* Rounder 11661-1888-2 BK01.

Drifting Blues. Charles Brown 1945 (28) *The Complete Aladdin Recordings of Charles Brown.* Mosaic MD5-153.

Mill Man Blues. Billy Bird 1928 (28) da 3534-2.

Three Ball Slues. Pearl Traylor 1951 (29) *The OKeh Rhythm & Blues Story 1940–1957.* Epic/OKeh/Legacy 48912.

Doggin' Me Blues. Lillian Glinn 1927 (31) *Complete Recorded Works in Chronological Order.* Document 5184.

How Many More Years. Howlin' Wolf 1951 (31) *His Best.* MCA Chess.

Joe Louis Is the Man. Joe Pullum 1935 (36) *Complete Recorded Works in Chronological Order Vol. 2.* Document 5394.

Joe Louis Blues. Carl Martin 1935 (36) *Complete Recorded Works in Chronological Order.* Document 5229.

Gang of Brownskin Women. Papa Harvey Hull 1927 (38–39) *The Songster Tradition.* Document 5045.

My Monday Woman Blues Tk. 3. Jim Jackson 1928 (38–39) *Complete Recorded Works in Chronological Order Vol. 1.* Document 5114.

Southern Can is Mine. Willie McTell 1931 (41) *Complete Recorded Works in Chronological Order Vol. 1.* Document 5006.

Bad Luck and Trouble. Lightnin' Hopkins 1951 (46) *Jake Head Boogie.* Ace CDCHD 697.

Drinking Shine. Elder Charlie Beck 1930 (48) *Preachin' the Gospel: Holy Blues.* Columbia/Legacy CK 46779.

God Don't Like It. Rosetta Tharpe 1943 (48) *Complete Recorded Works in Chronological Order Vol. 2.* Document 5335.

God Don't Like It. Anderson Johnson 1950s (48) *God's Mighty Hand: Gospel Evangelists.* Heritage HT CD 09.

Walk With Me Lord. One String Jones 1960 (49) *One String Blues.* Takoma CDTAK 1023.

If I Could Hear My Mother Pray. Georgia Tom 1934 (49) *Complete Recorded Works in Chronological Order Vol. 2.* Document 6022.

If I Could Only Hear My Mother Pray Again. Anderson Johnson 1950s (49) *God's Mighty Hand: Gospel Evangelists.* Heritage HT CD 09.

If I Could Hear My Mother Pray Again. Mahalia Jackson 1947 (49) *Gospels, Spirituals, and Hymns.* Columbia /Legacy C2K 47083.

Old Ship of Zion. Hallway H. S. Quartet 1941 (50) *Negro Religious Field Recordings.* Document 5312.

Old Ship of Zion. Roberta Martin 1949 (50).

Old Ship of Zion. Rev. Benjamin Osborne 1950s (50).

The Lord's Prayer. Mahalia Jackson 1952 (50) *The Apollo Sessions.* Pair PCD-2-1332.

You Never Miss Your Water. Lightnin' Hopkins 1962 (50) *The Complete Prestige/Bluesville Recordings.* Prestige 7PCD-4406-2.

Jump Back Honey. Hadda Brooks 1952 (53–54) *The OKeh Rhythm & Blues Story.* Epic/OKeh/Legacy 48912.

Mellow Down Easy. Little Walter 1954 (53–54) *Chess Blues.* MCA/Chess CHD4-9340.

De Blind Man Stood On De Road. Morris Brown Q'T 1939 (54) *Vocal Quartets Vol. 1.* Document 5537.

Blind Bartemus. T. T. Rose 1927 (54) *Gospel Singers and Preachers.* Document 5585.

Old Blind Barnabus. John Lee Hooker 1949 (54) *The Unknown John Lee Hooker.* Flyright CD57.

Highway No. 61 Blues. Jack Kelly 1933 (59) *Complete Recorded Works in Chronological Order.* Document 6005.

Ain't No Grave. Bozie Sturdivant 1942 (88) *Negro Religious Field Recordings.* Document 5312.

Satan, Your Kingdom. Blind Joe Taggart 1931 (89) *Complete Recorded Works in Chronological Order Vol. 2.* Document 5154.

Satan, Your Kingdom. Spartanburg Famous Four 1938 (89) *Carolina Gospel Quartets Vol. 1.* Document 5445.

Please Don't Go. Big Joe Williams (89).

Good Rocking Tonight. Wynonie Harris 1948 (101) *Good Rockin' Tonight.* Proper P1179.

Sixty Minute Man. The Dominoes 1951 (102).

Adell, Sandra. *Double-Consciousness/Double Bind: Theoretical Issues in Twentieth-Century Black Literature.* Champaign-Urbana: U of Illinois P, 1994.

———. "Speaking of Ma Rainey/Talking about the Blues." In *May All Your Fences Have Gates: Essays on the Drama of August Wilson.* Ed. Alan Nadel. Iowa City: U of Iowa P, 1994. 51–66.

Agamben, Giorgio. *Homo Sacer: Sovereign Power and Bare Life.* Trans. Daniel Heller-Roazen. Palo Alto: Stanford U P, 1999.

Ambush, Benny Sato. "Culture Wars." *African American Review* 31.4 (1997): 579–586.

Anderson, Elijah. *Code of the Street: Decency, Violence, and the Moral Life of the Inner City.* New York: W.W. Norton, 1999.

Andrews, Williams L., Frances Smith Foster, and Trudier Harris, eds. *The Oxford Companion to African American Literature.* London: Oxford U P, 1997. 781–783.

Austin, Mildred. "Anybody Here Want to Try My Cabbage." 1928. *Female Blues Singers Vol. 1: A/B.* Document 5505.

Baker, James. "Iron Head" and "De Blue Goose." Library of Congress, 1933.

Baldwin, James. "Many Thousands Gone." In *Collected Essays.* Ed. Toni Morrison. New York: Library of America, 1998. 19–34.

Barnes, Sandra. "Yoruba: Political Representation in Old States and New Nations." In *Portraits of Culture.* Ed. Melvin Ember, Carol R. Ember, and David Levinson. New Jersey: Prentice Hall, 1996. 25–50.

———, ed. *Africa's Ogun: Old World and New.* 2nd ed. Bloomington: Indiana UP, 1997.

Barthold, Bonnie. *Black Time: Fiction of Africa, the Caribbean, and the United States.* New Haven: Yale UP, 1981.

Beale Street Sheiks. "You Shall." 1927. *Frank Stokes' Complete Paramount Recordings in Chronological Order.* Document DOCD 5012.

Benjamin, Walter. *Illuminations: Essays and Reflections.* New York: Schocken, 1969.

Bigsby, C. W. E. *The Cambridge Companion to August Wilson.* Cambridge Companion to Literature. Cambridge: Cambridge UP, 2007.

"Black in America: The Black Man." CNN Documentary. July 24, 2008.

Bogan, Lucille. "Shave 'Em Dry." 1935. *Complete Recorded Works in Chronological Order Vol. 3.* Document BDCD 6038.

Bogle, Donald. *Toms, Coons, Mulattos, Mammies and Bucks.* New York: Continuum, 2002.

Book of Revelation: Scripture's Crescendo and Culmination. "Apocalyptic Literature and Revelation." http://www.osl.cc/believe/revhome.htm.

Boothe, Demico. *Why Are So Many Black Men in Prison?* Bloomington, Indiana: Xlibris, 2006.

Boskin, J. *Sambo: The Rise and Demise of an American Jester.* New York: Oxford UP, 1986.

Bourdieu, Pierre. *In Other Words: Essays Towards a Reflexive Sociology.* Stanford, California: Stanford UP, 1990.

Bourne, Randolph. *The State.* 1918. New York: Resistance Press, 1946.

Branch, William. *Crosswinds: An Anthology of Black Dramatists in the Diaspora.* Bloomington: Indiana University Press, 1993.

Brantley, Ben. "Wilson's Gems, Memory's Ocean." *New York Times.* 20 May 2007. http://www.nytimes.com/

Brockett, Oscar. *The Essential Theater.* 6th ed. Austin, Texas: Harcourt Brace, 1996. 256–307.

Broonzy, Big Bill. "Ash Hauler." 1935. *Complete Recorded Works in Chronological Order. Vol. 4.* Document 5126.

Brown, Othum. "Ora Nelle Blues." 1947. *Chicago Boogie!* P-Vine PCD-1888. (Original version of song later recorded as "That's All Right.")

Bryer, Jackson R., and Mary C. Hartig. *Conversations with August Wilson.* Literary Conversation Series. Jackson: UP of Mississippi, 2006.

Carroll, Grace. *Environmental Stress and African Americans: The Other Side of the Moon.* Westport, Connecticut: Praeger, 1998.

Carter, Stephen L. *Integrity.* New York: Basic, 1996.

Cashmore, Ellis. *The Black Culture Industry.* London: Routledge, 1997.

Clark, Keith. *Black Manhood in James Baldwin, Ernest J. Gaines, and August Wilson.* Champaign-Urbana: U of Illinois P, 2002.

Davis, Gary. "Death Don't Have No Mercy." 1960. *Harlem Street Singer.* Prestige-Bluesville OBCCD-547.

Dawson, M. C. *Behind the Mule: Race and Class in African American Politics.* Princeton: Princeton UP, 1994.

DeMott, Benjamin. "Put on a Happy Face: Masking the Differences between Blacks and Whites." In *Gender through the Prism of Difference.* Ed. Maxine Baca Zinn, Pierrette Hongdageneu-Sotelo, and Michael A. Messner. Boston: Allyn and Bacon, 2000. 358–365.

Dezell, Maureen. "A 10-Play Odyssey Continues with *Gem of the Ocean.*" In *Conversations with August Wilson.* Ed. Jackson R. Bryer and Mary C. Hartig. Jackson: UP of Mississippi, 2006. 253–56.

Dorsey, Georgia Tom. "If I Could Hear My Mother Pray Again." 1934. *Complete Recorded Works in Chronological Order. Vol. 2.* Document BDCD 6022.

Drewel, Henry John. "Performing the Other: Mami Wata Worship in Africa." *TDR* 32.2 (1988): 161.

DuBois, W. E. B. "Krigwa Players Little Theater: The Story of a Little Theatre Movement." *Crisis Magazine,* July 1926. 134-136.

———. *The Philadelphia Negro: A Social Study.* 1899. Philadelphia: U of Pennsylvania P, 1996.

———. *The Souls of Black Folks.* Chicago: A. C. McClurg, 1903.

———. "The Talented Tenth" in *African-American Social & Political Thought 1850–1920.* New Brunswick: Howard Brotz Transaction Publishers, 1999. 518–533.

Durkheim, Emile. *The Division of Labor.* London: Free Press, 1997.

Dyer, Richard. *White.* New York: Routledge, 1997.

Dyson, Michael Eric. "In a Color-Blind Society, We Can Only See Black and White." *Gender through the Prism of Difference.* Ed. Maxine Baca Zinn, Pierrette Hongdageneu-Sotelo, and Michael A. Messner. Boston: Allyn and Bacon, 2000. 475–480.

Easton, Amos. "The Death of Leroy Carr." 1935. *Complete Recorded Works in Chronological Order. Vol. 4.* Document 5264.

Elam, Harry J., Jr. "August Wilson's Women." In *May All Your Fences Have Gates: Essays on the Drama of August Wilson.* Ed. Alan Nadel. Iowa City: U of Iowa P, 1994. 165–182.

———. "*Gem of the Ocean* and the Redemptive Power of History." In *The Cambridge Companion to August Wilson.* Ed. Christopher Bigsby. Cambridge: Cambridge UP, 2007. 75–89.

———. *The Past as Present in the Drama of August Wilson.* Ann Arbor: U of Michigan P, 2006.

Eliade, Mircea. *The Myth of the Eternal Return.* Princeton: Princeton UP, 2005.

Ellison, Ralph. *Invisible Man.* 2nd ed. New York: Vintage, 1995.

———. "Remembering Richard Wright." *Going to the Territory.* New York: Vintage, 1987. 198–216.

Eng, David. *Racial Castration: Managing Masculinity in Asian America.* Durham, North Carolina: Duke UP, 2001.

Entman, Robert M. "African Americans According to TV News." *Gender through the Prism of Difference.* Ed. Maxine Baca Zinn, Pierrette Hongdageneu-Sotelo, and Michael A. Messner. Boston: Allyn and Bacon. 2000. 372–376.

Feingold, Michael. "August Wilson's Bottomless Blackness." *The Village Voice* 39 (27 November 1984): 117–118.

Fishman, Joan. "Romare Bearden, August Wilson, and the Traditions of African Performance." In *May All Your Fences Have Gates: Essays on the Drama of August Wilson.* Ed. Alan Nadel. Iowa City: U of Iowa P, 1994. 133–149.

Frazier, E. Franklin. *Black Bourgeoisie.* Glencoe, Illinois: Free Press, 1961.

Freedman, Samuel. "Leaving His Imprint on Broadway." *New York Times,* November 22, 1987.

Freud, Sigmund. *Beyond the Pleasure Principle.* Trans. C. J. M. Hubback. E-book: Digireads, 2008.

———. *Civilization and Its Discontents.* Ed. and trans. James Strachey. London: W.W. Norton, 1989.

———. "Reflections upon War and Death." In *Character and Culture.* Ed. Philip Rieff. New York: Collier Books, 1963. 107–133.

Fuller, Blind Boy. "I Crave My Pig Meat." 1939. *Complete Recorded Works in Chronological Order. Vol. 5.* Document 5095.

Gaffney, Floyd. "Ma Rainey's Black Bottom." In *Masterpieces of African American Literature.* Ed. Frank N. Madill. New York: Harper Collins, 1992. 269–272.

Gaither, Bill. "Champ Joe Louis (King of the Gloves)." 1938. *Complete Recorded Works in Chronological Order. Vol. 3.* Document 5253.

Gandy, Oscar H., Jr. *Communication and Race.* London: Arnold Press, 1998.

Gates, Henry Lewis, Jr. "The New Chitlin' Circuit." *New Yorker.* February 3, 1997. 44–55.

———. "TV's Black World Turns — But Stays Real." In *Race, Class and Gender.* Ed. Margaret L. Anderson and Patricia Hill Collins. Belmont, California: Wadsworth Publishing, 1992. 310–316.

Gibbs, Jewelle Taylor. *Young, Black, and Male in America: An Endangered Species.* New York: Auburn House Paperbacks, 1988.

Giddens, Anthony. *Capitalism and Modern Social Theory.* Cambridge: Cambridge University Press, 1971. 84–85.

Girard, Rene. *Violence and the Sacred.* Trans. Patrick Gregory. Baltimore: Johns Hopkins UP, 1977.

Glaude, Eddie. *In A Shade of Blue: Pragmatism and the Politics of Black America.* Chicago: U of Chicago P, 2007.

Glenn, Rhonda. "Paving the Rhodes for Other African-American Golfers." http://www.usga.org/news/2007/february/rhodes.html.

Graham, Laurie. *Singing the City: The Bonds of Home in an Industrial Land-scape.* Pittsburgh: U of Pittsburgh P, 1998.

Graham, Lawrence Otis. *Our Kind of People: Inside America's Black Upper Class.* New York: Harper Perennial, 2000.

Grant, Nathan. "Men, Women and Culture: A Conversation with August Wilson." *American Drama* 5.2 (1996): 100–122.

Green, Tara T. "Speaking of Voice and August Wilson's Women." In *August Wilson and Black Aesthetics.* Ed. Sandra G. Shannon and Dana A. Williams. New York: Palgrave Macmillan, 2004. 145–158.

Hall, Stuart. "Gramsci's Relevance for the Study of Race and Ethnicity." *Journal of Communication Inquiry* 10.2 (1986): 5–27.

Hallsway High School Quartet. "Old Ship of Zion." 1941. *Negro Religious Field Recordings.* Document 5312.

Hansberry, Lorraine. *"A Raisin in the Sun" and "The Sign in Sydney Brustein's Window."* New York: Signet Books, 1958.

Harris, Wynonie. "Good Rocking Tonight." 1947. *Wynonie Harris v. Roy Brown: Battle of the Blues.* Charly CD 37.

Harrison, Paul Carter. "August Wilson's Blues Poetics." In *August Wilson: Three Plays.* Ed. Paul Carter Harrison. Pittsburgh: U of Pittsburgh P, 1991.

———. "The Crisis of Black Theater Identity." *African American Review* 31. 4 (1997): 567–578.

———. *The Drama of Nommo.* New York: Grove Press, 1972.

———. "Mother/Word: Black Theatre in the African Continuum: Word/Song as Method." In *Totem Voices: Plays from the Black World Repertory.* Ed. Paul Carter Harrison. New York: Grove Press, 1989.

Harvey, A. E. *A Companion to the New Testament.* 2nd ed. Cambridge: Cambridge UP, 2004.

Haskins, James. *Black Theater in America.* New York: Thomas Crowell, 1982.

Henderson, Rosa. "Black Star Line." 1924. *Complete Recorded Works in Chronological Order. Vol. 2.* Document 5402.

———. "West Indies Blues." 1924. *Complete Recorded Works in Chronological Order. Vol. 2.* Document 5402.

Hernton, Calvin. *Sex and Racism in America.* New York: Grove Press, 1965.

Herrington, Joan. "Birth, Baptism and Resurrection: August Wilson and the Blues." In *The Playwright's Muse.* New York: Routledge, 2002. 53–69.

———. "*Jitney*: August Wilson's Round Trip." In *I Ain't Sorry for Nothin' I Done: August Wilson's Process of Playwrighting.* New York: Limelight, 1998. 113–130.

———. "*King Hedley II*: In the Midst of All This Death." *The Cambridge*

Companion to August Wilson. Ed. Christopher Bigsby. New York: Cambridge UP, 2007. 169–182.

Hickman, Lee. "Is It OK . . . to Play Golf?" *The Guardian*. http://www.guardian.co.uk/money/2006/jan/24/ethicalmoney.ethicalliving.

Holland, Sharon Patricia. *Raising the Dead: Readings of Death and (Black) Subjectivity*. Durham: Duke UP, 2000.

Holmes, Wright. "Alley Special." 1947. *Alley Special*. Collectables 5320.

hooks, bell. *We Real Cool: Black Men and Masculinity*. New York: Routledge, 2003.

"Hottentot Venus Goes Home." BBC. April 29, 2002.

House, Son. "Delta Blues." 1941. *Legends of Country Blues*. JSP 7715.

———. "Preachin' the Blues: Part 1." 1930. *Legends of Country Blues*. JSP 7715.

Hughes, Langston, and Milton Meltzer. *Black Magic: A Pictorial History of the Negro in American Entertainment*. Englewood Cliffs, New Jersey: Prentice Hall, 1970.

Hull, Papa Harvey, and Long Cleve Reed. "Gang of Brown Skin Women." 1927. *The Songster Tradition*. Document 5045.

Hutchinson, Earl Ofari. *The Assassination of the Black Male Image*. New York: Simon and Schuster, 1997.

Ife, Zadia. "The African Diasporan Ritual Mode." In *The African Aesthetic: Keeper of the Traditions*. Ed. Kariamu Welsh-Asante. New York: Praeger, 1994. 32–51.

Jahn, Janheinz. "From 'Blues: The Conflict of Cultures.'" In *Write Me a Few of Your Lines: A Blues Reader*. Ed. Steven C Tracy. Amherst: U of Massachusetts P, 1999. 28–31.

———. *A History of Neo-African Literature*. New York: Grove Press, 1968.

James, C. L. R. *The Black Jacobins: Toussaint L' Ouverture and the San Domingo Revolution*. New York: Random House, 1963. 235–237.

Jefferson, Blind Lemon. "Broke and Hungry." 1926. *All the Classic Sides*. JSP 7706.

Johnson, Lemuel. *The Devil, the Gargoyle, and the Buffoon: The Negro as Metaphor in Western Literature*. Fort Washington, New York: Kennikat Press, 1969.

Johnson, Lil. "Anybody Want to Buy My Cabbage?" 1935. *Complete Recorded Works in Chronological Order. Vol. 1*. Document 5307.

———. "Winner Joe (The Knock-Out King)." 1936. *Complete Recorded Works in Chronological Order. Vol. 1*. Document 5307.

Johnson, Ralph Arthur. "World without Workers: Prime Time's Presentation of Labor." *Labor Studies Journal* 5 (1981): 200.

Jones, Chris. "Golf: An Emotional End to Wilson's Play Cycle." *Chicago Tribune*, January 25, 2007. http://archives.chicagotribune.com/2007/jan/25/news/chi0701240434jan25.

Jones, Maggie. "Anybody Here Want to Try My Cabbage?" 1924. *Complete Recorded Works in Chronological Order. Vol. 1.* Document 5348.

Kalish, Richard A., and David K. Reynolds. *Death and Ethnicity: A Psychocultural Study.* Los Angeles: University of Southern California Press, 1976.

Kansas Joe and Memphis Minnie. "Preacher's Blues." 1931. *Complete Recorded Works 1929–1934 in Chronological Order. Vol. 2.* Document 5029.

Keil, Charles. *Urban Blues.* Chicago: U of Chicago P, 1966.

Kibler, M. Alison. *Rank Ladies.* Chapel Hill: U of North Carolina P, 1999.

Kitano, H. H. L. *Race Relations.* Englewood Cliffs, New Jersey: Prentice-Hall, 1991.

Kluckhohn, Clyde. "Myths and Rituals: A General Theory." In *Myth and Literature: Contemporary Theory and Practice.* Ed. John B. Vickery. Omaha: U of Nebraska P, 1966. 33–44.

Korten, David. *The Post Corporate World: Life after Capitalism.* San Francisco: Berrett-Koehler, 1999.

Krasner, David. "*Jitney*, Folklore and Responsibility." In *The Cambridge Companion to August Wilson.* Ed. Christopher Bigsby. Cambridge: Cambridge UP, 2007. 158–168.

Kubrin, Charis E., and Ronald Weitzer. "Retaliatory Homicide: Concentrated Disadvantage and Neighborhood Culture." *Social Problems* 50: 2 (2003): 157–180.

Lacan, Jacques. "The Mirror Stage as Formative of the Function of the I." In *Écrits: A Selection.* New York: W. W. Norton and Company, 1977. 1–7.

Lahr, John. "Been Here and Gone." In *The Cambridge Companion to August Wilson.* Ed. Christopher Bigsby. Cambridge: Cambridge UP 2007. 28–51.

———. "Hill Street Blues." *New Yorker.* http://www.newyorker.com/archive/2005/05/16/050516crth_theatre.

Larsen, Nella. *"Quicksand" and "Passing."* New Brunswick: Rutgers UP, 1986.

Lee, Matthew R., and Graham C. Ousey. "Counterbalancing Disadvantage? : Residential Integration and Urban Black Homicide." *Social Problems* 54: 2 (2007): 240–262.

Lincoln, C. E. "The Absent Father Haunts the Negro Family." *New York Times Magazine.* November 28, 1965. 60, 172–176.

Lipsyte, Robert. "Introduction to the American Edition." *Beyond a Boundary.* Durham: Duke UP, 1983.

Livingston, Dinah. "Cool August: Mr. Wilson's Red-Hot Blues." In *Conversa-*

tions with August Wilson. Ed. Jackson R. Bryer and Mary C. Hartig. Jackson: UP of Mississippi, 2006. 38–60.

Madhubuti, Haki. *Tough Notes: A Healing Call.* Chicago: Third World Press, 2002.

Malcolm X. *Malcolm X Speaks.* Ed. George Breitman. New York: Ballantine Books, 1965.

Marable, Manning. "The Black Male: Searching beyond Stereotypes." In *Gender through the Prism of Difference.* Ed. Maxine Baca Zinn, Pierrette Hongdageneu-Sotelo and Michael A. Messner. Boston: Allyn and Bacon, 2000. 251–257.

Marquis, Donald M. *In Search of Buddy Bolden: First Man of Jazz.* Baton Rouge: Louisiana State UP, 1978.

Marx, Karl. "Economic and Philosophic Manuscripts of 1844." In *The Marx-Engels Reader.* Ed. Robert C. Tucker. New York: W. W. Norton, 1978. 66–125.

Massey, Douglas S., and Nancy A. Denton. *American Apartheid: Segregation and the Making of the Underclass.* Cambridge: Harvard UP, 1998.

Mbiti, John S. *African Religions and Philosophy.* New York: Anchor Books, 1969.

McCoy, Viola. "You Don't Know My Mind." 1924. *Complete Recorded Works in Chronological Order. Vol. 2.* Document 5417.

McGary, Howard. "Alienation and the African-American Experience." In *African American Perspectives and Philosophical Traditions.* Ed. John P. Pittman. New York: Routledge, 1977. 282–296.

McGhee, Brownie. "The Death of Blind Boy Fuller #1 and #2." 1941. *The Complete Brownie McGhee.* Columbia/Legacy. C2K 52933.

McLean, Albert F. "Genesis of Vaudeville: Two Letters from B. F. Keith." *Theatre Survey 1* (1960): 82–95.

Memphis Minnie. "Ma Rainey." 1940. *Complete Recorded Works in Chronological Order. Vol. 5.* Document 6012.

Mincy, Ronald. *Black Males Left Behind.* Washington, D.C.: Urban Institute Press, 2006.

Mississippi Sheiks. "He Calls That Religion." 1932. *Complete Recorded Works in Chronological Order. Vol. 3.* Document 5085.

Molette, Carlton. "Ritual Drama in the Contemporary Black Theater." *The Black Scholar* 25.2 (1995): 24–31.

Moody-Adams, Michele M. "Race, Class, and the Social Construction of Self-Respect." In *African American Perspectives and Philosophical Traditions.* Ed. John P. Pittman. Routledge, New York: 1977. 251–266.

Moore, Sally F., and Barbara G. Myerhoff, eds. *Secular Ritual.* Assen/Amsterdam: Van Gorcum and Comp. B.V., 1977.

Morris Brown Quartet. "De Blind Man Stood on De Road and Cried." 1939. *Vocal Quartets Vol. 1: A/B/C.* Document 5537.

Morton, Jelly Roll. "Buddy Bolden's Blues." 1938. *The Complete Library of Congress Recordings by Alan Lomax.* Rounder 11661-1888-2 ST01.

———. "Buddy Bolden's Blues." 1939. *Last Sessions: The Complete General Recordings.* Commodore 403.

Moyers, Bill. "August Wilson: Playwright." *Conversations with August Wilson.* Ed. Jackson R. Bryer and Mary C. Hartig. Jackson: UP of Mississippi, 2006. 61–80.

Nadel, Alan. *Invisible Criticism: Ralph Ellison and the American Canon.* Iowa City: U Iowa P, 1987.

———. "*Ma Rainey's Black Bottom*: Cutting the Historical Record, Dramatizing a Blues CD." *The Cambridge Companion to August Wilson.* Ed. Christopher Bigsby. Cambridge, UK: Cambridge UP, 2007. 102–112.

———, ed. *May All Your Fences Have Gates: Essays on the Drama of August Wilson.* Iowa City: U of Iowa P, 1994.

Neal, Mark Anthony. "Confessions of a ThugNiggaIntellectual." *SeeingBlack. com.* http://www.seeingblack.com/2003/x091203/thugnig.shtml.

———. *New Black Man.* New York: Routledge, 2006.

Nora, Pierre. "Between Memory and History: Les Lieux de Memoire." *Representations* 26 (Spring 1989): 7–25.

Obama, Barack. "Speech on Race." *New York Times,* March 18, 2007.

Oliphant, Dave. *Texan Jazz.* Austin: University of Texas Press, 1996.

Parenti, Michael. *Make Believe Media: The Politics of Entertainment.* New York: St. Martin's, 1992.

Parks, Suzan-Lori. "The Light in August." *American Theater,* November 2005: 22+.

Patterson, Orlando. *Slavery and Social Death: A Comparative Study.* Cambridge, Massachusetts: Harvard UP, 1982.

Pereira, Kim. *August Wilson and the African-American Odyssey.* Champaign-Urbana: U of Illinois P, 1995.

Pieterse, J. *White on Black.* New Haven, Connecticut: Yale UP, 1992.

Powell, Richard J. *Black Art and Culture in the 20th Century.* London: Thames and Hudson, 1997.

Powers, Kim. "An Interview with August Wilson." *Theater* 16 (Fall/Winter 1984): 50–55.

Rashad, Phylicia. "Riding the Waves of History: Gem of the Ocean." *American Theatre* 24:8 (2007): 43.

Rawson, Christopher. "Obituary: August Wilson, Pittsburgh Playwright

Who Chronicles Black Experience." *Pittsburgh Post-Gazette*, October 3, 2005. http://www.post-gazette.com/pg/05276/581786.stm.

Richards, Lloyd. "Introduction." In *Fences*. By August Wilson. New York: Signet, 1986. vii–viii.

Richards, Sandra L. "Yoruba Gods on the American Stage: August Wilson's *Joe Turner's Come and Gone.*" *Research in African Literatures* 30.4 (December 1999): 92–105.

Roach, Joseph. *Cities of the Dead: Circum-Atlantic Performances*. New York: Columbia UP, 1996.

Roach, Max. "Jazz." In *African American Literary Criticism 1773–2000*. Ed. Hazel Arnett Ervin. New York: Twayne Publishers, 1999. 113–116.

Robeson, Paul. "King Joe Parts 1 and 2." 1941. *Count Basie: My Old Flame*. Centurion Jazz IECJ315.

Rogers, Jimmy. "That's All Right." 1950. *The Complete Chess Recordings*. MCA/Chess CHD2 9372. (See Othum Brown entry.)

Rorty, Richard. *Contingency, Irony, and Solidarity*. Cambridge, UK: Cambridge UP, 1989.

———. "Justice as a Larger Loyalty." In *Cosmopolitics: Thinking and Feeling beyond the Nation*. Ed. Pheng Cheah and Bruce Robbins. Cultural Politics series. Minneapolis: U of Minnesota P, 1998. 45–58.

Rosen, Carol. "August Wilson: Bard of the Blues." In *Conversations with August Wilson*. Ed. Jackson R. Bryer and Mary C. Hartig. Jackson: UP of Mississippi, 2006. 188–203.

Rothstein, Mervyn. "Round Five for the Theatrical Heavyweight." *New York Times*, April 15, 1990: 1+.

Rushing, Jimmy. "Boogie Woogie." 1936. *The Complete Decca Recordings*. GRP611.

Said, Edward. *Beginnings: Intention and Method*. 2nd ed. New York: Columbia UP, 2004.

Sainer, Arthur. *The New Radical Theatre Notebook*. New York: Applause, 1977.

Savran, David. "August Wilson." In *Conversations with August Wilson*. Ed. Jackson R. Bryer and Mary C. Hartig. Jackson: UP of Mississippi, 2006. 19–37.

———. *In Their Own Words: Contemporary American Playwrights*. New York: Theater Communications Group, 1988.

Shannon, Sandra G. *The Dramatic Vision of August Wilson*. Washington, DC: Howard UP, 1995.

———. "'Ain't I A Woman?' Sojourner Truth's Question Revisited in August Wilson's Female Characters." *MAWA Review* 14.1 (June 1999): 1–8.

———. "August Wilson Explains His Dramatic Vision: An Interview." In *Conversations with August Wilson*. Ed. Jackson R. Bryer and Mary C. Hartig. Jackson: UP of Mississippi, 2006. 118–154.

———. "The Ground on Which I Stand: August Wilson's Perspective on African American Women." In *May All Your Fences Have Gates: Essays on the Drama of August Wilson*. Ed. Alan Nadel. Iowa City: U of Iowa P, 1994. 150–164.

———. "The Long Wait: August Wilson's *Ma Rainey's Black Bottom*." *Black American Literature Forum* 25 (1991): 135–146.

———. "A Transplant That Did Not Take: August Wilson's Views on the Great Migration." *African American Review* 31.4 (Winter 1997): 659–666.

———, and Dana A. Williams. "A Conversation with August Wilson." In *August Wilson and Black Aesthetics*. Ed. Sandra G. Shannon and Dana A. Williams. New York: Palgrave Macmillan, 2004. 187–195.

Sheppard, Vera. "August Wilson: An Interview." In *Conversations with August Wilson*. Ed. Jackson R. Bryer and Mary C. Hartig. Jackson: UP of Mississippi, 2006. 101–117.

Soyinka, Wole. *Myth, Literature and the African World*. New York: Cambridge, 1976.

Staples, Robert. "The Illusion of Racial Equality: The Black American Dilemma." In *Gender through the Prism of Difference*. Ed. Maxine Baca Zinn, Pierrette Hongdageneu-Sotelo, and Michael A. Messner. Boston: Allyn and Bacon, 2000. 481–490.

Starke, Rosa. "Slave Narrative." In *Bullwhip Days: The Slaves Remember — An Oral History*. Ed. James Mellon. New York: Avon Books, 1988. 136.

Sturdivant, Bozie. "Ain't No Grave Can Hold My Body Down." 1942. *Negro Religious Field Recordings*. Document 5312.

Taggart, Blind Joe. "Satan Your Kingdom Must Come Down." 1931. *Complete Recorded Works in Chronological Order. Vol. 2*. Document 5154.

Taylor, Regina. "That's Why They Call It the Blues." *American Theatre* 13.2 (1996): 18–23.

Tharpe, Rosetta. "God Don't Like It." 1943. *Complete Recorded Works in Chronological Order. Vol. 2*. Document 5335.

Thomas, Jesse. "Baby Face" and "Blue Goose Blues." 1929. *Ramblin' Thomas and the Dallas Blues Singers*. Document 5107.

Tracy, Steven C. *Langston Hughes and the Blues*. Champaign-Urbana: U of Illinois P, 1988.

———, ed. *Write Me a Few of Your Lines: A Blues Reader*. Amherst: U of Massachusetts P, 1999.

Usekes, Cigdem. "'We's the Leftovers': Whiteness as Economic Power and Exploitation in August Wilson's Twentieth-Century Cycle of Plays." *African American Review* 37.1 (2003): 115–125.

Van Gennep, Arnold. *The Rites of Passage.* Trans. Monika B. Vizedom and Gabrielle L. Caffee. Chicago: U of Chicago P, 1960.

Vickery, John B., ed. *Myth and Literature.* Lincoln: U of Nebraska P, 1966.

Ward, Billy, and the Dominoes. "Sixty Minute Man." 1951. *Sixty Minute Man.* Rev-Ola CRREV 32.

Washboard Walter. "Wasn't It Sad about Lemon." 1930. *John Byrd and Walter Taylor.* Da CD 3517-2.

Washington, Booker T. "The Death of Bessie Smith." 1939. *Walter Davis: Complete Recorded Works in Chronological Order. Vol. 5.* Document 5285.

Wells, Junior. "You Lied to Me." 1966. *It's My Life, Baby!* Vanguard 73120.

Welsh-Asante, Kaiamu, ed. *The African Aesthetic.* Westport, Connecticut: Greenwood Press, 1993.

Western, Bruce. *Punishment and Inequality in America.* New York: Russell Sage Foundation Publications, 2007.

Wigley, Mark. "Untitled: The Housing of Gender." In *Sexuality and Space.* Ed. Beatriz Colomina. Princeton: Princeton Architectural Press, 1992. 327–389.

Wilson, August. "American Histories: Chasing Dreams and Nightmares: Sailing the Stream of Black Culture." *New York Times*, April 23, 2000, sec. 2.1.

———. *Fences.* New York: Plume Books, 1986.

———. *Gem of the Ocean.* New York: Theater Communications Group, 2006.

———. "The Ground on Which I Stand." *Callaloo* 20.3 (1997): 493–503.

———. *The Ground on Which I Stand.* New York: TCG Group, 2001.

———. *Jitney.* New York: Overlook P, 2003.

———. *Joe Turner's Come and Gone.* New York: Plume, 1988.

———. *King Hedley II.* New York: Theater Communications Group, 2005.

———. *Ma Rainey's Black Bottom.* New York: Samuel French, 1985.

———. *The Piano Lesson.* New York: Plume, 1990.

———. *Radio Golf.* New York: Theater Communications Group, 2007.

———. *Seven Guitars.* New York: Penguin Press, 1996.

———. *Two Trains Running.* New York: Plume, 1993.

Wilson, William Julius. *The Truly Disadvantaged: The Inner City, the Underclass, and Public Policy.* Chicago: U of Chicago P, 1987.

A World of Ideas with Bill Moyers: August Wilson. Prod. Public Affairs Television. New York, N.Y., 1988. PBS Video 1989.

Wright, Richard. "Blueprint for Negro Literature." In *Amistad 2.* Ed. John A. Williams and Charles F. Harris. New York: Vintage Books, 1971. 3-20.

NOTES ON CONTRIBUTORS

HERMAN BEAVERS is associate professor of English at the University of Pennsylvania. He is the author of the chapbook *A Neighborhood of Feeling* and the critical study *Wrestling Angels into Song: The Fictions of Ernest J. Gaines and James Alan McPherson*. His poems have appeared most recently in *Cross Connect, Peregrine*, and *Callaloo*. During the 2009–2010 academic year he was a visiting fellow in African American Studies at Princeton University.

YVONNE CHAMBERS has devoted nearly 30 years to practicing law but never lost her interest in theater. She currently lives in Columbus, Ohio, takes theater classes at Ohio State University, and serves as a volunteer play reader with the Contemporary American Theatre Company.

SOYICA DIGGS COLBERT, assistant professor of English at Dartmouth College, has published articles on James Baldwin, Alice Childress, and August Wilson. She is currently working on a book that examines how the physical space of the theater and the discursive space of the page relate to the dislocation enacted by trans-Atlantic slavery.

HARRY J. ELAM, JR. is the Olive H. Palmer Professor in the Humanities at Stanford University. He is the author of *Taking It to the Streets: The Social Protest Theater of Luis Valdez and Amiri Baraka* and *The Past as Present in the Drama of August Wilson* and is coeditor of *African American Performance and Theater History* and *Black Cultural Traffic: Crossroads in Performance and Popular Culture*. His articles have appeared in *American Drama, Modern Drama, Theatre Journal*, and *Text and Performance Quarterly*, as well as journals in Israel, Taiwan, and Poland, and in several critical anthologies.

NATHAN GRANT is an associate professor of English at Saint Louis University and editor of *African American Review*. He is the author of *Masculinist Impulses: Toomer, Hurston, Black Writing and Modernity*, and has also written several articles and book chapters on African American literature, theater, film, television, and popular culture.

DAVID LACROIX is an independent scholar and researcher. He has taught at Wake Forest University and the University of Kentucky. A specialist in African American literature, his work includes articles on Gayl Jones and Octavia Butler.

BARBARA LEWIS is director of the William Monroe Trotter Institute for the Study of Black History and Culture at the University of Massachusetts–Boston, where she holds a joint appointment as associate professor in Africana Studies and English. Her original drama has been presented at festivals and on professional stages nationally and internationally. From 2000 to 2002, she edited the journal *Black Renaissance/ Renaissance Noire*. For over fifteen years, she covered the arts scene in New York, writing for *Essence*, the *Amsterdam News,* the *Soho Weekly News*, and *Ms.* Magazine.

ALAN NADEL, William T. Bryan Professor of American Literature and Culture at the University of Kentucky, is the author of *Invisible Criticism: Ralph Ellison and the American Canon, Containment Culture, Flatlining on the Field of Dreams: Cultural Narratives in the Films of President Reagan's America*, and *Television in Black-and-White America: Race and National Identity* and the editor of *May All Your Fences Have Gates: Essays in the Drama of August Wilson*. His essays and reviews have appeared in numerous journals, including *American Literary History, Henry James Review, American Drama, Theater, Modern Fiction Studies, College Literature, Film Quarterly, Georgia Review*, and *Centennial Review*.

DONALD E. PEASE, Avalon Professor of Humanities at Dartmouth College, is the author of *The New American Exceptionalism* and *Visionary Compacts: American Renaissance Writings in Cultural Context* and the coeditor of several books, including *American Renaissance Rediscovered* and *Cultures of U.S. Imperialism*. He founded the Dartmouth Institute for the Future of American Studies and has been awarded the Guggenheim, NEH, Ford, Mellon, and Hewlett fellowships.

SANDRA G. SHANNON, professor of African American studies at Howard University, is the author of *The Dramatic Vision of August Wilson, August Wilson's Fences: A Reference Guide*, and coeditor of *August Wilson and Black Aesthetics*. A past editor of *Theatre Topics Journal* and past president of the Black Theatre Network, her publications on August Wilson have appeared in *The Influence of Tennessee Williams: Essays on Fifteen American Playwrights, August Wilson: A Casebook*, and *African American Performance and Theater History: A Critical Reader*, among other places.

VIVIAN GIST SPENCER is professor of English and Theatre Arts at Anne Arundel Community College in Arnold, Maryland. Other recent publications include an essay on August Wilson's "Urban Entrepreneurs," which illustrates the economic success of Wilson's characters in the industrial North despite Wilson's contention of the black exodus from the South being a cultural tragedy.

ANTHONY STEWART is associate professor in the English Department at Dalhousie University. His main research interest is twentieth- and twenty-first-century African American Literature and Culture. He is the author of *George Orwell, Doubleness, and the Value of Decency* and *You Must Be a Basketball Player: Rethinking Integration in the University.*

STEVEN C. TRACY is professor of Afro-American Studies at the University of Massachusetts Amherst. He is the author, editor, or coeditor of *Langston Hughes and the Blues, Going to Cincinnati: A History of the Blues in the Queen City, A Brush with the Blues, A Historical Guide to Langston Hughes, A Historical Guide to Ralph Ellison, Write Me a Few of Your Lines: A Blues Reader,* and the 16-volume *Collected Works of Langston Hughes,* among other books. A blues singer and harmonica player, he currently performs with his band Steve Tracy and the Crawling Kingsnakes and with the King Bees.

DANA A. WILLIAMS is chair and professor of African American Literature in the Department of English at Howard University. She is the author of *In the Light of Likeness — Transformed: The Literary Art of Leon Forrest,* the coeditor of *August Wilson and Black Aesthetics,* and the editor of *Contemporary African American Fiction: New Critical Essays*; *African American Humor, Irony, and Satire: Ishmael Reed, Satirically Speaking*; and *Conversations with Leon Forrest.*

KIMMIKA L. H. WILLIAMS-WITHERSPOON is an associate professor of Urban Theater at Temple University. She is the winner of a PEW Charitable Trust fellowship in scriptwriting, the DaimlerChrysler "Spirit of the Word" National Poetry Competition, and a Lila Wallace Creative Arts fellowship. A twice-returning playwright with the Minneapolis Playwrights' Center and Pew Charitable Trusts Playwrights Exchange, she is author of *The Secret Messages in African American Theater: Hidden Meaning Embedded in Public Discourse* and has contributed articles to such journals as *Conciousness, Theatre, Literature and the Arts 2007, Mass Media Research: International Approaches,* and *African American Rhetoric(s): Interdisciplinary Perspectives.*

INDEX

This selective index — intended to assist the reader who uses this book to research specific plays or critical perspectives — identifies only the places where specific plays are *discussed*, not merely mentioned, and those critics and theorists used to advance an essay's argument. The index, moreover, refers to the texts of the essays, omitting references that appear only in footnotes or bibliographies.

Gramley Library
Salem Academy and College
Winston-Salem, N.C. 27108